Scalable and Distributed Machine Learning and Deep Learning Patterns

J. Joshua Thomas
UOW Malaysia KDU Penang University College, Malaysia

S. Harini
Vellore Institute of Technology, India

V. Pattabiraman
Vellore Institute of Technology, India

A volume in the Advances in
Computational Intelligence and
Robotics (ACIR) Book Series

Published in the United States of America by
    IGI Global
    Engineering Science Reference (an imprint of IGI Global)
    701 E. Chocolate Avenue
    Hershey PA, USA 17033
    Tel: 717-533-8845
    Fax: 717-533-8661
    E-mail: cust@igi-global.com
    Web site: http://www.igi-global.com

Library of Congress Cataloging-in-Publication Data

Names: Thomas, J. Joshua, 1973- editor. | Sriraman, Harini, 1982- editor. |
    Venkatasubbu, Pattabiraman, 1976- editor.
Title: Scalable and distributed machine learning and deep learning patterns
    / edited by J. Joshua Thomas, Harini Sriraman, Pattabiraman
    Venkatasubbu.
Description: Hershey, PA : Engineering Science Reference, [2024] | Includes
    bibliographical references and index. | Summary: "By the end of this
    book, you will have the knowledge and abilities necessary to construct
    and implement a distributed data processing pipeline for machine
    learning model inference and training. Reduced time costs in machine
    learning result in shorter model training and model updating cycle wait
    times. Distributed machine learning enables ML professionals to reduce
    model training and inference time drastically. With the aid of this
    helpful manual, you'll be able to use your Python development experience
    and quickly get started with the creation of distributed ML, including
    multi-node ML systems"-- Provided by publisher.
Identifiers: LCCN 2023017936 (print) | LCCN 2023017937 (ebook) | ISBN
    9781668498040 (hardcover) | ISBN 9781668498057 (ebook)
Subjects: LCSH: Machine learning. | Deep learning (Machine learning) |
    Algorithms.
Classification: LCC Q325.5 .S275 2024 (print) | LCC Q325.5 (ebook) | DDC
    006.3/1--dc23/eng/20230816
LC record available at https://lccn.loc.gov/2023017936
LC ebook record available at https://lccn.loc.gov/2023017937

This book is published in the IGI Global book series Advances in Computational Intelligence and Robotics
(ACIR) (ISSN: 2327-0411; eISSN: 2327-042X)

British Cataloguing in Publication Data
A Cataloguing in Publication record for this book is available from the British Library.

All work contributed to this book is new, previously-unpublished material.
The views expressed in this book are those of the authors, but not necessarily of the publisher.

For electronic access to this publication, please contact: eresources@igi-global.com.

Advances in Computational Intelligence and Robotics (ACIR) Book Series

ISSN:2327-0411
EISSN:2327-042X

Editor-in-Chief: Ivan Giannoccaro, University of Salento, Italy

MISSION

While intelligence is traditionally a term applied to humans and human cognition, technology has progressed in such a way to allow for the development of intelligent systems able to simulate many human traits. With this new era of simulated and artificial intelligence, much research is needed in order to continue to advance the field and also to evaluate the ethical and societal concerns of the existence of artificial life and machine learning.

The **Advances in Computational Intelligence and Robotics (ACIR) Book Series** encourages scholarly discourse on all topics pertaining to evolutionary computing, artificial life, computational intelligence, machine learning, and robotics. ACIR presents the latest research being conducted on diverse topics in intelligence technologies with the goal of advancing knowledge and applications in this rapidly evolving field.

COVERAGE

- Artificial Life
- Machine Learning
- Artificial Intelligence
- Automated Reasoning
- Robotics
- Brain Simulation
- Pattern Recognition
- Computer Vision
- Computational Logic
- Cyborgs

IGI Global is currently accepting manuscripts for publication within this series. To submit a proposal for a volume in this series, please contact our Acquisition Editors at Acquisitions@igi-global.com or visit: http://www.igi-global.com/publish/.

Titles in this Series

For a list of additional titles in this series, please visit:
http://www.igi-global.com/book-series/advances-computational-intelligence-robotics/73674

Handbook of Research on Thrust Technologies' Effect on Image Processing
Binay Kumar Pandey (Department of Information Technology, College of Technology, Govind Ballabh Pant University of Agriculture and Technology, India) Digvijay Pandey (Department of Technical Education, Government of Uttar Pradesh, India) Rohit Anand (G.B. Pant DSEU Okhla-1 Campus, India & Government of NCT of Delhi, New Delhi, India) Deepak S. Mane (Performance Engineering Lab, Tata Research, Development, and Design Center, Australia) and Vinay Kumar Nassa (Rajarambapu Institute of Technology, India)
Engineering Science Reference • © 2023 • 542pp • H/C (ISBN: 9781668486184) • US $350.00

Multi-Disciplinary Applications of Fog Computing Responsiveness in Real-Time
Debi Prasanna Acharjya (Vellore Institute of Technology, India) and Kauser Ahmed P. (Vellore Institute of Technology, India)
Engineering Science Reference • © 2023 • 280pp • H/C (ISBN: 9781668444665) • US $270.00

Global Perspectives on Robotics and Autonomous Systems Development and Applications
Maki K. Habib (The American University in Cairo, Egypt)
Engineering Science Reference • © 2023 • 405pp • H/C (ISBN: 9781668477915) • US $360.00

Stochastic Processes and Their Applications in Artificial Intelligence
Christo Ananth (Samarkand State University, Uzbekistan) N. Anbazhagan (Alagappa University, India) and Mark Goh (National University of Singapore, Singapore)
Engineering Science Reference • © 2023 • 220pp • H/C (ISBN: 9781668476796) • US $270.00

Handbook of Research on Deep Learning Techniques for Cloud-Based Industrial IoT
P. Swarnalatha (Department of Information Security, School of Computer Science and Engineering, Vellore Institute of Technology, India) and S. Prabu (Department Banking Technology, Pondicherry University, India)
Engineering Science Reference • © 2023 • 432pp • H/C (ISBN: 9781668480984) • US $335.00

For an entire list of titles in this series, please visit:
http://www.igi-global.com/book-series/advances-computational-intelligence-robotics/73674

701 East Chocolate Avenue, Hershey, PA 17033, USA
Tel: 717-533-8845 x100 • Fax: 717-533-8661
E-Mail: cust@igi-global.com • www.igi-global.com

Table of Contents

Detailed Table of Contents

Chapter 1

Mekala Ramasamy, Bannari Amman Institute of Technology, India
Agila Harshini T, Vellore Institute of Technology, Chennai, India
Mohanraj Elangovan, K.S. Rangasamy College of Technology, India

For a number of reasons, distributed computing is crucial to machine learning and deep learning models. In the beginning, it makes it possible to train big models that won't fit in a single machine's memory. Second, by distributing the burden over several machines, it expedites the training process. Thirdly, it enables the management of vast amounts of data that may be dispersed across multiple devices or kept remotely. The system can continue processing data even if one machine fails because of distributed computing, which further improves fault tolerance. This chapter summarizes major frameworks Tensorflow, Pytorch, Apache spark Hadoop, and Horovod that are enabling developers to design and implement distributed computing models using large datasets. Some of the challenges faced by the distributed computing models are communication overhead, fault tolerance, load balancing, scalability and security, and the solutions are proposed to overcome the abovementioned challenges.

Chapter 2

Aswathy Ravikumar, Vellore Institute of Technology, India
Harini Sriraman, Vellore Institute of Technology, India

Distributed deep learning is a branch of machine intelligence in which the runtime of deep learning models may be dramatically lowered by using several accelerators. Most of the past research reports the performance of the data parallelism technique of DDL. Nevertheless, additional parallelism solutions in DDL must be investigated, and their performance modeling for specific applications and application stacks must be reported. Such efforts may aid other researchers in making more informed judgments while creating a successful DDL algorithm. Distributed deep learning strategies are becoming increasingly popular as they allow for training complex models on large datasets in a much shorter time than traditional training methods. TensorFlow, a popular open-source framework for building and training machine learning models, provides several distributed training strategies. This chapter provides a detailed evaluation of the different TensorFlow strategies for medical data. The TensorFlow distribution strategy API is utilized to perform distributed training in TensorFlow.

Chapter 3

Balaji V., Vellore Institute of Technology, Chennai, India
Sivagami M., Vellore Institute of Technology, India

The weather data generated, processed, and collected by the sensor or shared by IoT devices and mobile devices has significantly increased weather data collection in daily life. The data generation speed also accelerated, and a vast amount of data has been collected and stored in distributed databases, improving weather forecasting. Still, the conventional processing method for massive data is distributed and centralized computing, and this chapter looks into how distributed machine learning techniques help as to increase the processing speed. Some distributed frameworks that play a significant role in massive data, like MapReduce, have been trained and tested to resolve various machine learning problems in a distributed environment. The aim of this chapter will provide different information about datasets, issues, platforms, and optimized approaches in a distributed environment. So, researchers can use and deploy new techniques in machine learning algorithms. It helps the researchers develop new strategies in distributed computing environments.

Chapter 4

Agila Harshini Thangavel, Vellore Institute of Technology, Chennai, India

The Internet of Medical Things (IoMT) collects and transfers healthcare data over the network using sensors, software applications, and Edge devices. A greater number of Healthcare devices are being manufactured and there are various challenges like Interoperability, Security, Scalability, and privacy. IoMT devices are used to monitor and deliver treatments to patients remotely. For IoMt devices to reach their full potential the challenges need to be addressed. Healthcare devices when compromised can harm patients by disrupting personal data.

Smart contactless airport baggage management and handling system is a problem solver that fits in maximum aspects of airport luggage security and management system. Thus, ensuring contactless airport management would result in Covid safety. Current baggage handling management systems (BHMS) are highly error prone. The idea proposed here ensures Covid safety and enhances the current BHMS with the power of algorithms. With the use of this software, a revolutionary idea targets the elimination of the involvement of airport staff during the check-in of a passenger. The authors have developed a system that allows every passenger to validate the details of their luggage four times and maintains security by generating a unique QR at separate checkpoints. They also developed the luggage sorting knapsack algorithm to ensure that the goods are placed efficiently and optimized in the luggage compartment.

Today every individual is expected to wear a mask, which poses a new challenge to security and surveillance of individuals for any governing body. Though notable work has been done in the area of face mask detection, there still exists a bottleneck of fast detection. Additionally, the complexity of features, size of frames, and inhomogeneity of data poses a challenge to achieve a model with high accuracy. And law offenders are quick to exploit this opportunity to their advantage. Through this work, the aim is to propose a system that combines Tiny YOLOv7 and Jestson Nano which is able to detect faces with or without mask based on the recently introduced Tiny YOLOv7 algorithm. The proposed system was able to achieve a mAP of 55.94% and an average IoU of 53.70%. The average precision achieved for people with masks was 83.80% and 79.67% for specific detection of the mask region. The model uses a total of 5.527 BFLOPs and was able to achieve an average FPS of 71.8, which ensures a higher throughput leading to a faster model both in terms of training and detection.

Stock analysis involves comparing a company's current financial statement to its financial statements in previous years to give an investor a sense of whether the company is growing, stable, or deteriorating. Stock market analysis helps in getting insights into a company's stock and to make better decisions in buying or selling shares in the stock market. This chapter proposes a method to analyze and predict stock market prices based on historical data of 4 MNCs namely, Amazon, Apple, Google, and Microsoft. The prediction is implemented using three models; namely, ARIMA model, Facebook's Prophet model, and lastly a self-constructed, stacked LSTM model. The results of the three models are compared and analyzed. Mean absolute error is used to analyze the performance of the models on real-time test data. The minimum loss achieved by Facebook Prophet Model is 2.445, by ARIMA Model is 10.782, and the Stacked LSTM Model achieved a minimum loss of 6.552.

Convolutional neural network (CNN) carries spatial information—not all nodes in one layer are fully connected to nodes in the next layer; weights are shared. The main goal of CNN is to process large image pixel matrix and try to reduce high matrix dimensions without losing information, and to simplify the network architecture with weight sharing, reducing the number of trainable parameters in the network, which helped the model to avoid overfitting and as well as to improved generalization and still to give high performance with desired accuracy. So, CNN has become dominant in various computer vision tasks and is attracting interest across a variety of domains involving image processing. This chapter focuses on the foundation of CNN, followed by architecture of CNN, activation functions, applications, and recent trends in CNN.

      Abhinav Koushik, Vellore Institute of Technology, Chennai, India
      Denisha Miraclin, Vellore Institute of Technology, Chennai, India
      Swapnil Patil, Wipro Technologies Ltd, Pune, India
      Milind Dangate, Vellore Institute of Technology, Chennai, India

Castings that are near to net forms are made using the extremely complex manufacturing technique known as die casting. Despite the method's lengthy history—more than a century—a system engineering method for characterizing it as well as the information that each cycle of die casting can create has not yet been completed. Instead, a tiny subset of knowledge deemed to be essential for die castings has attracted the attention of industry and academia. The majority of the research that has been published on artificial intelligence in die casting has a specific focus, which restricts its usefulness and efficacy in an industrial casting. This study will examine the die casting process through the perspective of systems design and show practical uses of machine learning. In terms of technical definition and how people interact with the system, the die casting process satisfies the criteria for complex systems. The die casting system is an adaptive, self-organizing network structure, according to the technical definition.

      Kiruthika V, Vellore Institute of Technology, Chennai, India
      Sheena Christabel Pravin, Vellore Institute of Technology, Chennai, India
      Rohith G, Vellore Institute of Technology, Chennai, India
      Aswin B., Vellore Institute of Technology, Chennai, India
      Ompirakash S, Vellore Institute of Technology, Chennai, India
      Danush Ram R, Vellore Institute of Technology, Chennai, India

Chatbots are becoming increasingly crucial in modern society. Typically, a large group of individuals will purchase train tickets together. This requires considerable effort and time. Multiple inquiries from a user are part of the booking procedure. In this research, the authors create an intelligent, user-friendly chatbot for booking train tickets in the native language. In this study, a Tamil-speaking chatbot is developed to assist with train ticket purchases. The authors employed NLP techniques to create an effective and user-friendly conversational interface. The above poll indicates that chatbots have been used in a variety of contexts with positive results. This method will make purchasing tickets much less of a burden for residents of remote areas, who will appreciate it. The ANN model is used to train the chatbot to discern the consumer's desires and respond accordingly. The proposed method has a success rate of 85% and will benefit consumers by expediting and simplifying ticket transactions.

Biometrics is an automatic identification of people with their physiological and behavioural characteristics. There are various modes used in biometrics, such as face, iris, retina, fingerprint, palmprint, palm vein, ear, handwriting, speech, gait, and so on. All these types of biometrics have some shortcomings. Palmprint identification is the biometric methodology used in this chapter, has several advantages over other biometric features which includes user friendliness, environment flexibility, and discriminating capacity. For several years, palmprint identification has been employed in a variety of applications. In the proposed system, the difference of block means approach is used to recognize palmprint which only requires fundamental operations (addition and subtractions), resulting in a significantly lower computing cost compared to existing systems. Even with low-resolution images, the palmprint authentication method yields substantially better results. CASIA Multispectral Palmprint database is used in the experiments. The proposed approach achieves better accuracy.

# Chapter 12

Credit scoring is used to divide applicants into two groups: those with good credit and those with bad credit. When a bank gets a loan request, borrowers with strong credit have a high likelihood of repaying debt. The likelihood of default is higher for applicants with bad credit. The profitability of financial organisations depends on the accuracy of credit scoring. Financial institutions will experience less of a loss if their credit scoring of applicants with poor credit is even 1 percent more accurate. This study seeks to solve this categorization issue by examining the risk of granting a loan to the applicant using the applicant's socioeconomic and demographic attributes from German credit data. In terms of overall accuracy, the authors evaluated the efficiency of several ML techniques like decision tree, logistic regression model, neural network, SVM, as well as random forest. The authors compared and evaluated several models for the model optimization process, integrating the impacts of balancing the AUC (area under the ROC curve)and accuracy values.

Nowadays, eye gaze tracking of real-world people to acknowledge what they are seeing in a particular page is trending; but its complexity is also growing fast, and the accuracy is not enough. In the proposed system, the image patch of the eye region is extracted from the input image using the Viola Jones algorithm for facial feature detection. Then SqueezeNet and U-Net are combined to train the model for pixel classification of iris and pupil from the eye image patch with a training dataset that contains manually labelled iris and pupil region. After extracting the iris and pupil features, the eye gaze tracking is formulated by using 2D pupil center extracted by applying Mean-Shift algorithm and 3D eyeball center. The system achieved an accuracy of 99.93% which is best comparable to the state-of-the-art methods.

Because of the subsurface's inherent geologic unpredictability, it is difficult to forecast the fate and transit of groundwater contaminants. To solve the equation for advection, dispersion, and reactivity, forecasting the flow of pollutants has been done using simplified geology and accepted assumptions. It may soon be possible to use extensive groundwater quality data from long-term polluted sites to feed machine learning algorithms that predict the spread of pollution plumes and enhance site management. The objective of this study was to first utilise extensive historical data from groundwater monitoring well samples to better understand the complex relationships between groundwater quality parameters, and then to construct a useful model for predicting the time until site closure.

Preface

Welcome to *Scalable and Distributed Machine Learning and Deep Learning Patterns*. In this edited reference book, we explore the exciting world of distributed machine learning and its applications in modern deep learning patterns. We, the editors, J. Joshua Thomas, Sriraman Harini, and V. Pattabiraman, are thrilled to present this practical guide that aims to empower machine learning professionals, researchers, and students with the knowledge and techniques needed to harness the power of distributed systems for faster model training and inference.

The field of machine learning has seen tremendous growth in recent years, with algorithms becoming increasingly sophisticated and capable of solving complex problems. However, one major challenge that has persisted is the time and computational costs associated with model training and inference. In this book, we address this challenge head-on and demonstrate how distributed machine learning can drastically reduce training times and inference latency, thus revolutionizing the way we approach machine learning applications.

Our focus in this book is on practicality. We aim to equip you with the skills to create distributed machine learning systems, including multi-node setups, using your Python development expertise. Starting with the fundamentals, we delve into how distributed systems function within the context of machine learning, and we explore their integration with cutting-edge deep learning models.

The journey begins with an understanding of data parallel and model parallel methodologies, enabling you to optimize the training and serving pipeline in local clusters or cloud environments. We leave no stone unturned as we guide you through a comprehensive exploration of bottlenecks in distributed model training and serving stages, offering instruction on the latest parallel schemes that ensure optimal performance.

Throughout this book, we emphasize hands-on learning, and we provide practical examples and case studies to illustrate the concepts discussed. We also explore the use of deep learning platforms to implement distributed model training and serving pipelines effectively. Furthermore, we delve into identifying and addressing system bottlenecks during concurrent model training and inference, ensuring that your distributed machine learning system performs at its best.

The content in this book is designed to cater to a wide range of readers. Whether you are an undergraduate or postgraduate student, a PhD scholar, an R&D professional, an industry expert, or an interdisciplinary research scholar, you will find valuable insights and techniques that apply to your specific domain. Moreover, this book serves as an indispensable resource for those involved in artificial intelligence, deep learning, and high-performance computing.

Topics covered in this book include machine learning with Spark, deep feedforward networks, convolutional neural networks, recurrent neural networks, autoencoders, generative adversarial networks, and many more. Additionally, we provide in-depth discussions on data parallelism, model parallelism, and a hybrid of both approaches, along with practical tips on hyperparameter tuning, learning rate adjustment, and model synchronization schemes.

We are confident that *Scalable and Distributed Machine Learning and Deep Learning Patterns* will be a valuable addition to your library. Whether you are a data scientist, machine learning engineer, or an ML practitioner in academia or industry, this book will help you leverage distributed systems to boost the speed and efficiency of your machine learning models.

As editors, we extend our gratitude to all the contributors who have made this book possible. We hope that you find this reference book insightful and transformative in your pursuit of advancing artificial intelligence and deep learning applications.

Let the journey into the world of scalable and distributed machine learning and deep learning patterns begin!

CHAPTER OVERVIEW

Chapter 1: Navigating the Landscape of Distributed Computing Frameworks for Machine and Deep Learning – Overcoming Challenges and Finding Solutions

In this opening chapter, authors Mekala Ramasamy and Agila Harshini T. shed light on the crucial role of distributed computing in the realm of machine learning and deep learning models. They emphasize the significance of distributed computing in overcoming several key challenges faced in modern data-intensive applications.

The chapter begins by highlighting the three fundamental reasons why distributed computing is indispensable for machine and deep learning. Firstly, it enables the training of large-scale models that cannot fit within the memory constraints of a single machine. Secondly, by distributing the computational load across multiple machines, it accelerates the training process, leading to reduced model training times. Thirdly, it facilitates the handling of vast amounts of data, which may be spread across various devices or stored remotely.

One of the significant advantages of distributed computing discussed in this chapter is its ability to enhance fault tolerance. The authors explain how, in a distributed system, even if one machine fails, the overall processing can continue without disruption, ensuring robustness and reliability.

The chapter then delves into a comprehensive summary of major frameworks such as Tensorflow, Pytorch, Apache Spark Hadoop, and Horovod. These frameworks are instrumental in enabling developers to design and implement distributed computing models, particularly when dealing with large datasets.

In addition to the benefits of distributed computing, the authors acknowledge that there are certain challenges associated with its adoption. Communication overhead, fault tolerance, load balancing, scalability, and security are among the key challenges addressed in this chapter. To provide practical solutions, the authors propose strategies to overcome these obstacles and ensure the efficient and effective implementation of distributed computing in machine and deep learning applications.

This chapter serves as a solid foundation for the subsequent chapters in the book, setting the stage for readers to understand the importance of distributed computing frameworks and the methods to address associated challenges. By exploring these concepts, readers will gain valuable insights into creating scalable and fault-tolerant machine learning and deep learning models using distributed computing approaches.

Chapter 2: Evaluation of the Distributed Strategies for Data Parallel Deep Learning Model in TensorFlow

In Chapter 2, authors Aswathy Ravikumar and Harini Sriraman focus on the domain of distributed deep learning and its potential to significantly reduce the runtime of deep learning models through the utilization of multiple accelerators. The chapter emphasizes the importance of exploring various parallelism techniques within the context of Distributed Deep Learning (DDL) to achieve optimized performance for specific applications and application stacks.

Traditionally, much of the research in the field has concentrated on the performance evaluation of the data parallelism technique in DDL. However, the authors recognize the need to investigate additional parallelism solutions and assess their effectiveness for various applications. By doing so, they aim to equip researchers with the knowledge and insights necessary to make informed decisions while designing successful DDL algorithms.

The popularity of distributed deep learning strategies is attributed to their ability to train complex models on vast datasets in significantly shorter times compared to traditional training methods. In this chapter, the authors focus on TensorFlow, a widely used open-source framework renowned for building and training machine learning models. TensorFlow provides a range of distributed training strategies, which are thoroughly evaluated and analyzed in the context of medical data.

The TensorFlow Distribution Strategy API plays a pivotal role in enabling distributed training within TensorFlow. The authors provide detailed insights into the functioning and implementation of this strategy, presenting a practical guide for readers to effectively leverage distributed deep learning with TensorFlow.

By delving into the nuances of distributed strategies for data parallel deep learning models, this chapter contributes valuable knowledge to the growing field of distributed deep learning. Researchers and practitioners interested in optimizing the performance of their deep learning models using TensorFlow will find this chapter a valuable resource. Through the authors' evaluation and analysis of various strategies, readers will gain a deeper understanding of how to apply distributed deep learning techniques to real-world scenarios, particularly in the context of medical data and related applications.

Chapter 3: A Study on Distributed Machine Learning Techniques for Large-Scale Weather Forecasting

In Chapter 3, authors Balaji V. and Sivagami M. delve into the realm of weather forecasting, where the vast amounts of data generated by sensors, IoT devices, and mobile devices have become instrumental in improving daily life. The increasing speed of data generation has led to the collection and storage of massive datasets in distributed databases, presenting new challenges and opportunities for weather forecasting.

Traditionally, the processing of such massive datasets has relied on distributed and centralized computing methods. However, the authors recognize the potential of distributed machine learning techniques to enhance the processing speed and efficiency in this context. They aim to explore and assess various distributed machine learning frameworks, with a particular focus on MapReduce, a significant player in handling large-scale data.

The central goal of this chapter is to provide valuable insights into datasets, challenges, platforms, and optimized approaches for utilizing distributed machine learning techniques in the domain of weather forecasting. By studying and presenting different methodologies and strategies, the authors seek to empower researchers and practitioners to leverage cutting-edge machine learning algorithms in distributed environments.

Through this study, the authors aim to contribute to the advancement of weather forecasting techniques and enable researchers to develop new strategies for distributed computing environments. By understanding the nuances of distributed machine learning in weather forecasting, readers can identify and deploy innovative techniques that can effectively handle the massive datasets in this field.

This chapter serves as a resourceful reference for researchers and professionals engaged in weather forecasting and those interested in leveraging distributed machine learning techniques to tackle large-scale data challenges. By adopting the insights and approaches outlined in this chapter, researchers can develop and implement new, efficient, and accurate strategies for weather forecasting in a distributed computing context.

Chapter 4: Distributed Deep Learning for Smart IoMT Challenges in the Healthcare Domain

In Chapter 4, author Agila Harshini T. focuses on the intersection of distributed deep learning and the Internet of Medical Things (IoMT) in the healthcare domain. The chapter explores the exciting potential of digital healthcare products, such as fitness trackers and heart monitors, which record real-time and biometric data. These products hold immense promise for transforming society digitally, offering faster emergency response and acute care while simultaneously reducing the energy consumption and carbon footprint of server farms.

The chapter highlights two crucial challenges in the IoMT domain: latency and cybersecurity. As IoMT devices deal with sensitive medical data and operate in real-time scenarios, minimizing latency and ensuring robust cybersecurity are of paramount importance. Traditional security mechanisms, such as encryption and multifactor authentication, can be resource-intensive in terms of energy consumption due to longer bit lengths. Additionally, storing encryption keys on devices can lead to potential compromise and security vulnerabilities.

To address these challenges, the chapter advocates for the adoption of a lightweight technique that combines energy efficiency and high security standards. By leveraging distributed deep learning methodologies, researchers and practitioners can develop innovative solutions that are well-suited for the energy-efficient and highly secure IoMT ecosystem.

By exploring distributed deep learning techniques in the context of smart IoMT devices, this chapter provides valuable insights into the future of healthcare. Readers will gain a deeper understanding of how distributed deep learning can contribute to the advancement of digital healthcare and enable the creation of efficient and secure IoMT devices. As digital healthcare continues to evolve, researchers and professionals will find this chapter an essential resource for designing cutting-edge solutions that address latency, energy efficiency, and cybersecurity challenges in the healthcare domain.

Chapter 5: Smart Distributed Contactless Airport Baggage Management and Handling System – Smart Baggage

In Chapter 5, authors Ritik Agarwal, Azam Siddiqui, Shaunak Deshpande, Nikhil Chandrashekhar Chapre, Anmol Mishra, Ansh Khattar, Aswathy Ravikumar, and Harini Sriraman present an innovative solution to revolutionize airport baggage management and handling. The chapter introduces the Smart Contactless Airport Baggage Management and Handling System, which addresses various aspects of airport luggage security and management.

The chapter emphasizes the importance of contactless airport management, particularly in light of the COVID-19 safety protocols. By reducing the need for physical interactions and minimizing the involvement of airport staff during passenger check-in, the proposed system ensures both efficiency and enhanced safety measures.

The authors highlight the limitations of current Baggage Handling Management Systems (BHMS), which are prone to errors. In response, they propose a sophisticated system powered by algorithms that significantly improves the current BHMS. The integration of smart algorithms adds a layer of intelligence to the baggage management process, optimizing operations and ensuring accuracy.

A key feature of the Smart Baggage system is its emphasis on passenger engagement and luggage security. Passengers are empowered to validate their luggage details multiple times, and the system generates unique QR codes at separate checkpoints, ensuring an added layer of security and traceability throughout the baggage handling process.

To optimize luggage compartment space utilization, the authors have also developed the luggage sorting Knapsack algorithm. This algorithm efficiently organizes and places goods within the luggage compartment, maximizing space utilization and streamlining the handling process.

The Smart Distributed Contactless Airport Baggage Management and Handling System presented in this chapter represents a comprehensive and advanced solution to the challenges faced in airport baggage management. By embracing innovative algorithms and contactless technologies, airports can enhance efficiency, security, and passenger experience.

Readers will gain valuable insights into the potential of smart distributed systems for revolutionizing airport baggage management. The chapter offers practical solutions that can be implemented to ensure a safe and seamless luggage handling process at airports, with a strong focus on the unique challenges posed by the COVID-19 pandemic.

Chapter 6: On the Detection of Faces With Mask Using Tiny YOLOv7 Algorithm

In Chapter 6, authors Akhil Kumar and Megha Singh address the pressing need for efficient face mask detection systems in the context of today's global requirement for mask-wearing. The chapter highlights the challenges faced by governing bodies in ensuring security and surveillance of individuals wearing masks. While notable work has been done in the area of face mask detection, there remains a need for fast and accurate detection methods, particularly due to the complexity of features, varying frame sizes, and heterogeneous data.

The authors propose a novel system that combines the power of the Tiny YOLOv7 algorithm with the Jestson Nano platform. This combination enables effective and efficient face mask detection, catering to real-world requirements. The system is designed to detect faces with or without masks, providing critical information for monitoring and security purposes.

The proposed system achieves commendable results, with a mean Average Precision (mAP) of 55.94% and an average Intersection over Union (IoU) of 53.70%. Notably, the system demonstrates a high average precision of 83.80% for detecting people wearing masks and 79.67% for specific detection of the mask region. These results underscore the accuracy and effectiveness of the proposed algorithm.

Furthermore, the authors emphasize the efficiency of the model, as it utilizes only 5.527 billion Floating-Point Operations (BFLOPs) and achieves an average Frames Per Second (FPS) of 71.8. This high throughput ensures faster model training and detection, making the system a practical and reliable choice for real-time applications.

By leveraging the Tiny YOLOv7 algorithm and the Jestson Nano platform, this chapter offers a robust solution to the face mask detection challenge faced by governing bodies and security agencies. The proposed system's ability to achieve accurate and fast face mask detection, along with its computational efficiency, makes it a valuable tool for ensuring compliance with mask-wearing regulations and enhancing public safety.

Readers will gain a comprehensive understanding of the Tiny YOLOv7 algorithm and its application to face mask detection. The chapter provides practical insights into building effective and efficient face mask detection systems, paving the way for improved security and surveillance in the context of mask-wearing requirements.

Chapter 7: Stock Market Analysis and Prediction Using ARIMA, Facebook Prophet, and Stacked Long Short-Term Memory Recurrent Neural Network

In Chapter 7, authors Parvathi R. and Xiaohui Yuan delve into the critical domain of stock market analysis and prediction. Stock analysis plays a pivotal role in assessing a company's financial health and growth potential, enabling investors to make informed decisions regarding buying or selling shares in the stock market. The chapter emphasizes the significance of gaining insights into a company's stock performance to facilitate better investment decisions.

The authors propose a comprehensive method for analyzing and predicting stock market prices using historical data from four multinational companies, namely, Amazon, Apple, Google, and Microsoft. To achieve this, they implemented three distinct models: the ARIMA (AutoRegressive Integrated Moving Average) model, Facebook's Prophet model, and a self-constructed, stacked Long Short-Term Memory Recurrent Neural Network (LSTM) model.

The chapter provides a detailed comparison and analysis of the results obtained from the three models. The performance of each model is assessed using Mean Absolute Error (MAE) on real-time test data. The minimum loss achieved by the Facebook Prophet Model is 2.445, by the ARIMA Model is 10.782, and the Stacked LSTM Model achieved a minimum loss of 6.552.

By leveraging these predictive models, investors and analysts can gain valuable insights into stock market trends and make data-driven decisions. The chapter's thorough analysis of the three models and their respective performances offers readers a comprehensive understanding of their capabilities and limitations in the context of stock market prediction.

The proposed method holds significant potential for enhancing the accuracy and effectiveness of stock market analysis and prediction. By leveraging historical data and advanced predictive models, investors can better navigate the complexities of the stock market and make informed investment choices.

Readers will find this chapter an invaluable resource for understanding and implementing various stock market prediction models, including ARIMA, Facebook Prophet, and stacked LSTM. The comparative analysis of the models on real-world data provides practical insights into their respective strengths and weaknesses. As a result, readers will be better equipped to utilize these models to gain actionable insights for effective stock market analysis and prediction.

Chapter 8: Convolution Neural Network – Architecture, Applications, and Recent Trends

In Chapter 8, authors Kalyanbi N. Satone, Chitra A. Dhawale, and Pranjali B. Ulhe delve into the domain of Convolutional Neural Networks (CNNs), a powerful class of neural networks designed specifically for image processing and computer vision tasks. Unlike traditional Feedforward Networks (FFNs), CNNs carry spatial information, enabling them to process large image pixel matrices effectively.

The chapter begins by highlighting the key architectural differences between CNNs and FFNs. In CNNs, not all nodes in one layer are fully connected to nodes in the next layer, and weights are shared across the network. This weight sharing simplifies the network architecture and reduces the number of trainable parameters, which, in turn, helps prevent overfitting and improves the model's generalization capabilities, leading to higher performance with desired accuracy.

The main goal of CNNs is to process large image pixel matrices while preserving important information and reducing high matrix dimensions. By leveraging convolutional layers, pooling layers, and activation functions, CNNs can efficiently process and analyze images, making them dominant in various computer vision tasks.

The chapter focuses on laying the foundation of CNNs, providing readers with a clear understanding of the fundamental concepts. Subsequently, it explores the architecture of CNNs, shedding light on how convolutional layers and pooling layers work together to extract meaningful features from images.

Activation functions, a crucial element in neural networks, are also discussed, as they play a pivotal role in introducing non-linearity and enhancing the expressive power of CNNs.

The chapter then delves into the diverse applications of CNNs, highlighting their wide-ranging utility in computer vision tasks. From image classification to object detection and semantic segmentation, CNNs have demonstrated remarkable performance and have become a go-to choice for image-related challenges.

Finally, the chapter explores recent trends in CNNs, emphasizing the ongoing advancements and innovations in this rapidly evolving field. As the demand for image processing and computer vision solutions continues to grow, CNNs remain at the forefront of research and development.

Readers will gain comprehensive insights into the architecture, functioning, and applications of Convolutional Neural Networks. The chapter serves as a valuable resource for both beginners and experts in the field, providing a solid foundation in CNNs and highlighting the recent trends that are shaping the future of computer vision and image processing.

Chapter 9: Die Casting Process Using Automated Machine Learning

In Chapter 9, author Milind Dangate explores the intricacies of the die casting process and its application in the context of automated machine learning. Die casting is a highly complex manufacturing technique used to create near-net forms of castings. Despite its century-long history, there is still a lack of a comprehensive system engineering approach to characterize the die casting process and the information generated during each cycle.

Traditionally, only a small subset of knowledge deemed essential for die castings has received attention from industry and academia. This limited perspective has restricted the usefulness and efficacy of research on artificial intelligence in die casting, particularly in industrial casting applications.

The chapter aims to bridge this gap by examining the die casting process from a systems design perspective and showcasing practical applications of machine learning. By leveraging automated machine learning techniques, researchers and practitioners can uncover valuable insights and optimize the die casting process for improved efficiency and performance.

The technical definition of the die casting process aligns with the criteria for complex systems, as it is an adaptive, self-organizing network structure. This complexity necessitates advanced approaches, such as automated machine learning, to effectively model and analyze the die casting process.

Through this study, readers will gain a deeper understanding of the die casting process and its potential applications in combination with machine learning techniques. By embracing automated machine learning, researchers can unlock new possibilities for optimizing and enhancing the die casting process, leading to more efficient and cost-effective manufacturing.

The chapter serves as a valuable resource for researchers, engineers, and industry professionals interested in the intersection of die casting and machine learning. It sheds light on the challenges and opportunities in automating the die casting process using advanced machine learning approaches, paving the way for innovative advancements in the field of manufacturing.

Chapter 10: A Chatbot-Based Strategy for Regional Language-Based Train Ticket Ordering Using a Novel ANN Model

In Chapter 10, authors Kiruthika V., Sheena Christabel Pravin, Rohith G., Aswin B., Ompirakash D., and Danush Ram R. present an innovative approach to train ticket booking using chatbots and a novel Artificial Neural Network (ANN) model. Chatbots have become increasingly vital in modern society, streamlining various processes and interactions. One such scenario is the purchase of train tickets, where a large group of individuals often book tickets together, requiring significant effort and time.

To address this challenge, the authors develop an intelligent chatbot designed to facilitate train ticket bookings in the native language, specifically focusing on Tamil-speaking users. The chatbot employs Natural Language Processing (NLP) techniques to create a user-friendly conversational interface, allowing users to interact naturally and effortlessly during the ticket booking process.

The study demonstrates the successful implementation of chatbots in various contexts with positive outcomes, validating their potential to simplify interactions and transactions for users. By enabling ticket booking in regional languages, this approach aims to alleviate the burden for residents of remote areas, providing them with a more accessible and convenient ticket booking experience.

The novel ANN model is instrumental in training the chatbot to comprehend user preferences and respond accordingly. With an impressive success rate of 85%, this chatbot-based strategy significantly expedites and simplifies ticket transactions, benefiting consumers with a seamless and efficient booking process.

This chapter offers valuable insights into the development and implementation of chatbots for regional language-based train ticket ordering. It serves as a practical guide for researchers and practitioners interested in leveraging NLP techniques and ANN models to create user-friendly and effective chatbot systems.

Readers will gain a comprehensive understanding of how chatbots can revolutionize train ticket booking processes, particularly in regional languages, catering to a wider range of users. The proposed approach showcases the potential of chatbots to enhance user experiences and streamline transactions, making it a valuable resource for those seeking to implement similar solutions in various domains.

Chapter 11: Authentication by Palmprint Using Difference of Block Means Code

In Chapter 11, authors G. Ananthi, Shenbagalakshmi G., Anisha Shruti, and Sandhiya G. present a novel approach to authentication using palmprints. Biometrics refers to the automatic identification of individuals based on their physiological and behavioral characteristics. Various biometric modes are employed, such as face, iris, retina, fingerprint, palmprint, palm vein, ear, handwriting, speech, and gait. While each biometric modality has its advantages, palmprint identification stands out in this study due to its user-friendliness, flexibility in different environments, and high discriminating capacity.

The proposed authentication system focuses on palmprint identification and utilizes the Difference of Block Means (DBM) code as its approach. This method has several advantages, as it requires only basic operations like addition and subtraction, resulting in significantly lower computing costs compared to existing systems. Additionally, the palmprint authentication method exhibits superior performance even with low-resolution images, making it a robust and efficient solution.

The authors conduct experiments using the CASIA Multispectral Palmprint database to evaluate the proposed approach's performance. The results demonstrate that the DBM code-based palmprint authentication achieves better accuracy compared to other existing methods.

This chapter offers valuable insights into the use of palmprints as a biometric authentication modality and showcases the effectiveness of the DBM code-based approach. Researchers and practitioners in the field of biometrics and authentication will find this chapter to be a valuable resource, as it presents an innovative and efficient method for palmprint identification.

Readers will gain a comprehensive understanding of the advantages of using palmprints for authentication and the practical implications of the DBM code-based approach. The proposed system's accuracy and low computing costs make it an attractive solution for various applications that require reliable and user-friendly biometric authentication.

Chapter 12: Credit Risk Analysis and Prediction

In Chapter 12, authors Akhil Raman Sarepalli and Maheshwari S. delve into the critical domain of credit risk analysis and prediction. Credit scoring plays a vital role in financial institutions, as it helps divide loan applicants into two groups: those with good credit and those with bad credit. This categorization is crucial in determining the likelihood of borrowers repaying their debt or defaulting on their obligations.

The profitability of financial organizations depends heavily on the accuracy of credit scoring. Even a small improvement in credit scoring accuracy, such as 1 percent, can significantly reduce losses for financial institutions. This study focuses on addressing this categorization issue by examining the risk associated with granting loans to applicants based on their socioeconomic and demographic attributes, using German credit data.

The authors employ various Machine Learning (ML) techniques, including decision trees, logistic regression, neural networks, Support Vector Machines (SVM), and random forests, to evaluate the efficiency of each model in credit risk prediction. They analyze the overall accuracy of these models and compare their performance for the model optimization process.

In the pursuit of creating robust credit risk prediction models, the authors also consider the impact of balancing the Area Under the ROC Curve (AUC) and accuracy values. The AUC is a crucial metric for evaluating the performance of binary classification models, and finding a balance between AUC and accuracy is essential for a well-rounded credit risk analysis.

This chapter serves as a valuable resource for researchers, practitioners, and financial institutions seeking to improve their credit risk analysis and prediction capabilities. By leveraging various ML techniques and optimizing model performance, financial organizations can make more informed lending decisions, mitigating the risk of default and improving their overall profitability.

Readers will gain comprehensive insights into the challenges and opportunities in credit risk analysis. The chapter's in-depth evaluation of multiple ML techniques and model optimization strategies provides practical guidance for implementing accurate credit scoring systems. As a result, financial institutions can enhance their risk management practices and ensure responsible lending practices.

Chapter 13: Eye Gaze Capture for Preference Tracking in a Scalable Environment

In Chapter 13, authors G. Ananthi, Shenbagalakshmi G., Pujaa M., and Amretha V. M. present a novel approach to eye gaze capture for preference tracking in a scalable environment. Eye gaze tracking, which involves monitoring the visual focus of real-world individuals on a specific page or object, is gaining popularity due to its fast-emerging applications. However, its complexity is also increasing, and achieving high accuracy remains a challenge.

The proposed system addresses this challenge by extracting the image patch of the eye region from the input image using the Viola Jones Algorithm for facial feature detection. The authors then combine SqueezeNet and U-Net to train the model for pixel classification of the iris and pupil from the eye image patch. The training dataset contains manually labeled iris and pupil regions.

After extracting the iris and pupil features, the system formulates eye gaze tracking by utilizing the 2D pupil center extracted through the Mean-Shift algorithm and the 3D eyeball center. This approach enables accurate and real-time tracking of eye gaze preferences.

The system achieved an impressive accuracy of 99.93%, comparable to state-of-the-art methods. This high accuracy makes it a valuable solution for eye gaze capture in various scalable environments, where precise preference tracking is critical.

This chapter offers valuable insights into the development of eye gaze capture systems and their applications in preference tracking. Researchers and practitioners in the fields of computer vision, human-computer interaction, and user preference analysis will find this chapter to be a valuable resource, as it presents an innovative and accurate method for eye gaze tracking.

Readers will gain a comprehensive understanding of the complexities and opportunities in eye gaze capture and preference tracking. The proposed system's high accuracy and scalability make it an attractive solution for various real-world applications, such as user preference analysis, usability testing, and interactive systems design.

Chapter 14: Groundwater Contamination Forecasting Using Automated Machine Learning

In Chapter 14, authors Milind Dangate and Deepak Chaudhari embark on the challenging task of forecasting groundwater contamination using automated machine learning. Groundwater contamination poses a significant environmental concern due to the complex and unpredictable nature of subsurface geology. Accurately predicting the fate and transport of contaminants in groundwater remains a difficult task, often requiring simplifications and assumptions.

To address this challenge, the authors propose a novel approach that leverages extensive groundwater quality data from long-term polluted sites to train machine learning algorithms. By feeding historical groundwater monitoring well samples into automated machine learning models, they aim to uncover complex relationships between groundwater quality parameters and develop a predictive model for estimating the time until site closure.

The study's main objective is twofold: first, to gain a comprehensive understanding of the intricate interplay between various groundwater quality parameters, and second, to construct a reliable model capable of forecasting the time required for site closure.

By utilizing automated machine learning, the authors aim to enhance site management practices and improve the prediction of pollution plume spread in groundwater. This approach has the potential to revolutionize groundwater contamination forecasting by harnessing the power of extensive data and sophisticated machine learning algorithms.

This chapter provides valuable insights into the application of automated machine learning in environmental sciences, particularly in the context of groundwater contamination. Researchers, environmental scientists, and professionals involved in site management and remediation will find this chapter to be a valuable resource, as it presents a promising methodology for addressing complex groundwater contamination challenges.

Readers will gain a comprehensive understanding of the potential of automated machine learning in forecasting groundwater contamination. The use of extensive historical data and machine learning algorithms holds the key to improving the accuracy of groundwater pollution plume predictions, ultimately contributing to more effective environmental management and conservation efforts.

IN SUMMARY

In closing, *Scalable and Distributed Machine Learning and Deep Learning Patterns* stands as a testament to the dynamic and transformative nature of the fields of machine learning, deep learning, and distributed computing. As editors, we take immense pride in presenting this remarkable collection of chapters, crafted by brilliant minds from around the world.

The journey through these chapters has been nothing short of inspiring, offering a glimpse into the forefront of technological advancements and novel methodologies. Each chapter has contributed valuable insights, ranging from intelligent chatbots and face mask detection to groundwater contamination forecasting and eye gaze capture. Together, they paint a vivid picture of the boundless possibilities that scalable and distributed systems offer in reshaping various industries and solving complex challenges.

As editors, we extend our heartfelt gratitude to all the authors for their dedication, expertise, and commitment to this project. Their collective contributions have created a valuable resource that will inspire researchers, practitioners, and students in their pursuit of cutting-edge solutions.

We are confident that the knowledge disseminated in these pages will propel future breakthroughs, fueling advancements in artificial intelligence, machine learning, and distributed computing. As the landscape of technology continues to evolve, we hope this book serves as a guiding light for transformative innovations across various domains.

Thank you for embarking on this enlightening journey with us. We trust that the insights gained from *Scalable and Distributed Machine Learning and Deep Learning Patterns* will inspire new ideas, collaborations, and solutions that shape the future of these dynamic fields.

J. Joshua Thomas
UOW Malaysia KDU Penang University College, Malaysia

S. Harini
Vellore Institute of Technology, India

V. Pattabiraman
Vellore Institute of Technology, India

Chapter 1

Navigating the Landscape of Distributed Computing Frameworks for Machine and Deep Learning:
Overcoming Challenges and Finding Solutions

Mekala Ramasamy
ⒾⒹ https://orcid.org/0000-0003-0889-9869
Bannari Amman Institute of Technology, India

Agila Harshini T
Vellore Institute of Technology, Chennai, India

Mohanraj Elangovan
K.S. Rangasamy College of Technology, India

ABSTRACT

For a number of reasons, distributed computing is crucial to machine learning and deep learning models. In the beginning, it makes it possible to train big models that won't fit in a single machine's memory. Second, by distributing the burden over several machines, it expedites the training process. Thirdly, it enables the management of vast amounts of data that may be dispersed across multiple devices or kept remotely. The system can continue processing data even if one machine fails because of distributed computing, which further improves fault tolerance. This chapter summarizes major frameworks Tensorflow, Pytorch, Apache spark Hadoop, and Horovod that are enabling developers to design and implement distributed computing models using

DOI: 10.4018/978-1-6684-9804-0.ch001

large datasets. Some of the challenges faced by the distributed computing models are communication overhead, fault tolerance, load balancing, scalability and security, and the solutions are proposed to overcome the abovementioned challenges.

1. INTRODUCTION

In order to get quick and precise results, significant computation must be applied to speech recognition and object recognition applications. By combining the pertinent qualities, multiscale CNNs effectively serve this type of work with less compute, fewer errors, and low memory needs. Parallel distributed training algorithms offer parallel computing for communication synchronisation, compression approaches, and system topologies, replacing the need for high processing environments like GPUs and TPUs for effective communication.

The main distributed computing frameworks in usage, issues affecting the results of distributed computing, and appropriate solutions are all covered in this chapter. The Local SGD (DaSGD with Delayed Averaging) technique is a synchronous execution model that necessitates workers to pause forward and back propagations, wait for gradients aggregated from all workers, and get weight updates prior to the next batch of jobs and offers trustworthy results.

The fundamental ideas of algorithms for deep learning and machine learning are examined one at a time before moving on to distributed computing.

Machine Learning: A subfield of artificial intelligence, machine learning enables computers to learn through data and gradually improve performance without explicit programming. It entails developing algorithms capable of seeing patterns and producing predictions or choices based on what input data they are given. These algorithms gain the ability to identify complex links and trends by being exposed to enormous datasets, which enables them to offer meaningful information and automate processes. Machine learning improves decision-making and enables computers perform jobs that used to be believed to be exclusively the domain of human intelligence in a number of industries, including banking, healthcare, marketing, and more.

Deep Learning is a specialised area of machine learning that was motivated by the neural networks in the human brain. To enable computers to learn on their own representations of data, complex simulated neural networks with multiple levels are constructed. By tackling challenging issues including image and language translation, speech recognition, and even engaging strategic games, deep learning has produced remarkable results in a variety of fields. These networks tend to be most efficient for jobs involving huge datasets because of their depth and complexity, which enable them to identify complex trends and hierarchies in data. Deep learning's capacity to automatically discover relevant characteristics from unstructured data has driven significant advances in AI and positioned it as a pillar of current machine learning research.

An approach in computer science called distributed computing makes use of numerous connected computers or other devices to operate as one cohesive system. This method allows for parallel execution and the effective use of resources by dividing and allocating tasks and processes within numerous network nodes. In order to collectively solve difficult problems that would be hard for a single machine to address, every node in the network provides its computational capacity. The application of distributed computing is widespread, with applications ranging from online services and big data processing to scientific simulations and data analysis. It offers advantages such enhanced performance, scalability, fault tolerance, and the capacity to handle challenging issues quickly compared to using a single machine. To assure the best performance and reliability, organising communication, synchronisation, and data propagation across distributed systems involves challenges that call for advanced algorithms and architectural considerations.

2. FRAMEWORKS FOR DISTRIBUTED DEEP LEARNING AND MACHINE LEARNING TECHNIQUES

2.1 Horovod and Tensorflow Frameworks for Deeplearning Models

Deep neural networks (DNNs) can be trained on big datasets using the distributed training framework presented by Alexandros Koliousis et al(2019). The approach combines Horovod, a solution for distributed training of DNNs that makes use of the cutting-edge ring-all reduce technique, with TensorFlow, a popular deep learning library. By dividing the training data among several workers, each of whom has a separate instance of the DNN model, the proposed system makes use of the power of data parallelism. Using the Horovod framework, which enables effective gradient aggregation and model update synchronisation, the workers communicate with one another. The authors demonstrate that the proposed framework significantly outperforms single-node training while maintaining high accuracy by evaluating its performance on a variety of deep learning models, such as convolutional neural networks (CNNs) and recurrent neural networks (RNNs).

The proposed framework surpasses existing distributed deep learning frameworks in terms of training time and scalability, such as the built-in distributed training in TensorFlow and the well-known All reduce-based framework, according to the authors' comparisons. Additionally, they offer helpful advice for utilising the suggested framework, such as the ideal worker configuration and batch size, and they illustrate its efficiency using a number of benchmark datasets. In conclusion, the paper introduces a helpful and effective distributed deep learning training framework that can be utilised to speed up the training of DNNs on big datasets and offers insightful information for machine learning researchers and practitioners.

2.2 Parameter Server Architecture for Distributed Learning Models

The distributed learning framework proposed by Mu li et al. (2014) uses a parameter server architecture to scale up machine learning algorithms on huge datasets. The suggested system centralises the model parameters on a parameter server rather than integrating them with the worker nodes. In order to aggregate and update the global model parameters, the parameter server receives asynchronous transmissions from the worker nodes that compute the gradients of the model parameters on their local data. The suggested framework can be utilised with a variety of machine learning algorithms, including logistic regression, support vector machines (SVMs), and deep neural networks. It is created to be scalable, fault-tolerant, and versatile.

The authors test the proposed framework's performance using a number of benchmark datasets and show that it significantly outperforms single-node training in terms of speed while retaining good accuracy. In addition, they demonstrate how the proposed framework outperforms competing distributed machine learning frameworks, such as Google's DistBelief and Apache Mahout, in terms of scalability and efficiency. The Distributed Machine Learning Toolkit (DMTK), which is open-source and freely accessible to researchers and practitioners, incorporates the suggested framework. In conclusion, the study makes a significant contribution to the field of distributed machine learning by presenting a new and efficient distributed learning framework that can be utilised to scale up machine learning algorithms on huge datasets.

2.3 DistBelief: A Framework for Distributed Deep Learning

A very scalable and effective framework for distributed deep learning is presented by Jeffrey Dean(2012), The authors contend that current deep learning models, which frequently need a lot of data and compute, are becoming increasingly sophisticated and massive, and standard deep learning frameworks are not well-suited to manage them. They suggest a brand-new framework called DistBelief to address this issue. DistBelief is made to function on massively distributed systems like clusters and data centres. DistBelief uses a variety of cutting-edge strategies, including data parallelism and model parallelism, to achieve excellent scalability and efficiency.

Model parallelism entails dividing the deep learning model among many machines, whereas data parallelism requires dividing the training data among various machines. Due to the effective distribution of compute and data across numerous machines, DistBelief is able to train large-scale deep learning models. When some of the machines malfunction while being trained, DistBelief also employs a mechanism called fault tolerance. Applying DistBelief to a variety of deep learning tasks, including speech recognition, image classification, and natural language processing, the authors show that it is effective. They contrast DistBelief's performance with that of other cutting-edge deep learning frameworks like Caffe and Theano. The authors demonstrate that, in terms of performance, DistBelief is on par with or outperforms existing deep learning frameworks.

The DistBelief framework's technical specifics are the main topic of this research. The parameter server and the workers are the two primary parts of the framework's architecture, which the authors discuss. The workers actually process the input while the parameter server keeps the model parameters and manages model updates. The communication protocols employed by DistBelief are also discussed in the paper. These protocols are designed to minimise communication overhead between the workers and the parameter server. The paper's conclusion features a discussion of DistBelief's existing limitations and potential future research options. They point out that the present DistBelief version does not scale well and does not support several deep learning models, such as recurrent neural networks.

Overall, by developing a highly scalable and effective framework for distributed deep learning, which makes a substantial contribution to the field of deep learning. The authors present evidence supporting the DistBelief framework's efficacy and offer technical information that may be useful to academics and practitioners who wish to employ DistBelief for deep learning tasks.

2.4 Horovod: Fast and Easy Distributed Deep Learning in TensorFlow

Alex Sergeev et al (2018) discusses the Horovod distributed deep learning framework, which aims to be quick, scalable, and simple to use. The Horovod framework makes use of a cutting-edge ring-allreduce method for effective gradient aggregation and synchronisation, which lowers communication costs and boosts model training's scalability. Convolutional neural networks (CNNs), recurrent neural networks (RNNs), and generative adversarial networks (GANs) are just a few of the deep learning models supported by the framework, which is also simple to combine with TensorFlow, a well-liked deep learning library. The Horovod framework achieves state-of-the-art performance in terms of training time and scalability, especially on large-scale distributed systems, according to the authors' evaluation of its performance on multiple benchmark datasets.

The authors also contrast the Horovod framework with existing distributed deep learning frameworks, such as distributed training incorporated into TensorFlow, and demonstrate how quickly and effectively it outperforms them. More specifically, they outline the ideal worker setup and batch size for the Horovod framework and show how well it performs in a variety of real-world deep learning applications, including image classification and natural language processing. In conclusion, the study makes a significant contribution to the field of deep learning by presenting a quick, scalable, and user-friendly distributed deep learning framework that can be utilised to speed up the training of deep neural networks on sizable datasets.

On heterogeneous computing systems, Venkatesh Kannan et al. (2019) presented a framework for distributed deep learning model training. To achieve great speed and scalability, the suggested framework uses a hybrid architecture that combines CPU and GPU clusters. Before proposing a communication protocol that facilitates effective data transfer and synchronisation between the clusters, the authors first provide a novel distribution approach that divides the data and the model parameters across the CPU and GPU clusters. The authors test the proposed framework's performance using a number of benchmark datasets and show that it significantly outperforms single-node training in terms of speed while retaining good accuracy.

The authors also compare the suggested framework to other distributed deep learning frameworks, such as the well-liked All reduce-based system and TensorFlow's built-in distributed training, and demonstrate that it performs better in terms of training time and scalability. A number of practical deep learning applications, including speech and picture recognition, are used to demonstrate the usefulness of the best arrangement of the number of CPU and GPU nodes. In conclusion, the paper describes a unique and efficient method for distributed deep learning model training on heterogeneous computing platforms and offers insightful information for machine learning researchers and practitioners.

2.5 Distributed Stochastic Gradient Descent (DSGD) in Deep Learning

A new technique to increase the communication efficiency of distributed stochastic gradient descent (DSGD) in deep learning is suggested by Zhengao Cai(2023)

The authors contend that because model changes are frequently sent between the workers and the parameter server, classic DSGD approaches have a significant communication overhead. They offer a communication-effective DSGD method that makes use of a cutting-edge method known as quantization-aware training to address this problem. In order to lower the precision of the model parameters and, as a result, the communication bandwidth needed to communicate them, this technique quantizes the model parameters during the training phase.

Integrating distributed stochastic gradient descent using gradient sparsification and adding a pooling operator to take into account ignored local gradient correlations is an innovative approach for improving distributed deep neural network training. The convergence rates of this approach, when added to error feedback, are comparable to those of standard SGD. Experimental results indicate significant reduction of uploaded gradient bits—up to orders of magnitude—while maintaining model accuracy for a variety of models, including CNN, LSTM, and ResNet. This innovation provides the possibility to greatly speed up training with little sacrifice in accuracy.

The authors used a variety of deep learning models to demonstrate the efficacy of this technique, obtaining notable increases in communication efficiency without sacrificing the precision of the trained models. A new communication-efficient DSGD technique, known as QSGD, is also introduced. It performs quantization-aware training utilising a stochastic gradient descent optimizer with a quantization step. The QSGD achieves significantly increased communication efficiency while keeping the same or superior convergence rates by comparing it to numerous cutting-edge DSGD algorithms. Overall, the paper offers a potential method for enhancing the DSGD's communication efficiency in deep learning, which may enable larger deep learning models to be trained more quickly and flexibly.

2.6 MXNet for Distributed Networks

A flexible and effective deep learning library named MXNet is presented by Tianqi Chen et al. (2015) and is intended to function on heterogeneous distributed networks. The authors contend that conventional deep learning libraries are inadequate to handle the growing complexity and scale of contemporary deep learning models, which call for a significant quantity of data and compute. The authors suggest MXNet, a novel framework that may operate on heterogeneous distributed systems like clusters and cloud computing platforms, in order to overcome this problem. MXNet uses a variety of cutting-edge strategies, including networked computing, multi-GPU training, and support for several programming languages, to achieve high flexibility and efficiency. Additionally, MXNet provides a hybrid deep learning approach that enables academics and industry professionals to mix imperative and symbolic programming models.Imperative programming is creating imperative code that represents the computations carried out by the model, whereas symbolic programming entails defining a computation graph that describes the forward and backward propagation of the deep learning model.

Utilising the advantages of both programming methods and achieving great flexibility and efficiency are both possible with the hybrid approach. The authors show how well MXNet performs on a variety of deep learning tasks, such as audio recognition, image classification, and natural language processing. They demonstrate that MXNet has scaling and efficiency levels that are on par with or better than those of other cutting-edge deep learning frameworks. The computation engine, the scheduling engine, the communication engine, and the storage engine are the four primary components of MXNet's architecture, which is also covered in the article. The deep learning models' actual computations are carried out by the computing engine. While the communication engine manages communication between the computers, the scheduling engine organises computation and data across numerous machines.

MXNet: makes an important contribution to the field of deep learning by offering a deep learning library that is flexible and efficient and is created to run on heterogeneous distributed systems. The authors present evidence supporting MXNet's efficacy and offer technical information that may be useful to academics and practitioners who wish to employ MXNet for deep learning tasks. MXNet is a useful tool for researchers and practitioners who want to train large-scale deep learning models effectively on heterogeneous distributed networks due to its flexibility and efficiency.

2.7 Tensorflow Framework for Machine Learning

A research paper by Martin Abadi et al. (2019) introduces TensorFlow, a scalable, adaptable, and effective machine learning framework. The authors contend that because large-scale machine learning models demand a lot of computational power, conventional machine learning methods are not well-suited to manage them. This problem is addressed by TensorFlow, which offers a scalable, distributed machine learning framework that can function on a variety of hardware, including CPUs, GPUs, and clusters. TensorFlow uses a variety of cutting-edge strategies, including data parallelism, model parallelism, and autonomous differentiation, to achieve high levels of scalability, efficiency, and adaptability. Model parallelism entails dividing the deep learning model among many machines, whereas data parallelism requires dividing the training data among various machines. TensorFlow can train large-scale machine learning models using these methods.

For the purpose of optimising the model during training, the gradients of the model parameters are computed using an automated differentiation technique. The authors use a variety of machine learning applications, including as speech recognition, image classification, and natural language processing, to show how effective TensorFlow is. They demonstrate that TensorFlow attains scaling and efficiency on par with or better than other cutting-edge machine learning systems. The dataflow graph, the execution engine, the distributed runtime, and the platform are the four primary parts of TensorFlow's architecture. The machine learning model's computation is represented by the dataflow graph, which enables effective distributed computation across various machines.

The computation is carried out by the execution engine, while machine communication is managed by the distributed runtime. The platform offers academics and practitioners a flexible and extendable interface to construct and personalise their machine learning models. The introduction of a scalable, adaptable, and effective machine learning system that can function on a variety of hardware in TensorFlow-Architecture which makes a substantial addition to the field of machine learning overall. Researchers and practitioners who desire to use TensorFlow for their machine learning jobs may benefit from the authors' demonstration of TensorFlow's effectiveness and technical specifics. For researchers and practitioners who want to train large-scale machine learning models effectively on a number of different data sets, TensorFlow is a great tool.

2.8 COTS:High Performance Computing

Deep learning on commercially available (COTS) high-performance computing (HPC) platforms is covered by Wei Tan et al. (2017). Deep learning models, according to the scientists, need a lot of processing power, and COTS HPC systems can help you get great performance at a reasonable price. Data parallelism, model parallelism, and hybrid parallelism are only a few of the distributed deep learning techniques covered in this study. Model parallelism entails dividing the deep learning model among many machines, whereas data parallelism requires dividing the training data among various machines. To take use of the advantages of both strategies, hybrid parallelism mixes data and model parallelism. The authors also go through MXNet, Caffe2, and TensorFlow, three deep learning frameworks that offer distributed training on COTS HPC systems.

The authors use COTS HPC systems to illustrate the efficiency of distributed deep learning, demonstrating that distributed training can result in noticeably quicker training periods than single-machine training. Additionally, they demonstrate how distributed training may be scaled to deep learning models and enormous datasets. The research also examines several issues and factors, including communication overhead, load balancing, and fault tolerance, while employing distributed deep learning on COTS HPC systems. According to the authors, these difficulties can be overcome by carefully planning and implementing systems and employing fault-tolerant strategies and communication protocol optimisation.

2.9 Distributed Data Parallelism in Deep Learning Using Multi-GPU

S. Zhang (2018) et al explored about the performance of data parallelism in deep learning utilising multi-GPU and multi-node training in their research work.The authors contend that data parallelism, which entails partitioning the training data among various devices and training the same model on each device, is a well-liked strategy for training large-scale deep learning models. In the research, convolutional neural networks (CNNs) and recurrent neural networks (RNNs) are used to examine the performance of data parallelism on multi-GPU and multi-node systems. The effectiveness of these strategies is assessed by the authors in terms of training time, communication costs, and scalability. The study's findings demonstrate that multi-node training for large-scale deep learning can perform better than multi-GPU training.

The authors also contend that data parallelism, which entails partitioning the training data among various devices and training the same model on each device, is a well-liked strategy for training large-scale deep learning models. In the research, convolutional neural networks (CNNs) and recurrent neural networks (RNNs) are used to examine the performance of data parallelism on multi-GPU and multi-node systems. The effectiveness of these strategies is assessed by the authors in terms of training time, communication costs, and scalability. The study's findings demonstrate that multi-node training for large-scale deep learning can perform better than multi-GPU training. The paper emphasises the potential of multi-node training to enhance the scalability and performance of deep learning models.

A unique pipeline parallelism-based strategy is described by Yanping Huang et al. (2019) for training huge neural networks, allowing for the efficient use of many accelerators to train models with trillions of parameters. The authors trained a variety of neural network models using this method, including transformer-based language models and convolutional neural networks, employing billions of parameters.

2.9.1 Parallelizing Convolutional Neural Networks

The hidden dimensions of parallelizing convolutional neural networks (CNNs) are explored by Song Han (2016). The authors contend that parallelization can offer a solution by dividing the computation among a number of processors or devices because CNNs are not well-suited to manage the growing quantity and complexity of contemporary image and video datasets.

The work investigates the hidden dimensions in CNN parallelization, that is, the aspects of computing that are not immediately apparent in the architecture of the data or the model. The channel dimension, the spatial dimension, and the batch dimension are only a few of the hidden dimensions that the authors name. The performance and scalability of CNN parallelization can be impacted by these dimensions, and the authors suggest numerous strategies to improve them.

The authors use CPU and GPU-based parallelization to show the efficacy of their methods on a number of CNN models, including VGG, ResNet, and Inception. They demonstrate how their methods can accelerate CNN parallelization by achieving almost linear speedups as the number of processors or devices increases.

In addition, the study examines a number of difficulties and factors to take into account while parallelizing CNNs, including load balancing, communication costs, and synchronisation. The authors contend that by carefully planning and implementing a system, these problems can be solved.

Overall, this work significantly advances the field of deep learning by investigating the hidden dimensions in CNN parallelization and offering solutions to enhance them. The technical information and insights presented by the authors should be useful to researchers and professionals that want to use CNN parallelization for their image and video processing activities. The study highlights how CNN parallelization can improve the usability and scalability of CNN models, but it also demonstrates the challenges that must be addressed in order to realise these benefits.

2.10 Gpipe Technique

Yanping huang et.al(2019) proposed a pipeline-like processing method, the GPipe technique which breaks the neural network into smaller micro-batches. As a result, since each accelerator is capable of processing portion of the micro-batches, many accelerators can be employed more efficiently. The usefulness of pipeline parallelism was increased by the authors' addition of dynamic pipeline scheduling, overlapping processing, and communication.

Previously thought to be impossible, training huge neural networks with billions of parameters is now possible thanks to pipeline parallelism. The authors also showed how the GPipe approach was able to achieve state-of-the-art performance on a variety of benchmarks despite its huge size.

Other researchers have been researching alternative methods for improving the efficiency and scalability of training enormous neural networks ever since the GPipe paper's release. The methods outlined in the GPipe research are anticipated to be used in future deep learning workloads as they can expedite and reduce the expense of training large models.

GPUs. Caffe-MPI uses a variety of cutting-edge strategies, including model parallelism, data parallelism, and pipelined communication, to achieve excellent scalability and efficiency. Using multiple GPUs to divide the DNN model is known as model parallelism.

2.11 Scalable Distributed DNN Training Using Commodity GPU Cloud Computing

Model parallelism divides the DNN model among numerous GPUs, as opposed to data parallelism, which distributes the training data across a number of GPUs. These two techniques effectively spread compute and data for massive DNN model training using several GPUs. Pipelined communication mixes communication and processing that might otherwise overlap in order to reduce communication overhead.

The success of Caffe-MPI is demonstrated by the authors using a range of DNN applications, including speech recognition and image classification. They show that scaling and efficiency achieved by Caffe-MPI are on par with or better than those of other state-of-the-art deep learning frameworks. The architecture of Caffe-MPI, which consists of a number of parts including a worker, a parameter server, and a communication module, is also covered in the paper. The parameter server keeps the model parameters and handles model updates while the worker uses the GPUs to perform the actual computation. The correspondence between the employees and the parameter server is handled by the communication module.

Overall, by creating a highly scalable and effective framework for distributed DNN training using commodity GPU cloud computing, " significantly advances the field of deep learning. Researchers and practitioners who want to employ Caffe-MPI for their DNN projects may find the technical information provided by the authors helpful. The authors also illustrate the efficiency of Caffe-MPI. Researchers and practitioners who want to train large-scale DNN models effectively on commodity GPU cloud computing platforms may consider Caffe-MPI due to its scalability and efficiency.

Ameet Talwalkar et al (2016) examines the difficulties and possibilities of distributed machine learning. The authors contend that distributed machine learning can offer a solution by distributing the computation and data across numerous machines. Traditional machine learning techniques, they claim, are not well-suited to handle the growing quantity and complexity of modern data sets. The paper discusses a number of difficulties with distributed machine learning, including load balancing, fault tolerance, and communication overhead. As the number of machines rises, communication overhead—the price of sending data and model updates between the machines—can create a bottleneck. The difficulty of evenly spreading computation and data across the computers to prevent underutilizing or overloading is known as load balancing.

Additionally, the authors go over a number of advantages of distributed machine learning, including the capacity to train bigger models, work with bigger datasets, and have improved accuracy. They discuss a number of distributed machine learning techniques, including asynchronous stochastic gradient descent (ASGD), model parallelism, and data parallelism. Model parallelism entails dividing the deep learning model among many machines, whereas data parallelism requires dividing the training data among various machines. In ASGD, the model is trained asynchronously on each machine without holding up the training process for the other machines to complete their calculations.

The authors also describe several distributed machine learning frameworks, such as TensorFlow, MXNet, and Caffe2, that provide support for distributed training on a variety of hardware architectures, including clusters and cloud platforms. The authors provide technical details and insights that could help researchers and practitioners who want to use distributed machine learning for their machine learning tasks. The study highlights the potential of distributed machine learning to improve the performance and scalability of machine learning models, but also emphasizes the challenges that need to be addressed to realize these benefits (A. Abirami, S. Palanikumar, 2023).

The table given below contains some state-of-the-art models or frameworks used in distributed computing.

3. APPLICATION DOMAINS OF DISTRIBUTED COMPUTING

It is widely accepted that the ImageNet Large Scale Visual Recognition Challenge is a benchmark in computer vision. To carry out object classification and detection tasks, deep neural networks must be trained and evaluated on a sizable collection of images. Large-scale model training on ImageNet needs distributed computation, and numerous research teams have deployed distributed architectures to win this battle.

i.   Transformers-based BERT (Bidirectional Encoder Representations) Pretraining:

BERT is a ground-breaking natural language processing model which succeeds in numerous NLP tasks. Training a big transformer model on a sizable amount of text data is required for pretraining BERT. Distributed computing is essential for accelerating the pretraining process because of the enormous scope of the model and the associated data set. Distributed frameworks have been deployed by research teams to train BERT on GPU or TPU clusters.

i.   Modern translation using neural machines models, such as the Transformer model, require distributed computing for training because of the model's complicated architecture and multiple concurrent corpora that are used. Although these models need a lot of computational resources, they achieve exceptional translation quality.

Table 1. Distributed computing frameworks and real-time use cases

Authors and year of Publication	Algorithm/ Framework used	Title of the work	Outcomes
Maoteng Zheng et al(2023)	Distributed bundle adjustment (DBA) method with block-based sparse matrix compression format (BSMC)	Distributed bundle adjustment with block-based sparse matrix compression for super large scale datasets	Decreases the memory constraints and runtime effectiveness for apps for retrieving images and videos
Jeroen G. S. Overschie et al(2022)	fseval,an opensource Pypi platform	fseval: A Benchmarking Framework for Feature Selection and Feature Ranking Algorithms	Enables reproducible experiments using built-in integration using a single configuration file.
Jason (Jinquan) Dai et al(2022)	Nebula-I	Nebula-I: A General Framework for Collaboratively Training Deep Learning Models on Low-Bandwidth Cloud Clusters	In Nebula-I, parameter-efficient training procedures, hybrid parallel computing techniques, and adaptive communication accelerating techniques are together applied to balance precision and communication efficiency.For jointly training deep learning models across remote heterogeneous clusters, it is accomplished utilising the PaddlePaddle deep learning framework.
Siyuan Zhuang et al	Hoplite:Task-based distributed framework	Hoplite: Efficient and Fault-Tolerant Collective Communication for Task-Based Distributed Systems	A layer of communication for task-oriented distributed systems that is effective and fault-tolerant, Asynchronous SGD, RL, and model serving workloads are accelerated by Hoplite by as much as 7.8x, 3.9x, and 3.3x, correspondingly.It promotes faster failure recovery and Low latency transfer is attained
Sandeep Singh et al	Mango	MANGO: A Python Library for Parallel Hyperparameter Tuning	The parallel hyperparameter tuning package developed for distributed computing clusters used in recent ML training pipelines. It demonstrates the abstraction offered by Mango, which makes it simple to describe intricate hyperparameter search areas, the target function, and the optimisation process.
Jiale Zhi et al(2022)	Fiber	Fiber: A Platform for Efficient Development and Distributed Training for Reinforcement Learning and Population-Based Methods	Utilising a substantial amount of heterogeneous computing gear, dynamically scaling algorithms to increase the use of resources effectiveness, and minimising the technical work necessary for making RL and population-based algorithms function on computer clusters are all things Fibre efficiently accomplishes.
Aamir Shaf et al(2021)	Dask	Efficient MPI-based Communication for GPU-Accelerated Dask Applications	On an internal cluster constructed with NVIDIA Tesla V100 GPUs for 1 to 6 Dask workers, MPI4Dask reduces the average execution times of the two programmes by 3.47 and 3.11 seconds, respectively.

continued on following page

Table 1. Continued

Authors and year of Publication	Algorithm/ Framework used	Title of the work	Outcomes
Ji Liu et al(2023)	Heterogeneous Parameter Server (HeterPS), composed of a distributed architecture and a Reinforcement Learning (RL)-based scheduling	HeterPS: Distributed Deep Learning With Reinforcement Learning Based Scheduling in Heterogeneous Environments	Utilising a reinforcement learning-based scheduling technique, each layer gets scheduled in accordance with the right kind of computing resource to save costs while maintaining the throughput limit.
Jiale Zhi et al(2020)	BigDL 2.0	BigDL 2.0: Seamless Scaling of AI Pipelines from Laptops to Distributed Cluster	It allows consumers to create end-to-end AI pipelines that can be transparently accelerated on a single node (with up to 9.6x speedup in our testing) and smoothly scaled out to a large cluster (over many hundreds of machines in practical cases) by Mastercard, Burger King, Inspur, etc.) being produced
Ming zhou et al(2021)	MALib	MALib: A Parallel Framework for Population-based Multi-agent Reinforcement Learning	Framework experiments with a variety of difficult tasks, like multi-agent According to Atari Games, MALib outperforms RLlib and OpenSpiel in multi-agent training tasks by a factor of 5 and at least 3, accordingly, on a single computer with 32 CPU cores. It results in significant levels of training task flexibility as compared to auto-curriculum policy combinations.
Liang Shen et al (2023)	SE-MOE	SE-MOE: A Scalable And Efficient Mixture-Of-Experts Distributed Training And Inference System	Elastic MoE training may effectively satisfy the requirements of NLP and CV tasks when combined with 2D prefetch, Fusion communication via Hierarchical storage, SE-MoE, MoE training, and inference system. It not only resolves the large model issue with inference and training but also provides competitive performance.

ii.   Complex mathematical models are used in climate and weather simulations, necessitating high-performance computing clusters. These models, which simulate the climate of the planet and solve partial differential equations, are essential for comprehending climate change as well as making wise policy decisions.

iii.   Particle Physics Simulations (LHC): Large volumes of data need to be processed and analysed as a result of experiments like those performed at the Large Hadron Collider (LHC). The data produced by the above experiments is processed and analysed using distributed computer grids, such as the Worldwide LHC computer Grid (WLCG).

iv.   Large amounts of genetic data are produced by genome sequencing, which must be analysed for a variety of reasons, including finding genes and genetic variants that have been related to particular diseases. For effectively processing and analysing these enormous datasets, distributed computing is essential.

v.   Simulations of autonomous cars' actions must be performed since they may act differently in various circumstances. Distributed simulators are used to model accurate traffic scenes and determine the manner in which automobiles react to other vehicles.

Nivash Jeevanantham (2023) listed the major frameworks used in current trends of distributed Computing and they are represented in the following Figure 1. Microsoft's DeepSpeed is a PyTorch-based project created for the distributed training of massive models. For models with billions of parameters, it introduces model parallelism and successfully handles memory issues by minimising computation, communication effectiveness, and memory footprint. In order to run TensorFlow on Apache Spark clusters, Yahoo developed TensorFlowOnSpark, which supports both synchronous and asynchronous development, model, and data parallelism, in addition to TensorFlow tools. Elephas is an extension of Keras that emphasises simplicity and quick prototyping for scalable distributed deep learning using Spark. Horovod streamlines distributed deep learning algorithms across GPUs or hosts and is compatible with the TensorFlow Keras, PyTorch, and Apache MXNet. A distributed deep learning language based on TensorFlow called Mesh TensorFlow (mtf) focuses on expressing and realising tensor computations across hardware. Deep learning on Apache Spark is facilitated by the BigDL framework.

4. CHALLENGES IN DISTRIBUTED COMPUTING IN ML AND DL MODELS AND SOLUTIONS

Communication bottleneck: A bottleneck may occur in the communication between various nodes or devices. This may occur when there is a significant volume of data being exchanged between nodes, which causes network congestion and increases delay. Using effective communication methods or minimising the amount of data that must be sent can help to mitigate this.

Computational bottleneck: The distributed ML devices can have an extensive range of processing power. As a result, some devices may compute their portion of the model significantly more slowly than others, creating a computational bottleneck. This can be reduced by using computing devices with comparable capabilities or by changing the workload distributed among the devices.

Figure 1. Major distributed computing frameworks used in applications

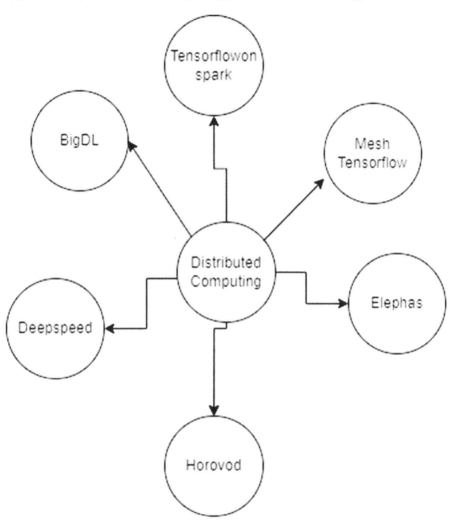

Data bottleneck: The performance of distributed ML models can be impacted by the quantity and quality of data. This may occur if certain devices only have a limited amount of data access or if the data is of poor quality. Data preparation methods ensuring that all devices have access to high-quality data can help to reduce this.

Bottleneck in synchronisation: In distributed ML, the model must be periodically synced to make sure that all devices are using the same version of the model. If the synchronisation process takes too long or if there are too many devices to synchronise, this could represent a bottleneck. By adopting effective synchronisation methods or limiting the number of devices that must be synchronised simultaneously, this can be lessened.

Security bottleneck: The adoption of encryption and other security measures might have an influence on performance. Security is a crucial factor in distributed machine learning. This can occur when there are too many devices to encrypt data for or when the encryption process takes too long. By employing effective encryption techniques or limiting the number of devices that must be encrypted simultaneously, this can be lessened.

5. ETHICAL IMPLICATIONS OF DISTRIBUTED COMPUTING

Data Privacy and Security: Data privacy and security are significant ethical issues that are raised by distributed computing, which includes processing and exchanging data across a network of connected machines. There is a higher danger of unauthorised access, breaches, or leakage as data is sent across and stored on several nodes. To protect sensitive information, it becomes essential to implement effective encryption, controls on access, and data protection laws. Maintaining data's integrity, confidentiality, and accessibility is morally right in order to maintain people's personal information safe and secure.

Impacts on Environment and Energy use: While distributed computing has an opportunity to increase resource utilisation and energy efficiency, it might have a negative impact on the environment. Large-scale networks can require an immense amount of energy resources to run, which increases their carbon footprint. It's crucial to find a balance between computing needs and environmental sustainability. We must investigate energy-efficient technologies, sources of renewable energy, and techniques to reduce distributed computing's negative environmental effects in order to ensure that technical advancements are consistent with ethical environmental behaviour.

Distributed computing can have a detrimental impact on the environment even if it has the ability to increase resource efficiency and reduce down on energy use. Running large distributed systems can require a lot of energy, increasing the carbon footprint. It's vital to strike a balance between the need for computing and environmental sustainability. In order to ensure that technological breakthroughs are in line with ethical ecological practises, we must investigate energy-efficient technologies, sources of clean energy, and mitigation methods to reduce distributed computing's environmental impact.

Ethics borders in cloud environment: In the sense that they might be interpreted in several ways, the rules are ambiguous or lack specificity. Hamith reza faragardi(2017) emphasizes the ethical concern and explained the limits in cloud domain.When there isn't any specific norm for a situation that currently arose, moral considerations become crucial. As a result, in order to reduce the ethical issues in the system, both rule-makers for Clouds and negotiators on terms and conditions agreements who are on the client side have to take into account as many situations as they can. As an illustration of this, it is likely stated in the negotiated degree of security that the provider of cloud services will notify you if someone attempts (successfully or unsuccessfully) to access user data.

Digital Divide and Fair Access: In distributed computing, the fair sharing of resources is a major ethical issue. The availability of cutting-edge hardware, fast internet, and current technology differs greatly between countries and socioeconomic levels. By limiting taking part in distributed computing efforts, the digital gap can worsen already existing disparities. The need to close this gap is highlighted by ethical issues in order to guarantee that everyone can benefit from distributed computing, regardless of the place they live or just how well equipped they are. Responsible deployment requires efforts that improve digital literacy, offer equal opportunities, and guarantee fair access.

6. SOLUTIONS FOR ADDRESSING THE CHALLENGES IN DISTRIBUTED COMPUTING

Communication bottleneck: Using effective communication protocols, such as parameter servers or all-reduce algorithms, that reduce the quantity of data that needs to be exchanged between nodes is one way to address the communication bottleneck.

Computing bottleneck: Using graphics processing units (GPUs) or other specialised hardware is a well-liked method of reducing the computational bottleneck

Data bottleneck: To reduce the data bottleneck, employ feature engineering, normalisation, and other data preprocess techniques to make sure that all devices have access to high-quality data. Using strategies like Data Parallelism, which replicates the model across many devices and trains each replica on a separate subset of data, is an additional option.

Security bottleneck: Encryption and other security measures can be used to safeguard data transmission between nodes in order to alleviate the security bottleneck.

Synchronization bottleneck: We can use asynchronous updates rather than synchronous updates to lessen the effects of the synchronisation bottleneck. As a result, each device can autonomously update its portion of the model without having to wait for other devices to finish.

7. IMPLEMENTATION OF DISTRIBUTED SENTIMENT ANALYSIS USING APACHE AS DISTRIBUTED COMPUTING FRAME WORK

The given below steps are explaining how to develop a sentiment analysis model using social media data using Apache framework.

1.   Apache Spark as a framework

Apache Spark acts as an open-source platform for distributed computing that offers high-level APIs for processing distributed data. It is made with speed, usability, and scalability in mind. The Resilient Distributed Dataset (RDD), the fundamental abstraction of Spark, is a distributed set of data that can be examined concurrently over a cluster of computers.

2.   Steps in Implementation:

Data preprocessing and partitioning in Step 1

Acquire social media data via several sources, then clean, tokenize, and get the text ready for analysis.

Reduce the preprocessed information into more manageable portions. These pieces will be distributed around the cluster via Spark.

Building the Sentiment Analysis Model in Step 2

Using labelled data, train a sentiment analysis model. Utilising machine learning algorithms such naive Bayes or support vector machines as well as Natural Language Processing (NLP) libraries like NLTK or spaCy are common techniques.

The trained model should be serialised and saved so that it may be disseminated to all Spark cluster nodes.

Spark Application in Step 3

Create a Spark application and configure it so that it can connect to your cluster.

Install the sentiment analysis model on each cluster node.

Read the preprocessed data into Spark RDDs from distributed storage (HDFS, Amazon S3, etc.).

Distributed Sentiment Analysis in Step 4

Apply the sentiment analysis model to each text input in the RDD using Spark's map transformation. Throughout the cluster, this procedure will be carried out in simultaneously.

Each text will be categorised as either good, negative, or neutral by the sentiment analysis algorithm.

Aggregation and visualisation in Step 5

Use Spark's built-in aggregation methods like reduceByKey or groupByKey to combine the results based on sentiment labels after sentiment analysis.

Bring the combined findings back to the driver nodes and generate visualisations like word clouds or bar charts using visualisation frameworks like Matplotlib and D3.js.

Code for Testing the Sentiment Analysis model

```
from pyspark.sql import SparkSession
from pyspark.ml import PipelineModel
# Initialize Spark session
spark = SparkSession.builder.appName("SentimentAnalysis").
getOrCreate()
# Load the trained model
model = PipelineModel.load("sentiment_model")
# Load new data for testing
new_data = spark.createDataFrame([
    (0, "This product is amazing"),
    (1, "I'm disappointed with the service"),
    # ... more test data
], ["id", "text"])
# Preprocessing: Tokenization and Stop Words Removal (similar
to training)
# Make predictions using the trained model
predictions = model.transform(new_data)
# Display the predictions
predictions.select("id", "text", "prediction").show()
# Stop the Spark session
spark.stop()
```

Monitoring and fault tolerance are step 6.

For tracking the development of our application, including utilisation of resources and job execution, Spark offers a web-based monitoring interface.

Spark also handles fault tolerance, improving the dependability of your distributed application by automatically rerunning failed jobs on available nodes.

8. CONCLUSION

To sum up, distributed computing has fundamentally changed how we handle and analyse enormous volumes of data, and frameworks such Hadoop, Spark, and TensorFlow taking the lead. These tools empower companies to gain new perspectives and make informed choices on an unprecedented level of scale. But even as we welcome these developments, it's critical to address ethical issues by putting in place strong security measures and encouraging responsible usage to stop misuse and violation of privacy.

Distributed computing has countless uses, from transforming industries like healthcare and banking to enriching entertainment. These frameworks are changing industries and broadening the possibilities of computation as they develop. Distributed computing sets the path for a future where complicated issues are resolved, fresh insights are found, and concerns are cooperatively managed through promoting responsible development and mitigation.

REFERENCES

Abadi, M., Agarwal, A., Barham, P., Brevdo, E., Chen, Z., Citro, C., Corrado, G. S., Davis, A., Dean, J., Devin, M., Ghemawat, S., Goodfellow, I., Harp, A., Irving, G., Isard, M., Jia, Y., Jozefowicz, R., Kaiser, L., Kudlur, M., & Zheng, X. (2016). TensorFlow: A System for Large-Scale Machine Learning. *Journal Name: Proceedings of the 12th USENIX Symposium on Operating Systems Design and Implementation* (OSDI '16) .

Abirami, A., & Palanikumar, S. A hybrid big-bang big-crunch optimization and deliberated deep reinforced learning mechanisms for cyber-attack detection. Computers and Electrical Engineering, Volume :109, Part B, 108773, 2023, ISSN 0045-7906, https://doi.org/ doi:10.1016/j.compeleceng.2023.108773

CaiZ.ChenA.LuoY.LiJ.T. "Communication-Efficient Distributed Stochastic Gradient Descent with Pooling Operator" Journal name:SSRN Year of Publication: 2023

Chen, T., Li, M., Li, Y., Lin, M., Wang, N., Wang, M., Xiao, T., Xu, B., Zhang, C., & Title, Z. Z. "MXNet: A Flexible and Efficient Machine Learning Library for Heterogeneous Distributed Systems" Journal Name: Proceedings of the 2015 ACM Symposium on Cloud Computing (SoCC '15) Volume: N/A Issue: N/A Year of Publication: 2015 Pages: 1-13

Jason Dai, Ding Ding, Dongjie Shi, Shengsheng Huang, Jiao Wang, Xin Qiu, Kai Huang, Guoqiong Song, Yang Wang, Qiyuan Gong, Jiaming Song, Shan Yu, Le Zheng, Yina Chen, Junwei Deng, Ge Song Title: BigDL 2.0: Seamless Scaling of AI Pipelines from Laptops to Distributed Cluster, Journal name: arXiv Volume:2204.01715 Year of Publication:2022

Dean, J., Corrado, G., Monga, R., Chen, K., Devin, M., & Mao, M. Marc'Aurelio Ranzato, Andrew Senior, Paul Tucker, Ke Yang, Quoc V. Le, and Andrew Y. Ng Title: "DistBelief: A Framework for Distributed Deep Learning" Journal Name: Proceedings of the 26th International Conference on Neural Information Processing Systems (NIPS '12) Volume: N/A Issue: N/A Year of Publication: 2012 Pages: 1-9

Faragardi HR. Title: Ethical Considerations in Cloud Computing Systems. Journal name: Proceedings. Year of Publication: 2017

Han, S., Mao, H., & Dally Title, W. J. "Exploring Hidden Dimensions in Parallelizing Convolutional Neural Networks" Journal Name: Proceedings of the 2016 ACM International Conference on Multimedia (MM '16) Volume: N/A Issue: N/A Year of Publication: 2016 Pages: 689-698

Yanping Huang, Youlong Cheng, Ankur Bapna, Orhan Firat, Derek Gilpin, and Mostafa Dehghani,"GPipe: Efficient Training of Giant Neural Networks using Pipeline Parallelism", Year of Publication: 2019

Kannan, V., Vijaykumar, N., & Title, G. J. "Towards Distributed Training of Deep Learning Models on Heterogeneous Computing Platforms" Journal Name: *Proceedings of the 33rd IEEE International Parallel and Distributed Processing Symposium Workshops (IPDPSW '19)*, 2019, Pages: 1109-1116

Alexandros Koliousis, Ilias Katsaroumpas, Peter Pietzuch, and Vladimir Vlassov Title: "Distributed Deep Learning Using TensorFlow and Horovod" IEEE Transactions on Parallel and Distributed Systems Volume: 30 Issue: 7 Year of Publication: 2019 Pages: 1533-1545

Li, M., Andersen, D. G., Smola, A., & Title, K. Y. "Scaling Distributed Machine Learning with the Parameter Server" Journal Name: Proceedings of the 11th USENIX Symposium on Operating Systems Design and Implementation (OSDI '14) Volume: N/A Issue: N/A Year of Publication: 2014 Pages: 583-598

Ji Liu, Zhihua Wu, Danlei Feng, Minxu Zhang, Xinxuan Wu, Xuefeng Yao, Dianhai Yu, Yanjun Ma, Feng Zhao and Dejing Dou Title:"HeterPS: Distributed deep learning with reinforcement learning based scheduling in heterogeneous environments" Journal name:Future Generation Computer Systems,Volume:148,Year of Publication:2023,Pages 106-117

Jeroen G. S. Overschie, Ahmad Alsahaf and George Azzopardi, " fseval: A Benchmarking Framework for Feature Selection and Feature Ranking Algorithms, Journal of Open Source software,Volume:7(79) Year of Publication: 2023

Sandha, S. S., Aggarwal, M., Fedorov, I., & Srivastava, M. Title: MANGO: A Python Library for Parallel Hyperparameter Tuning IEEE Proceedings ICASSP 2020, Year of Publication: 2021

Sergeev, A., Del Balso, M., Johnson, M., Ramanujam, N., Wang, T., Wang, Z., & Re, C. H. "Horovod: Fast and Easy Distributed Deep Learning in TensorFlow", Proceedings of the 2018 ACM SIGMOD International Conference on Management of Data (SIGMOD '18), Year of Publication: 2018,Pages: 27-39

Liang Shen, Zhihua Wu, WeiBao Gong, Hongxiang Hao, Yangfan Bai, HuaChao Wu, Xinxuan Wu, Jiang Bian, Haoyi Xiong, Dianhai Yu, Yanjun Ma Title:"SE-MOE: A Scalable And Efficient Mixture-Of-Experts Distributed Training And Inference System" Journal name: arXiv Volume:2205.10034 Year of Publication:2023

Ameet Talwalkar, Virginia Smith, Michael Jordan Title: "Distributed Machine Learning: Challenges and Opportunities" Journal Name: IEEE Big Data Volume: N/A Issue: N/A Year of Publication: 2016 Pages: 1-10

Tan, W., Wei, T., & Mailthody Title, V. S. "Deep Learning with COTS HPC Systems: Distributed Strategies and Frameworks" Journal Name: Proceedings of the 2017 ACM International Conference on Supercomputing (ICS '17) Volume: N/A Issue: N/A Year of Publication: 2017 Pages: 56-67

Yifei Wang, Wei Zhang, Jun Yuan, Xiaolong Wang, and Jie Liu Title: "Scalable Distributed DNN Training Using Commodity GPU Cloud Computing" Journal Name: IEEE Transactions on Parallel and Distributed Systems Volume: 30 Issue: 8 Year of Publication: 2019 Pages: 1813-1827

Yang Xiang, Zhihua Wu, Weibao Gong, Siyu Ding, Xianjie Mo, Yuang Liu, Shuohuan Wang, Peng Liu, Yongshuai Hou, Long Li, Bin Wang, Shaohuai Shi, Yaqian Han, Yue Yu, Ge Li, Yu Sun, Yanjun Ma, Dianhai Yu Title: "Nebula-I: A General Framework for Collaboratively Training Deep Learning Models on Low-Bandwidth Cloud Clusters" Journal Name: arXiv Volume:2205.09470 Year of Publication: 2022

Zhang, S., Yao, Z., Xu, S., Xu, S., Huang, J., Wang, Y., Zhang, C., & Zhuang, Y. (2018). Exploiting Data Parallelism in Deep Learning: A Comparative Study of Multi-GPU and Multi-Node Training. *IEEE Transactions on Parallel and Distributed Systems Volume*, 29(11), 2527–2540. doi:10.1109/TPDS.2018.2840098

Zhang, W., Iqbal, S., Wu, S., Zhang, J., Bao, Y., Huang, C., Zhan, J., & Title, D. Q. (2018, November). Scalable Distributed DNN Training Using Commodity GPU Cloud Computing. *Journal Name:IEEE Transactions on Parallel and Distributed Systems Volume*, 29(11), 2427–2442.

Zheng, M., Chen, N., Zhu, J., Zeng, X., Qiu, H., Jiang, Y., Lu, X., & Qu, H. Distributed bundle adjustment with block-based sparse matrix compression for super large scale datasets" arXiv:2307.08383 Year of Publication: 2023

Zhi, J., Wang, R., Clune, J., & Stanley, K. O. Title:"Fiber: A Platform for Efficient Development and Distributed Training for Reinforcement Learning and Population-Based Methods"Journal name: arXiv Volume:2003.11164 Year of Publication:2020 A. Shafi, J. Hashmi, H. Subramoni and D. Panda, Title:"Efficient MPI-based Communication for GPU-Accelerated Dask Applications"Journal name: 2021 IEEE/ACM 21st International Symposium on Cluster, Cloud and Internet Computing (CCGrid) Year of Publication: 2021, Pages: 277-286

Ming Zhou, Ziyu Wan, Hanjing Wang, Muning Wen, Runzhe Wu, Ying Wen, Yaodong Yang, Weinan Zhang, Jun Wang Title:"MALib: A Parallel Framework for Population-based Multi-agent Reinforcement Learning", Journal name: arXiv Volume:2106.07551 Year of Publication:2022

Siyuan Zhuang, Zhuohan Li, Danyang Zhuo, Stephanie Wang, Eric Liang, Robert Nishihara, Philipp Moritz, Ion Stoica, Title:Hoplite: efficient and fault-tolerant collective communication for task-based distributed systems SIGCOMM 2021 Year of Publication: 2021 Pages 641–656

Chapter 2
Evaluation of the Distributed Strategies for Data Parallel Deep Learning Model in TensorFlow

Aswathy Ravikumar

https://orcid.org/0000-0003-0897-6991
Vellore Institute of Technology, India

Harini Sriraman

https://orcid.org/0000-0002-2192-8153
Vellore Institute of Technology, India

ABSTRACT

Distributed deep learning is a branch of machine intelligence in which the runtime of deep learning models may be dramatically lowered by using several accelerators. Most of the past research reports the performance of the data parallelism technique of DDL. Nevertheless, additional parallelism solutions in DDL must be investigated, and their performance modeling for specific applications and application stacks must be reported. Such efforts may aid other researchers in making more informed judgments while creating a successful DDL algorithm. Distributed deep learning strategies are becoming increasingly popular as they allow for training complex models on large datasets in a much shorter time than traditional training methods. TensorFlow, a popular open-source framework for building and training machine learning models, provides several distributed training strategies. This chapter provides a detailed evaluation of the different TensorFlow strategies for medical data. The TensorFlow distribution strategy API is utilized to perform distributed training in TensorFlow.

DOI: 10.4018/978-1-6684-9804-0.ch002

INTRODUCTION

Deep learning has emerged as an effective method for dealing with a wide variety of challenging issues in a variety of fields, including machine vision, natural language processing, and recognition of speech, to name a few (Baby, 2014; Harini et al., 2022; John et al., 2021; Ravikumar et al., 2022; Robin et al., 2021). As deep learning models have increased in size and complexity over the past few years, it has become increasingly clear how essential it is to make use of distributed computing platforms to effectively train these models. According to Abadi et al. (2016), TensorFlow, considered one of the most renowned deep learning frameworks, provides customers with a distributed computing API. Thanks to this API, users can train large models in a distributed manner using several machines.

TensorFlow is widely employed in a wide variety of fields because to the numerous benefits it offers in deep learning (Muhammad Jaleed Khan et al., 2018; Zhang & Wei, 2020). This is because TensorFlow can be applied to a large range of problems. This is because Google was the one that initially built TensorFlow. On the other hand, TensorFlow is highly restricted for a single processing node, particularly when the size of the data set rises (Andrade & Trabasso, 2017; Bekeneva et al., 2020). As the size of the data set grows, the limits of TensorFlow become more and more apparent. How to overcome this barrier for TensorFlow to expand efficiently on ultra-large-scale systems, enhance the training pace of deep learning through parallelism, minimize the time required for training, improve the accuracy of both training and testing and apply deep learning to new domains. Sk et al. (2017) and Zhang et al. (2019) found that it significantly impacts the solving of challenging situations, which can have far-reaching implications.

Distributed data parallelism and distributed strategies are important concepts in machine learning when working with large datasets that cannot be processed on a single machine (Dean et al., n.d.). In TensorFlow, these concepts are implemented to enable training of machine learning models on distributed systems. Distributed data parallelism is a technique used to distribute the training of a model across multiple devices or machines. This is achieved by breaking the input data into multiple pieces and processing them in parallel on each device or machine. The model weights are then averaged across all devices or machines to produce the final model. Distributed strategies in TensorFlow are a set of tools and techniques used to distribute training and inference across multiple devices or machines. These strategies include data parallelism, model parallelism, and parameter servers. Data parallelism involves distributing the input data across multiple devices or machines and training the model on each device or machine. Model parallelism(Chen et al., 2019) involves distributing the model across multiple devices or machines and training different parts of the model on each device or machine. Parameter servers

(Li et al., n.d.)involve separating the model parameters from the computation and storing them on separate devices or machines. Using distributed data parallelism and distributed strategies in TensorFlow can greatly speed up the training of machine learning models and enable training on large datasets that would otherwise not be feasible on a single machine.

In this chapter, we will evaluate various distributed strategies for data parallelism in TensorFlow. Data parallelism is a common technique used in distributed deep learning, where large datasets are partitioned across multiple machines and each machine trains the model on a subset of the data. We will explore different strategies for data parallelism in TensorFlow, including synchronous and asynchronous training, and evaluate their performance on a large-scale deep learning model. Our aim is to provide insights into the strengths and weaknesses of each strategy, and help users choose the most appropriate strategy for their specific use case.

DISTRIBUTED AND PARALLEL COMPUTING

Distributed computing is a technique that allows a group of computers to work together in a coordinated manner to solve a common problem, rather than relying on a single large computer. This approach divides a task into smaller subtasks that are then distributed to multiple computers. The computers work on their assigned subtasks and send their results back to a central controller, which combines the results to produce the final output. This technique offers benefits such as improved performance, reliability, scalability, and fault tolerance of computing systems. It allows computing resources to be scaled up or down as per demand and is particularly useful for large-scale data processing and computationally intensive tasks. Distributed computing systems such as clusters, grids, and cloud computing platforms require specialized software and hardware to ensure effective communication and management of the distributed environment.

Parallel computing is another type of computing where multiple processors or computing units work together to solve a computational problem. It involves breaking a large problem into smaller sub-problems that can be solved simultaneously, and then combining the results to produce a final solution. Parallel computing can be achieved through various approaches, including shared-memory multiprocessing, distributed-memory multiprocessing, and GPU acceleration. Shared-memory multiprocessing involves multiple processors accessing a shared memory space, while distributed-memory multiprocessing involves multiple processors working on separate memory spaces that communicate through a network. GPU acceleration involves using the graphics processing unit to offload certain types of computations that are optimized for certain types of calculations.

Parallel computing finds applications in various fields such as scientific simulations, data analysis, and machine learning, to name a few. It offers significant performance improvements over serial computing, especially for problems that involve large datasets or complex calculations. However, implementing parallel computing can be a challenging task that requires careful consideration of factors such as load balancing, data partitioning, and communication overhead. To take advantage of parallel computing, software developers need to use specialized libraries and frameworks such as MPI (Message Passing Interface), OpenMP, and CUDA. These tools provide the necessary abstractions and APIs for managing parallelism and ensuring that multiple processors or computing units work together efficiently.

DISTRIBUTED DEEP LEARNING

Distributed deep learning is a subfield of deep learning that involves training deep neural networks across multiple machines or devices in a distributed computing environment. The goal of distributed deep learning is to reduce the time and resources required to train large and complex models by allowing the workload to be split across multiple machines or devices (Bekeneva et al., 2020; Ben-Nun & Hoefler, 2018; Dai et al., 2019).

Figure 1. Distributed computing

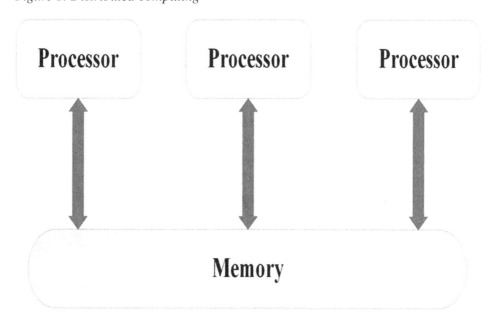

Figure 2. Parallel computing

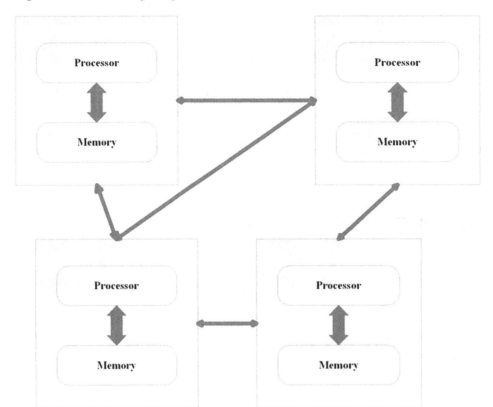

Distributed deep learning requires specialized software and hardware to manage the distributed environment and ensure that the different components of the system are communicating and working together effectively. Some popular frameworks for distributed deep learning include TensorFlow (Abadi et al., n.d.), PyTorch, and Horovod (Sergeev & Del Balso, 2018).

Distributed deep learning has many benefits, including the ability to train larger and more complex models, faster training times, and the ability to process larger datasets. However, it also has its challenges, including increased communication overhead and the need for careful load balancing and fault tolerance to ensure that the distributed system remains stable and efficient(Ravikumar et al., 2023; Ravikumar & Sriraman, 2023a).

In this chapter we will be exploring more about data parallelism and the different distributed strategies in TensorFlow.

Data Parallelism

Data parallelism is a technique used in distributed computing and deep learning to train machine learning models on large datasets. In data parallelism, the data is split across multiple machines or devices, and each machine or device trains a copy of the model on its assigned subset of the data.

The goal of data parallelism is to accelerate the training process and reduce the time required to train large models by allowing the workload to be split across multiple machines or devices. This technique is particularly useful when the dataset is too large to fit into memory on a single machine or device.

Data parallelism requires specialized software and hardware to manage the distributed environment and ensure that the different components of the system are communicating and working together effectively. Some popular frameworks for data parallelism include TensorFlow, PyTorch, and Horovod.

Data parallelism has many benefits, including faster training times and the ability to process larger datasets. However, it also has its challenges, including increased communication overhead and the need for careful load balancing and fault tolerance to ensure that the distributed system remains stable and efficient.

Synchronous and asynchronous data parallelism are two common approaches to parallelize deep learning models across multiple devices or processors in a distributed computing environment (Ravikumar & Sriraman, 2023b, 2023c).

Synchronous data parallelism is a technique where multiple devices or processors work together to compute the gradients for a batch of data in parallel, but they wait for all the gradients to be computed before updating the model parameters. In synchronous data parallelism, the batch size is typically divided equally among the devices, and each device computes the forward and backward passes independently. Once all the devices have computed the gradients, they are averaged, and the model parameters are updated accordingly. Synchronous data parallelism is easy to implement and guarantees that all devices have the same model parameters at any given time.

Asynchronous data parallelism is a technique where multiple devices or processors work independently to compute the gradients for different batches of data, and they update the model parameters as soon as they compute the gradients. In asynchronous data parallelism, there is no need to wait for all the gradients to be computed, and each device may have a different version of the model parameters at any given time. Asynchronous data parallelism can be more efficient than synchronous data parallelism when there are significant variations in the time required to compute gradients for different batches of data.

Both synchronous and asynchronous data parallelism have their advantages and disadvantages, and the choice between them depends on the specific requirements of the deep learning application and the available computing resources.

DISTRIBUTED STRATEGIES IN TENSOR FLOW

Distributed training in TensorFlow involves splitting a large dataset and distributing the training workload across multiple devices or machines to accelerate the training process. Distributed training is particularly useful for training large-scale machine learning models, such as deep neural networks, on large datasets. TensorFlow supports distributed training through its TensorFlow Distributed API, which provides several strategies for distributing training across multiple devices or machines. These strategies include data parallelism, model parallelism, and a combination of the two.

Data parallelism involves replicating the model across multiple devices or machines and splitting the training data across them. Each device or machine trains on a different portion of the data and updates the model parameters in parallel, which accelerates the training process. Model parallelism, on the other hand, involves splitting the model across multiple devices or machines and computing the forward and backward passes in parallel. To use the TensorFlow Distributed API, you will need to set up a TensorFlow cluster, which consists of one or more TensorFlow servers and one or more TensorFlow clients. The servers handle the distribution of training across devices or machines, while the clients submit the training jobs to the cluster. Once the cluster is set up, you can use the Distributed API to define the model and the distribution strategy. TensorFlow will then automatically distribute the training workload across the devices or machines in the cluster and aggregate the results to update the model parameters.

Tensorflow Distributed Architecture

TensorFlow has a distributed architecture that enables the training of large-scale models across multiple devices, such as GPUs or CPUs. The distributed architecture of TensorFlow provides several benefits, including increased computation power, reduced training time, and better model accuracy.

The distributed architecture of TensorFlow consists of the following components:

Parameter Server: The parameter server stores and manages the parameters of the machine learning model. It receives updates from the workers and distributes the updated parameters to all workers **(Li, 2014)**.

Workers: The workers are responsible for executing the computations of the machine learning model. Each worker runs a copy of the model and communicates with the parameter server to update and retrieve the parameters.

Cluster Manager: The cluster manager is responsible for managing the communication between the parameter server and the workers. It ensures that the workers are synchronized and that the model is trained efficiently.

Master: The master is a special type of worker that controls the training process. It is responsible for creating and managing the workers, as well as monitoring the training process.

TensorFlow provides several APIs for implementing the distributed architecture, including the tf.distribute.Strategy API, which enables distributed training across multiple devices. The tf.estimator API provides a high-level interface for training and evaluating TensorFlow models using a distributed architecture.

Environment Configuration

The experimental setup for implementing the distributed strategies was done in Colab GPU using MNIST dataset for a novel CNN designed. Colab GPU (Graphics Processing Unit) is a cloud-based GPU provided by Google Colaboratory (Colab) that allows users to run deep learning models and other computationally intensive tasks. Colab GPU offers several benefits for deep learning tasks, such as faster training times and the ability to handle larger datasets. Colab provides access to a single NVIDIA Tesla K80 GPU with 12GB of VRAM, or a single NVIDIA Tesla T4 GPU with 16GB of VRAM, depending on availability. Users can access the Colab GPU by creating a new notebook and selecting "GPU" as the hardware accelerator. The GPU can then be used to train deep learning models in frameworks such as TensorFlow and PyTorch. Colab also supports distributed training using TensorFlow's tf.distribute API, which allows users to train models on multiple GPUs or TPUs.

To configure a Google Colab GPU for running distributed strategies in TensorFlow on the MNIST dataset for a Convolutional Neural Network (CNN), you can follow these steps:

- First, ensure that you are using a GPU runtime in Google Colab. You can check this by going to "Runtime" in the menu bar and selecting "Change runtime type." Then, choose "GPU" from the "Hardware accelerator" dropdown.
- Install TensorFlow and other required packages. Import the necessary libraries.

Figure 3. Importing libraries

```
import tensorflow_datasets as tfds
import tensorflow as tf
import os
```

- Load the MNIST dataset and prepare it for training. The MNIST dataset has been widely used in the development and testing of image classification algorithms, particularly in the context of deep learning and CNN.

Figure 4. Data preparation

```
datasets, info = tfds.load(name='mnist', with_info=True, as_supervised=True)
mnist_train, mnist_test = datasets['train'], datasets['test']
# You can also do info.splits.total_num_examples to get the total number of examples in the dataset.
num_train_examples = info.splits['train'].num_examples
num_test_examples = info.splits['test'].num_examples
```

- Define the distributed strategy.
- Build the CNN model-Note that we are using the strategy.scope() context manager to define the model, which ensures that the model is replicated across all available GPUs.

Figure 5. CNN model

```
Model: "sequential_1"
```

Layer (type)	Output Shape	Param #
conv2d_1 (Conv2D)	(None, 26, 26, 32)	320
max_pooling2d_1 (MaxPooling 2D)	(None, 13, 13, 32)	0
flatten_1 (Flatten)	(None, 5408)	0
dense_2 (Dense)	(None, 64)	346176
dense_3 (Dense)	(None, 10)	650

```
Total params: 347,146
Trainable params: 347,146
Non-trainable params: 0
```

- Train the model

Figure 6. Model fitting

```
model.fit(train_dataset, epochs=EPOCHS, callbacks=callbacks)
```

- Evaluate the model:

Figure 7. Model evaluation

```
eval_loss, eval_acc = model.evaluate(eval_dataset)
print('Eval loss: {}, Eval accuracy: {}'.format(eval_loss, eval_acc))
```

Strategies

The DistributionStrategy API facilitates the distribution of training duties across multiple computers. The DistributionStrategy API is intended to grant the use of current models and code. To facilitate distributed training, users only need minimal modifications to models and code (***TensorFlow*, n.d.**). tf.distribute.Strategy is the primary distributed training technique in TensorFlow. This method allows you to distribute the training of your model across multiple devices. It is designed to be simple to use, to provide effective out-of-the-box performance, and to facilitate easy strategy switching.

Mirrored Strategy

tf.distribute.MirroredStrategy makes it possible to execute synchronous, distributed instructions across multiple GPUs that are located on a single computer. It produces one copy of the model for each GPU device in the system. Each replica contains a copy of all of the model's variables. These variables, when taken as a whole, make up the concept variable known as MirroredVariable. Applying identical changes helps to preserve the alignment of these variables.

The utilization of effective all-reduce algorithms allows for the transmission of variable changes between devices. The all-reduce operation combines tensors on all devices, making them available on those devices. It is a combined strategy that is exceptionally effective and has the potential to cut synchronization overhead by a significant amount. Numerous all-reduce algorithms and implementations are available, and their availability is contingent on the connection between the devices. The default all-reduce implementation for NVIDIA GPUs is the NVIDIA NCCL library. In addition, the user has the choice of choose one of a few extra solutions or coming up with their own unique solution to the problem. The tf.distribute operation, as well as the HierarchicalCopyAllReduce one.In addition to the tf.distribute option, the ReductionToOneDevice option includes two other possibilities.By default, the approach used is called NcclAllReduce.

Multiworker Mirrored Strategy

tf.distribute.MultiWorkerMirroredStrategy closely resembles MirroredStrategy. It employs synchronous distributed training across a number of agents, each of which may possess multiple GPUs. It utilizes CollectiveOps for the multi-worker communication system for synchronizing variables. Multi-worker configuration is one of the most notable differences between multi-worker and multi-GPU training.

Figure 8. Mirrored strategy working

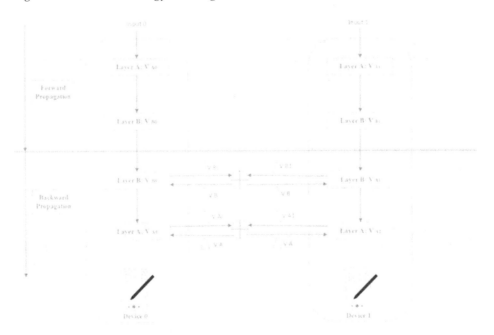

Figure 9. Mirrored strategy code snippet

```
strategy = tf.distribute.MirroredStrategy()
with strategy.scope():
  model = tf.keras.Sequential([
      tf.keras.layers.Conv2D(32, 3, activation='relu', input_shape=(28, 28, 1)),
      tf.keras.layers.MaxPooling2D(),
      tf.keras.layers.Flatten(),
      tf.keras.layers.Dense(64, activation='relu'),
      tf.keras.layers.Dense(10)
  ])
```

The "TF_CONFIG" environment variable in TensorFlow is the standard technique for assigning the cluster configuration to each worker in the cluster.

Central Storage Strategy

Synchronous training is available through CentralStorageStrateg. Variables are not copied; rather, they are stored on the central processing unit and operations are reproduced on each local graphics processing unit. If there is only one GPU available, then that GPU will be given responsibility for all of the variables and operations. This will produce an instance of the Central storage strategy that makes full use of all of the available processing power (including CPU and GPU). The aggregation of changes to variables on duplication will take place before the application.

One Device Strategy

tf.distribute.OneDeviceStrategy is a storage strategy that stores every variable and computation on one device. In OneDeviceStrategy, all variables generated within its scope are explicitly set on the fixed device.

Figure 10. Multi worker mirrored strategy code snippet

```
strategy = tf.distribute.MultiWorkerMirroredStrategy()
with strategy.scope():
  model = tf.keras.Sequential([
      tf.keras.layers.Conv2D(32, 3, activation='relu', input_shape=(28, 28, 1)),
      tf.keras.layers.MaxPooling2D(),
      tf.keras.layers.Flatten(),
      tf.keras.layers.Dense(64, activation='relu'),
      tf.keras.layers.Dense(10)
  ])
```

Figure 11. Central storage strategy code snippet

```
strategy = tf.distribute.experimental.CentralStorageStrategy()
with strategy.scope():
  model = tf.keras.Sequential([
      tf.keras.layers.Conv2D(32, 3, activation='relu', input_shape=(28, 28, 1)),
      tf.keras.layers.MaxPooling2D(),
      tf.keras.layers.Flatten(),
      tf.keras.layers.Dense(64, activation='relu'),
      tf.keras.layers.Dense(10)
  ])
```

Figure 12. One device strategy code snippet

```
strategy = tf.distribute.OneDeviceStrategy(device="/gpu:0")
with strategy.scope():
  model = tf.keras.Sequential([
      tf.keras.layers.Conv2D(32, 3, activation='relu', input_shape=(28, 28, 1)),
      tf.keras.layers.MaxPooling2D(),
      tf.keras.layers.Flatten(),
      tf.keras.layers.Dense(64, activation='relu'),
      tf.keras.layers.Dense(10)
  ])
```

Parameter Server Strategy

A popular data-parallel method for improving model training on different devices at the same time is using parameter server training. Employees and parameter servers comprise a training cluster for parameter servers. Variables are created on parameter servers, and employees at each phase read and modify them.

Figure 13. Parameter server strategy code snippet

```
    tf.distribute.cluster_resolver.TFConfigClusterResolver(),
    variable_partitioner=variable_partitioner)
 coordinator = tf.distribute.experimental.coordinator.ClusterCoordinator(
    strategy)
with strategy.scope():
  model = tf.keras.Sequential([
      tf.keras.layers.Conv2D(32, 3, activation='relu', input_shape=(28, 28, 1)),
      tf.keras.layers.MaxPooling2D(),
      tf.keras.layers.Flatten(),
      tf.keras.layers.Dense(64, activation='relu'),
      tf.keras.layers.Dense(10)
  ])
```

TPU Strategy

Tensor Processing Units (TPUs) are Google's custom-developed application-specific integrated circuits (ASICs) used to accelerate machine learning workloads. They are designed to speed up matrix operations, which are central to neural network computations. TensorFlow provides high-level APIs to leverage TPUs with its tf.distribute strategy. tf.distribute is a TensorFlow API to distribute training across multiple devices. It allows researchers to use distributed training strategies with minimal code changes.

```
strategy = tf.distribute.get_strategy()
```

TensorFlow program first detects if any TPUs are available. If TPUs are detected, the program connects to the TPU and initializes it. Then it sets up a TPU distribution strategy (tf.distribute.experimental.TPUStrategy). When TPUs aren't available, it defaults to a strategy that works on CPUs and single GPUs.

After the strategy is defined, a model is created and compiled within the strategy's scope. This means that the model's training will be distributed according to the strategy.

The primary advantage of using TPUs in TensorFlow is that they can provide significant acceleration for machine learning tasks, allowing models to train more quickly and to handle larger datasets. By leveraging TPUs via the tf.distribute API, you can greatly reduce the time and computational resources needed to train deep learning models.

FUTURE SCOPE

Knowing How Different Network Topologies Affect Performance: Analyzing the effects of various network topologies on data-parallel deep learning is one potential future research. This could include contrasting totally linked, ring, and hierarchical systems, for instance. The study will provide knowledge on how to employ various topologies to enhance communication effectiveness and training efficiency.

Adaptive Strategies: Creating adaptive strategies that can automatically change the configuration based on the model, dataset, and hardware environment is another intriguing field for future research. Depending on the situation, these solutions could entail dynamically adjusting the workforce, batch size, or learning rate.

Model parallelism separates the model, whereas data parallelism distributes the dataset among numerous devices. A potential way to scale up training and boost resource efficiency for bigger models could be to investigate a hybrid parallelism technique that includes elements of both model and data parallelism.

Federated Learning: Federated Learning, a recent development in distributed deep learning, decentralizes the learning process and makes on-device training possible. Future studies might assess the efficacy of various distributed techniques in a federated learning environment.

Elastic Training and Fault Tolerance: Another issue that future research may tackle is the issue of fault tolerance. The likelihood of a worker failing likewise grows as distributed deep learning scales. To lessen the effects of worker failures and build a more reliable distributed learning framework, researchers can look at developing new tactics or improving current ones. Additionally, allowing for the dynamic addition and removal of workers—also known as elastic training—could increase the flexibility and effectiveness of these systems.

Cross-Framework Generalization: Future study may look at how distributed techniques might be used and improved in other deep learning frameworks, such as PyTorch or MXNet, even if the present research focuses on TensorFlow. As a result, the effectiveness and application of these tactics would be more thoroughly understood.

Real-World Applications and Case Studies: Lastly, it would be beneficial to research how these tactics are used in the real world. This can entail cooperating with sectors or groups that have abundant computational capacity and distinctive data difficulties. Such partnerships could provide light on the potential and difficulties that come with putting distributed deep learning methodologies into reality.

Energy Efficiency: As we go into a time where energy consumption is becoming a bigger problem, distributed solutions' power efficiency has to be a top priority. Future studies might examine the energy effectiveness of different methods, offering advice on how to conduct extensive training with the least possible negative environmental impact.

CONCLUSION

In machine learning, distributed strategies for data parallel deep learning models in TensorFlow are an essential area of research. These strategies enable the efficient distribution of data and computation across multiple processors, making the training of deep learning models quicker and more scalable. In this evaluation, we examined the efficacy of these GPU-based deep learning model training strategies on the MNIST dataset. In this evaluation, we trained a convolutional neural network (CNN) using TensorFlow on the MNIST dataset and compared the efficacy of several distributed strategies for data parallelism. Distributed strategies for data parallel deep learning models can increase training efficiency and scalability significantly. Synchronous training was the most effective strategy for the MNIST dataset, resulting in quicker and more accurate training. Researchers and practitioners working on large-scale deep learning models can benefit from these findings, as they provide guidance on the most effective distributed strategies to employ for their applications.

REFERENCE

Abadi, M., Agarwal, A., Barham, P., Brevdo, E., Chen, Z., Citro, C., Corrado, G. S., Davis, A., Dean, J., Devin, M., Ghemawat, S., Goodfellow, I., Harp, A., Irving, G., Isard, M., Jia, Y., Jozefowicz, R., Kaiser, L., Kudlur, M., & Zheng, X. (2016). *TensorFlow: Large-Scale Machine Learning on Heterogeneous Distributed Systems* (arXiv:1603.04467). arXiv. https://arxiv.org/abs/1603.04467.

Adek, R. T., & Ula, M. (2020). A Survey on The Accuracy of Machine Learning Techniques for Intrusion and Anomaly Detection on Public Data Sets. *2020 International Conference on Data Science, Artificial Intelligence, and Business Analytics (DATABIA)*. IEEE. 10.1109/DATABIA50434.2020.9190436

Andrade, D., & Trabasso, L. G. (2017). An OpenCL framework for high performance extraction of image features. *Journal of Parallel and Distributed Computing*, *109*, 75–88. doi:10.1016/j.jpdc.2017.05.011

Baby, K. (2014). *Big Data: An Ultimate Solution in Health Care.*

Bekeneva, Y., Petukhov, V., & Frantsisko, O. (2020). Local image processing in distributed monitoring system. *Journal of Physics: Conference Series*, *1679*(3), 032048. doi:10.1088/1742-6596/1679/3/032048

Ben-Nun, T., & Hoefler, T. (2018). *Demystifying Parallel and Distributed Deep Learning: An In-Depth Concurrency Analysis* (arXiv:1802.09941). arXiv. https://arxiv.org/abs/1802.09941

Chen C.-C. Yang C.-L. Cheng H.-Y. (2019). Efficient and Robust Parallel DNN Training through Model Parallelism on Multi-GPU Platform. *ArXiv:1809.02839 [Cs]*. https://arxiv.org/abs/1809.02839

Dai, J., Wang, Y., Qiu, X., Ding, D., Zhang, Y., Wang, Y., Jia, X., Zhang, C., Wan, Y., Li, Z., Wang, J., Huang, S., Wu, Z., Wang, Y., Yang, Y., She, B., Shi, D., Lu, Q., Huang, K., & Song, G. (2019). BigDL: A Distributed Deep Learning Framework for Big Data. *Proceedings of the ACM Symposium on Cloud Computing*, (pp. 50–60). ACM. 10.1145/3357223.3362707

Dean, J., Corrado, G. S., Monga, R., Chen, K., Devin, M., Le, Q. V., Mao, M. Z., Ranzato, M., Senior, A., Tucker, P., Yang, K., & Ng, A. Y. (n.d.). *Large Scale Distributed Deep Networks*. 11.

Distributed training with TensorFlow. (n.d.). TensorFlow Core. https://www.tensorflow.org/guide/distributed_training

Harini, S., Ravikumar, A., & Keshwani, N. (2022). Malware Prediction Analysis Using AI Techniques with the Effective Preprocessing and Dimensionality Reduction. In J. S. Raj, K. Kamel, & P. Lafata (Eds.), *Innovative Data Communication Technologies and Application* (pp. 153–169). Springer Nature Singapore. doi:10.1007/978-981-16-7167-8_12

How the pytorch freeze network in some layers, only the rest of the training? (2019, February 26). PyTorch Forums. https://discuss.pytorch.org/t/how-the-pytorch-freeze-network-in-some-layers-only-the-rest-of-the-training/7088?page=2

John, J., Ravikumar, A., & Abraham, B. (2021). Prostate cancer prediction from multiple pretrained computer vision model. *Health and Technology*, *11*(5), 1003–1011. doi:10.100712553-021-00586-y

Khan, M. J., Yousaf, A., Abbas, A., & Khurshid, K. (2018). Deep learning for automated forgery detection in hyperspectral document images. *Journal of Electronic Imaging*, *27*(5), 053001. doi:10.1117/1.JEI.27.5.053001

Li, M. (2014). Scaling Distributed Machine Learning with the Parameter Server. *Proceedings of the 2014 International Conference on Big Data Science and Computing - BigDataScience '14*. ACM. 10.1145/2640087.2644155

Li, M., Zhou, L., Yang, Z., Li, A., Xia, F., Andersen, D. G., & Smola, A. (n.d.). *Parameter Server for Distributed Machine Learning*. 10.

Ravikumar, A., & Sriraman, H. (2023a). A Novel Mixed Precision Distributed TPU GAN for Accelerated Learning Curve. *Computer Systems Science and Engineering*, *46*(1), 1. doi:10.32604/csse.2023.034710

Ravikumar, A., & Sriraman, H. (2023b). Attenuate Class Imbalance Problem for Pneumonia Diagnosis Using Ensemble Parallel Stacked Pre-Trained Models. *Computers. Materials & Continua, 75*(1), 1. doi:10.32604/cmc.2023.035848

Ravikumar, A., & Sriraman, H. (2023c). Real-time pneumonia prediction using pipelined spark and high-performance computing. *PeerJ. Computer Science, 9*, e1258. doi:10.7717/peerj-cs.1258 PMID:37346542

Ravikumar, A., Sriraman, H., Lokesh, S., & Maruthi Sai Saketh, P. (2023). Identifying Pitfalls and Solutions in Parallelizing Long Short-Term Memory Network on Graphical Processing Unit by Comparing with Tensor Processing Unit Parallelism. In S. Smys, K. A. Kamel, & R. Palanisamy (Eds.), *Inventive Computation and Information Technologies* (pp. 111–125). Springer Nature Singapore. doi:10.1007/978-981-19-7402-1_9

Ravikumar, A., Sriraman, H., Saketh, P. M. S., Lokesh, S., & Karanam, A. (2022). Effect of neural network structure in accelerating performance and accuracy of a convolutional neural network with GPU/TPU for image analytics. *PeerJ. Computer Science, 8*, e909. doi:10.7717/peerj-cs.909 PMID:35494877

Robin, M., John, J., & Ravikumar, A. (2021). Breast Tumor Segmentation using U-NET. *2021 5th International Conference on Computing Methodologies and Communication (ICCMC)*, 1164–1167. 10.1109/ICCMC51019.2021.9418447

Sergeev, A., & Del Balso, M. (2018). *Horovod: Fast and easy distributed deep learning in TensorFlow* (arXiv:1802.05799). arXiv. https://arxiv.org/abs/1802.05799

Sk, O., Santosh, K., Halder, C., Das, N., & Roy, K. (2017). Word-Level Multi-Script Indic Document Image Dataset and Baseline Results on Script Identification. *International Journal of Computer Vision and Image Processing, 7*(2), 81–94. doi:10.4018/IJCVIP.2017040106

TensorFlow. (n.d.). TensorFlow. https://www.tensorflow.org/

Zhang, S., Ren, X., Luo, L., Guo, T., & Liang, X. (2019). Logging-based identification and evaluation of karst fractures in the eastern Right Bank of the Amu Darya River, Turkmenistan. *Natural Gas Industry B, 6*. Advance online publication. doi:10.1016/j.ngib.2019.01.008

Zhang, S., & Wei, C. (2020). Deep learning network for UAV person re-identification based on residual block. *Science China. Information Sciences, 63*(7), 179203. doi:10.100711432-018-9633-7

Chapter 3
A Study on Distributed Machine Learning Techniques for Large–Scale Weather Forecasting

Balaji V.

(iD) https://orcid.org/0009-0005-9140-8486
Vellore Institute of Technology, Chennai, India

Sivagami M.
Vellore Institute of Technology, India

ABSTRACT

The weather data generated, processed, and collected by the sensor or shared by IoT devices and mobile devices has significantly increased weather data collection in daily life. The data generation speed also accelerated, and a vast amount of data has been collected and stored in distributed databases, improving weather forecasting. Still, the conventional processing method for massive data is distributed and centralized computing, and this chapter looks into how distributed machine learning techniques help as to increase the processing speed. Some distributed frameworks that play a significant role in massive data, like MapReduce, have been trained and tested to resolve various machine learning problems in a distributed environment. The aim of this chapter will provide different information about datasets, issues, platforms, and optimized approaches in a distributed environment. So, researchers can use and deploy new techniques in machine learning algorithms. It helps the researchers develop new strategies in distributed computing environments.

DOI: 10.4018/978-1-6684-9804-0.ch003

INTRODUCTION

The origins of human history: human have always aimed to predict and learn the world and strive to make better predictions. The weather is known as fluctuation in the daily atmosphere (Jain & Jain, 2017). Weather data like precipitation, temperature, pressure, wind speed, direction, humidity, air pressure, etc., collected from the different metrological departments from radar observation, sea-level observation, ground-level observation, and various data observations show the current weather status. Weather forecasting plays a vital role in many people's daily lives (Leu et al., 2014). It will impact many fields like marine trade, agriculture, aquaculture, industry, mining irrigation, etc.,

The enormous value of the dataset is utilized in various fields like geographical, industry, agriculture, and education (Thusoo et al., 2010). This chapter mainly concentrates on geographical data like NETCDF and Radar data. Parallel computing is complicated in the database and the cost is high in procedure to implement structured query language for developing the machine learning models. Data has categorized into three types there are structured (Standard format), semi-structured (Sensor data and Radar data), unstructured data (multimedia data), and reason for data growth by the database parallelization(Al-kahtani & Karim, 2017).

Machine learning approaches are applied in various applications and areas, such as robotics, natural language processing, clustering(Yeo et al., n.d.), and document classification(Shahid et al., 2019). Massive data like terabytes are applying the machine learning model increased drastically and the cost is also high for optimization by parallel computing. Distributed computing is concrete in the machine learning model; it will divide the workload among the serval computational machine to complete the work(Neumeyer et al., 2010).

Distributed Systems

Distributed systems are a combination of various nodes or machines that must have computational capabilities and communicate with each other, as shown in Fig 2. The data transfer between the machine is performed through the network with efficient bandwidth with N number of resources. In a distributed system, the single node failure cannot affect a network's overall communication and reliability; it will improve data transmission and easy access with nodes at the maximum workload. The distributed systems must ensure minimum communication cost with nodes and utilize the system's computational capability.

Generally, MapReduce and Hadoop approaches are exploited to implement the large-scale model in machine learning algorithms. The Hadoop system is most

Figure 1. Machine learning aspects

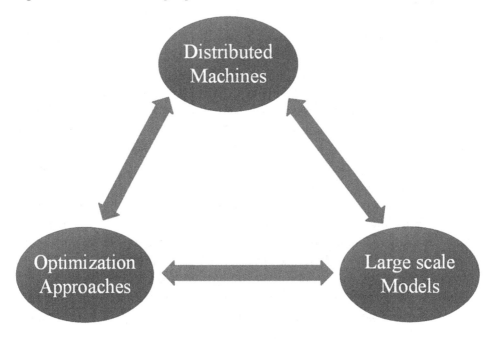

prevalent in MapReduce approaches. Apache Spark, Apache Storm, Apache Mahout, and Apache Kafka are distributed streaming computing paradigms.

Related Work

MLlib(Hung et al., 2018) is a Python-compatible machine-learning library built to run on Spark. Like dislib, MLlib provides an API reminiscent of scikit-learn, catering to developers with limited expertise in the domain. Nevertheless, the primary differences between dislib and MLlib can be found in their respective execution frameworks.

SystemML (Agrawal et al., 2019; Ghoting et al., 2011) is scalable and more flexible in the distributed environment specially designed for declarative machine learning, operating on both MapReduce (Dean & Ghemawat, 2008) and Spark (Farki & Noughabi, 2023). Declarative machine learning (DML) is a core usage that allows the manipulation of mathematical and linear algebra primitives on matrices. The SystemML runtime analyzes DML scripts, determining the most efficient execution strategy, and then generates a sequence of MapReduce or Spark jobs to perform parallel processing of the application. Users can enjoy significant flexibility in building diverse machine-learning algorithms using R and Python syntax in DML.

DAAL4PY (Mohindru et al., 2022) is a Python-based machine learning library that exhibits more similarities with dislib than previously mentioned libraries. Its

Figure 2. Distributed system

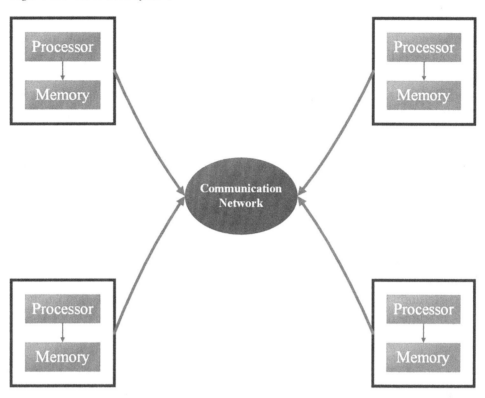

user-friendly interface supports models such as principal component analysis, Linear regression, K-means clustering, etc. Additionally, DAAL4PY provides an estimator-based interface for specific algorithms like K nearest neighbors, Decision tree classifier, and Random forest classifier. To achieve parallel execution, DAAL4PY relies on MPI(Gropp et al., 1996), making it particularly suitable for HPC clusters.

PyCOMPSs (Tejedor et al., 2017) is a programming model based on tasks, aiming to create ease and access to parallel and distributed Python applications. It is classified into two parts: the programming model and the runtime. Through simple annotations provided by the programming model, developers can identify potential areas of parallelism within their real-time applications. During process run time, PyCOMPSs will be annotated and automatically allocates computation across the available resources, effectively streamlining the process of parallel execution.

Meteorological Datasets

There are various meteorological datasets available for computing by machine learning model. The dataset will contain NETCDF, gridded binary files, radar data, and satellite data in weather forecasting; metrological departments in various countries will collect the data from different meteorological departments. There were structured, semi-structured, and unstructured data, three different data utilized for classification(Sonntag & Profitlich, 2019) and clustering(Yeo et al., n.d.).

Approaches of Machine Learning Algorithms

Machine learning approaches learn to predict or make decisions depending on data. We classified the machine learning algorithms based on three characteristics.

- **Feedback:** While learning algorithms, system feedback is given during that time.
- **Method:** When we were giving feedback to the algorithm, the nature of Machine learning model evaluation will occur.
- **Purpose:** The appropriate result for a particular algorithm.

Feedback: The feedback is training a model or algorithm; it will provide feedback as data to gradually improve the model or algorithms. There are different types of feedback(Arulkumaran et al., 2017). Supervised learning is a dataset consisting of labeled data to train the algorithm that will predict or classify outcomes accurately. The input data will feed to the model; it will adjust weight until it fitted the model, which occurs in the cross-validation process. Unsupervised learning is a dataset consisting of unlabeled data to train the algorithm to classify or associate the data. Semi-supervised learning will train the model with small amounts of labeled data and a large amount of unlabeled data.

Method: The method helps machine learning algorithms to expand performance itself based on input data; it will increase the accuracy. So, we identified the five different groups of machine learning methods.

1) Evolutionary algorithms(Gong et al., 2015) are specific to the genetic algorithm it will learn and iterate based on the evolution.
2) Stochastic gradient descent algorithms have the most common training approaches are take in machine learning models consisting of the support vector machine(F. Zhang & O'Donnell, 2020), perceptron(Agirre-Basurko et al., 2006; P. Zhang et al., 2020), Artificial neural networks(Dike et al., 2018), Deep neural networks(Haidar & Verma, 2018), Convolutional neural networks(Boonyuen

et al., 2018), recurrent neural networks(Wang et al., 2021), Hopfield networks, self-organizing feature maps, stochastic neural networks(Shin et al., 2019), auto-encoders, generative adversarial networks.

3) Rule-based machine learning(Weiss & Indurkhya, 1995) consists of a set of rules to represent the problems in a small part. The rule-based has particular conditions that must be satisfied in this model. Some models represent association rule learning, and decision trees(N et al., 2016) are taken in rule-based algorithms, and

4) Topic models(Blei, 2012) are most applied in text data; it is statical models for finding and mapping the data. The topic models consist of three categories: latent Dirichlet allocation, latent semantic analysis, naïve Bayes classifiers, and probabilistic latent semantic indexing.

5) Matrix factorization models (Simm et al., 2017)are applied to find the missing values in matrix-structured data or latent factors. Matrix factorization approaches have been used in many recommender systems like user-item ratings and drug compound-target protein matrix.

Purpose(Kwon et al., 2019): Machine learning algorithms are used for various purposes, such as predicting the probability of an event occurring and classifying the image. Therefore, the following methods like regression, classification, anomaly detection, clustering, dimensionality reduction, and representation learning.

Hyperparameter Optimization

Many Machine learning algorithms we discussed in the previous section have a massive impact on hyperparameter optimization. For example, stochastic gradient descent, a choice of the batch size, the initialization of the algorithm or model, the learning rate, etc. In machine learning algorithm and dataset has optimal values of hyperparameters that are different for a problem. Many algorithms will optimize the parameters automatically in the distributed machine-learning techniques that loop execution across several machine-learning algorithms. These include

1) First-order algorithms: The first-order algorithms are mainly based on the gradient-based optimization methods; they are used for gradient objective functions concerning the hyperparameter tuning and will update them every iteration. First-order algorithms use at least one derivate function that will map the parameter's value to the accuracy in machine learning algorithms using that parameter. Stochastic dual coordinate ascent and stochastic gradient descent(Byrd et al., 2016) are examples of first-order algorithms.

2) Second-order Techniques: The second-order algorithms also like to go beyond on gradient and consider that the curvature of the objective function depends on the hyperparameters. Second-order techniques are used for any second-derivate function that will map the parameter's value to the accuracy in machine learning algorithms using that parameter. Examples are Newton's method(Albersmeyer & Diehl, 2010) and the Quasi-Newton method(Byrd et al., 2016).

3) Random Search: The random search will use a random trail choice for sample hyperparameter values, which often gives a better result than a grid search(Bischl et al., 2023).

Combining Multiple Machine Learning Algorithms: Ensemble Methods

A unique machine learning model will not provide enough accuracy to solve weather forecasting problems. To resolve these issues, we can combine two or more models called ensemble learning. For example, to increase the performance and reduce the time complexity of not only distributed computing and parallel computing but there was also another process to requires training a model in two different stages: first, where data has stored in local sites, and second will aggregate over impressive results of the first(Ji & Ling, n.d.). This type of aggregation will be achieved when we apply ensemble methods.

There were various ways to perform ensemble learning, such as:

1) **Bagging**(Opitz & Maclin, n.d.): Bagging is a technique that can improve the accuracy and performance of machine learning algorithms. This technique can be applied to the original dataset, considering the average of all algorithms processed and giving an ensemble model. This technique works efficiently for high-dimensional datasets and minimizes overfitting as well. It deals with bias-variance trade-offs and reduces the variance of the prediction model.

2) **Boosting**(Opitz & Maclin, n.d.): The limitation of bagging is that it can't deal with the errors that have happened by individual algorithms. Boosting technique can be used to build strong classifiers with sequential learning. It overcomes the underfitting issue by reducing bias.

3) **Bucketing:**(Alfaro et al., 2020) It will train all possible models and eventually select the best-performing single model. When the bucket model is tested with one model, it cannot produce a better model in the set and will perform best in evaluating the many models.

4) **Stacking:**(Gu et al., 2022) Stacking differs from the ensemble method of bagging and boosting. The process will predict from the multiple nodes and

build combined new models. The final model is used to predict the value from the tested dataset.

5) **Learning Classifier systems:** It is mainly taken part in learning approaches. The learning classifier system will iterate over the data point from the data; in each iteration, the entire learning process is taken part. Depending on the data, various attributes will change the performance of learning classifier systems, Such as Pittsburgh-style vs. Michigan-style architecture(Orriols-Puig et al., 2009), incremental learning vs. batch learning(Clearwater et al., 1989), supervised learning vs. reinforcement learning (Kaelbling et al., 1996), and strength-based vs. accuracy-based(Wilson, 1995).

6) **Voting:**(Tavana et al., 2023) It is the easiest ensemble method in machine learning. It is a method of the combination of multiple unique models to make a final prediction. The classification voting problems consists of two types: hard voting and soft voting.

Distributed Machine Learning Ecosystem

The machine learning algorithm has been applied for Heterogeneous distributed machine learning with the help of structured data. Nowadays, knowledge-based machine learning for real-time applications has enhanced the distributed computing process. Distributed computing will be utilized more than one processor for calculation and analysis. The graphics processing and central processing units are the best-suited processors for heterogeneous computing.

However, similar topics like weather forecasting analysis, to predict the weather aspects are increasingly essential and become important to predict as fast as the technology matures provide information to the people. The main problem is that processing an enormous amount of data on cluster nodes is not restricted by a machine-learning approach. However, this study has been focused on a long time in distributing the data in the machine and database research has been taken part. There were popular general-purpose distributed frameworks like Apache Spark that had the opportunity to execute machine learning. Fig 3 shows the ecosystem of distributed machine learning.

The distributed computing in machine learning, there were two primary ways of partitioning across the machines. There are classified as the Data-Parallel method and the Model-Parallel method(Peteiro-Barral & Guijarro-Berdiñas, 2013; Verbraeken et al., 2021). These two methods can be applied simultaneously in distributed machine learning(Xing et al., 2016). The data will be partitioned as N times to worker nodes in the system in the data-parallel method. Fig 4(a) shows the data parallel approaches. All worker nodes will apply a similar algorithm to various datasets. It will be single coherent output that will be generated naturally. The model-Parallel method is a copy of

Figure 3. Ecosystem of distributed machine learning

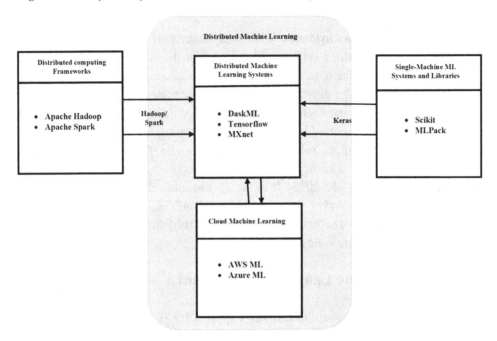

whole datasets that will be processed to worker nodes and works for different machine learning models. Fig 4(b) shows the model parallel approaches. It will aggregate all the models. It cannot be applied automatically to every algorithm. The model generally cannot split up the parameters. It will train different instances of the same model and aggregates the output of all trained models, like ensembling models shown in Fig 4.

Approaches of the Distributed Machine Learning

Another design of distributed machine learning will be deployed, which is a machine within the cluster where organized. The topology is designed in different distribution degrees, and the system is implemented. Fig 5 shows four different possible topologies, Baran's(Baran, 1962) generally distributed communication networks. The possible topologies were centralized and decentralized systems and Fully distributed systems.

- **Centralized systems:** It is a hierarchical approach; aggregation will happen with a single central location, as shown in Fig 5(a).
- **Decentralized systems:** Is allowed to intermediate aggregation. Either model will be replicated in consistent updates in all nodes in tree topologies, as

Figure 4. The distributed machine learning in parallelism. The data parallel will train multiple instances of a similar model on various training datasets into subsets, while the model parallel will allocate a single model to various nodes.

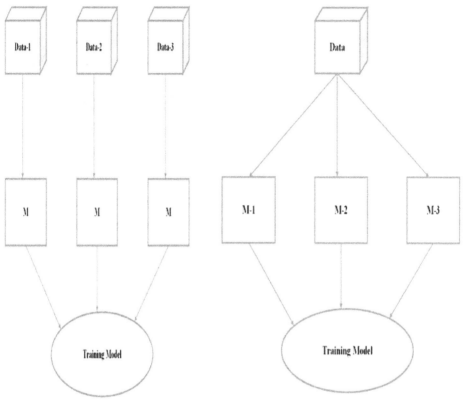

Figure 4(a) Data-Parallel

Figure 4(b) Model-Parallel

shown in Fig 5(c). Or the partitioned model will be shared over two or more parameter servers, as shown in Fig 5(b).

- **Fully Distributed Systems:** This network consists of independent nodes; it will ensemble the problem and give solutions together and no specific roles will be assigned to any nodes or machine, as shown in Fig 5(d).

Topologies

Several different topologies have most popular in distributed machine learning clusters, such as Trees, Rings, Parameter servers, and Peer to Peer.

Figure 5. Distributed machine learning topologies

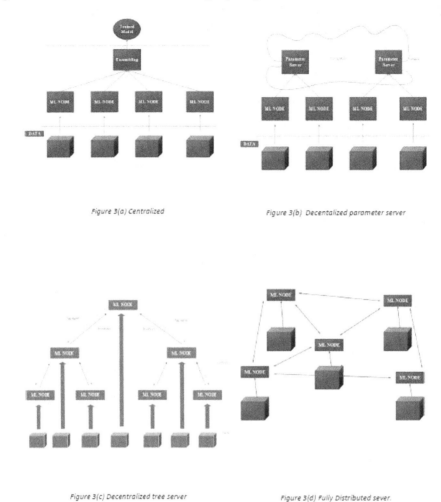

Figure 3(a) Centralized

Figure 3(b) Decentralized parameter server

Figure 3(c) Decentralized tree server

Figure 3(d) Fully Distributed sever.

- **Trees:** These topologies have many advantages that are easier to scalable and manageable, and each node communicates with the parent and child nodes only. An example tree will accumulate from their local nodes from their children nodes and pass the result to overall parent nodes(Levitin & Dai, 2007).
- **Rings:** These topologies do not provide efficient support for broadcasting in the communication nodes or systems, and the communication with systems or minimum overhead. It only communicates with neighbor nodes and synchronizes the messages. An example of ring topologies is used between the two or more GPUs on a unique machine(Lin et al., 2001).

- **Parameter server:** The parameter server was a decentralized set of worker nodes and a centralized set of primary nodes that will be maintained with a shared state. In this, all model parameters will be shared on every parameter server; it is all write and read by a key-value store. It has the main advantage is it will be shared in global memory(Cui et al., 2016; Wei et al., 2015).
- **Peer-to-Peer:** In a fully centralized state and fully distributed model, every node will have its own copy of the parameter and directly communicate with each other(Foster & Iamnitchi, 2003). The main advantage of these topologies is high scalability and eliminating node failure in the machine is easy(Androutsellis-Theotokis & Spinellis, 2004).

Implementation of Distributed Machine Learning for Large Weather Forecasting Using Dask ML

1) Dataset Description

The dataset consists of around ten years of data from 2008 to 2017 of daily weather observations from different locations in Australia. It consists of 24 attributes in this dataset. The dataset is in the form of CSV, and the size of the dataset is 13.5 MB.

2) Dask Machine Learning

Dask ML is a library parallel and distributed machine learning library that can be used with the XGBoast and sci-kit-learn to predict models and massive datasets. Dask can process thousands of terabytes of data efficiently. It will enable the faster execution of large datasets like NetCDF and multidimensional data and accelerate and scale pipelines or workflows. Dask emphasizes the following: flexible, scale-up, scale-down, faster, familiar, etc. DaskMl performs distributed computation across the dask cluster to harness the power of the n number of nodes, making it feasible when also handling massive datasets.

Dask ML works with the following collections in Python for handling large datasets:

- **Dask Arrays:** It will split the extensive data into chunks. Chucks will parallelize the computations. Dask Arrays helps parallelize the operations involved in feature engineering and pre-processing.
- **Dask Dataframes:** It is designed to handle large memory datasets divided into n partitions that can process data in parallel. It will effectively manage large datasets and also parallelize computations effectively.

- **Dask Bags:** It is a parallel and distributed version of Python lists. It will be designed to handle unstructured data like CSV, Text data, and JSON files and will process in parallel across multiple cores or distributed computing clusters.

3) Environment configuration Dask ML

   The Environment configuration of dask ML can be done in Google-colab, and also install Anaconda environment in Jupiter notebook. Google-colab is a cloud-based environment. Both environments allow us to execute machine learning and also daskML.

- Install daskML and necessary other packages in the environment.

Figure 6. Install DaskML and Import Libaries

```
!pip install dask==2.22.0
!pip install dask distributed --upgrade
import pandas as pd
import numpy as np
from datetime import datetime
)
import dask
import dask.dataframe as dd
import dask.array as da
from dask.distributed import Client, progress
import joblib
```

- The weather dataset has been loaded for training. The weather dataset consists of 24 attributes and 142193 entities. The size of the file consists of 13.5 MB. They were dataset loaded with the panda's data frame in Fig 9, showing the loaded time has been high compared to the daskML data frame in Fig 10. The DaskMl loaded time is less and more efficient.

Figure 7. Dataset loaded with pandas data frame

```
start_time = datetime.now()
df = pd.read_csv('/content/drive/MyDrive/Dataset/weatherAUS.csv')
time_elapsed = datetime.now() - start_time
print('Time elapsed (h:mm:ss){}'.format(time_elapsed))

Time elapsed (h:mm:ss)0:00:01.631097
```

Figure 8. Dataset loaded with daskMl data frame

```
start_time = datetime.now()
full_data = dd.read_csv('/content/drive/MyDrive/Dataset/weatherAUS.csv')
time_elapsed = datetime.now() - start_time
print('Time elapsed (h:mm:ss){}'.format(time_elapsed))

Time elapsed (h:mm:ss)0:00:00.043399
```

- The loaded dataset is partitioned in the block size of “2.3 MB.” The total dataset size is “13.5 MB.” It has been split as a six-block, shown in Fig 11.

Figure 9. Partitioned has a different block

```
import dask.dataframe as dd
df = dd.read_csv('/content/drive/MyDrive/Dataset/weatherAUS.csv', blocksize='2.3MB')
df.visualize()
```

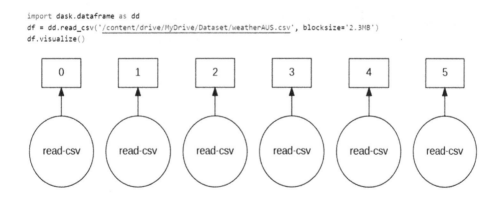

- The step-Up of the Dask distributed cluster.

Figure 10. Dask distributed cluster

```
from dask.distributed import Client
client = Client(n_workers=4, threads_per_worker=1)
client
```

```
/usr/local/lib/python3.10/dist-packages/distributed/node.py:182: UserWarning: Port 8787 is already in use.
Perhaps you already have a cluster running?
Hosting the HTTP server on port 32817 instead
  warnings.warn(
INFO:distributed.scheduler:State start
INFO:distributed.scheduler:  Scheduler at:     tcp://127.0.0.1:38289
INFO:distributed.scheduler:  dashboard at:     http://127.0.0.1:32817/status
INFO:distributed.nanny:         Start Nanny at: 'tcp://127.0.0.1:38399'
INFO:distributed.nanny:         Start Nanny at: 'tcp://127.0.0.1:40537'
INFO:distributed.nanny:         Start Nanny at: 'tcp://127.0.0.1:42189'
INFO:distributed.nanny:         Start Nanny at: 'tcp://127.0.0.1:46259'
INFO:distributed.scheduler:Register worker <WorkerState 'tcp://127.0.0.1:38059', name: 3, status: init, memory: 0, processing: 0>
INFO:distributed.scheduler:Starting worker compute stream, tcp://127.0.0.1:38059
INFO:distributed.core:Starting established connection to tcp://127.0.0.1:33190
INFO:distributed.scheduler:Register worker <WorkerState 'tcp://127.0.0.1:44765', name: 0, status: init, memory: 0, processing: 0>
INFO:distributed.scheduler:Starting worker compute stream, tcp://127.0.0.1:44765
INFO:distributed.core:Starting established connection to tcp://127.0.0.1:33188
INFO:distributed.scheduler:Register worker <WorkerState 'tcp://127.0.0.1:40285', name: 1, status: init, memory: 0, processing: 0>
INFO:distributed.scheduler:Starting worker compute stream, tcp://127.0.0.1:40285
INFO:distributed.core:Starting established connection to tcp://127.0.0.1:33186
INFO:distributed.scheduler:Register worker <WorkerState 'tcp://127.0.0.1:38673', name: 2, status: init, memory: 0, processing: 0>
INFO:distributed.scheduler:Starting worker compute stream, tcp://127.0.0.1:38673
INFO:distributed.core:Starting established connection to tcp://127.0.0.1:33194
INFO:distributed.scheduler:Receive client connection: Client-dd997534-0bf2-11ee-808f-0242ac1c000c
INFO:distributed.core:Starting established connection to tcp://127.0.0.1:33206
```

Client
Client-dd997534-0bf2-11ee-808f-0242ac1c000c
Connection method: Cluster object   **Cluster type:** distributed.LocalCluster
Dashboard: http://127.0.0.1:32817/status
▶ **Cluster Info**

- Training Model

Figure 11. Training model

```
X_train, X_test, y_train, y_test = train_test_split(X, y, test_size=0.2, random_state=42)
```

- Evaluate the model Logistic Regression as described in Fig 12, the DaskML cluster connection and distributed computations, and also how to predict and evaluate the model

Figure 12. Evaluation model

```
from dask.distributed import Client
# Connect to the Dask cluster
client = Client('http://127.0.0.1:32817/status')
# Perform distributed computations
X_train = client.persist(X_train)  # Persist data on the cluster
model = LogisticRegression()
model.fit(X_train, y_train)
# Make predictions
y_pred = model.predict(X_test)
# Evaluate the model
accuracy = (y_pred == y_test).mean().compute()
```

CONCLUSION

Distributed machine learning can optimize a massive database provided by various users and will be predicted efficiently. They were two approaches that already existed frameworks distributed systems like Hadoop and MapReduce. In this chapter, the distributed strategies for the data parallel using the machine learning model in DaskML. These strategies are more efficient for computation in the efficiency, resulting in more scalable and faster training of a machine learning model. The Evaluation was examed the effectiveness of these strategies in training a distributed machine-learning model on the weather dataset. In the evaluation process, we trained as logistic regression on the daskML in the weather dataset. The model has been compared with machine learning and DaskML with the model of the logistic regression algorithm. The DaskML has performed highly scalable and efficiently in the vast dataset compared to machine learning. These results can be helpful to researchers on large-scale weather forecasting in machine learning models. It is the most effective distributed strategy for some other applications. The distributed machine-learning approaches are supervised and unsupervised, and reinforcement learning is performed efficiently in several forms of data and structured, unstructured, and semi-structured data.

REFERENCES

Agirre-Basurko, E., Ibarra-Berastegi, G., & Madariaga, I. (2006). Regression and multilayer perceptron-based models to forecast hourly O3 and NO2 levels in the Bilbao area. *Environmental Modelling & Software*, *21*(4), 430–446. doi:10.1016/j.envsoft.2004.07.008

Agrawal, P., Arya, R., Bindal, A., Bhatia, S., Gagneja, A., Godlewski, J., Low, Y., Muss, T., Paliwal, M. M., Raman, S., Shah, V., Shen, B., Sugden, L., Zhao, K., & Wu, M.-C. (2019). Data Platform for Machine Learning. *Proceedings of the 2019 International Conference on Management of Data*, (pp. 1803–1816). ACM. 10.1145/3299869.3314050

Al-kahtani, M. S., & Karim, L. (2017). An Efficient Distributed Algorithm for Big Data Processing. *Arabian Journal for Science and Engineering*, *42*(8), 3149–3157. doi:10.100713369-016-2405-y

Albersmeyer, J., & Diehl, M. (2010). The Lifted Newton Method and Its Application in Optimization. *SIAM Journal on Optimization*, *20*(3), 1655–1684. doi:10.1137/080724885

Alfaro, J. C., Aledo, J. A., & Gámez, J. A. (2020). *Averaging-Based Ensemble Methods for the Partial Label Ranking Problem.*, doi:10.1007/978-3-030-61705-9_34

Androutsellis-Theotokis, S., & Spinellis, D. (2004). A survey of peer-to-peer content distribution technologies. *ACM Computing Surveys, 36*(4), 335–371. doi:10.1145/1041680.1041681

Arulkumaran, K., Deisenroth, M. P., Brundage, M., & Bharath, A. A. (2017). Deep Reinforcement Learning: A Brief Survey. *IEEE Signal Processing Magazine, 34*(6), 26–38. doi:10.1109/MSP.2017.2743240

Baran, P. (1962). *On Distributed Communications Networks.* RAND Corporation. doi:10.7249/P2626

Bischl, B., Binder, M., Lang, M., Pielok, T., Richter, J., Coors, S., Thomas, J., Ullmann, T., Becker, M., Boulesteix, A., Deng, D., & Lindauer, M. (2023). Hyperparameter optimization: Foundations, algorithms, best practices, and open challenges. *WIREs Data Mining and Knowledge Discovery, 13*(2). doi:10.1002/widm.1484

Blei, D. M. (2012). Probabilistic topic models. *Communications of the ACM, 55*(4), 77–84. doi:10.1145/2133806.2133826

Boonyuen, K., Kaewprapha, P., & Srivihok, P. (2018). Daily rainfall forecast model from satellite image using Convolution neural network. *2018 International Conference on Information Technology (InCIT)*, (pp. 1–7). IEEE. 10.23919/INCIT.2018.8584886

Byrd, R. H., Hansen, S. L., Nocedal, J., & Singer, Y. (2016). A Stochastic Quasi-Newton Method for Large-Scale Optimization. *SIAM Journal on Optimization, 26*(2), 1008–1031. doi:10.1137/140954362

Clearwater, S. H., Cheng, T.-P., Hirsh, H., & Buchanan, B. G. (1989). INCREMENTAL BATCH LEARNING. In *Proceedings of the Sixth International Workshop on Machine Learning* (pp. 366–370). Elsevier. 10.1016/B978-1-55860-036-2.50093-X

Cui, H., Zhang, H., Ganger, G. R., Gibbons, P. B., & Xing, E. P. (2016). GeePS. *Proceedings of the Eleventh European Conference on Computer Systems*, (pp. 1–16). ACM. 10.1145/2901318.2901323

Dean, J., & Ghemawat, S. (2008). MapReduce. *Communications of the ACM, 51*(1), 107–113. doi:10.1145/1327452.1327492

Dike, H. U., Zhou, Y., Deveerasetty, K. K., & Wu, Q. (2018). Unsupervised Learning Based On Artificial Neural Network: A Review. *2018 IEEE International Conference on Cyborg and Bionic Systems (CBS)*, (pp. 322–327). IEEE. 10.1109/CBS.2018.8612259

Farki, A., & Noughabi, E. A. (2023). Real-Time Blood Pressure Prediction Using Apache Spark and Kafka Machine Learning. *2023 9th International Conference on Web Research (ICWR)*, 161–166. 10.1109/ICWR57742.2023.10138962

Foster, I., & Iamnitchi, A. (2003). *On Death*. Taxes, and the Convergence of Peer-to-Peer and Grid Computing. doi:10.1007/978-3-540-45172-3_11

Ghoting, A., Krishnamurthy, R., Pednault, E., Reinwald, B., Sindhwani, V., Tatikonda, S., Tian, Y., & Vaithyanathan, S. (2011). SystemML: Declarative machine learning on MapReduce. *2011 IEEE 27th International Conference on Data Engineering*, (pp. 231–242). IEEE. 10.1109/ICDE.2011.5767930

Gong, Y.-J., Chen, W.-N., Zhan, Z.-H., Zhang, J., Li, Y., Zhang, Q., & Li, J.-J. (2015). Distributed evolutionary algorithms and their models: A survey of the state-of-the-art. *Applied Soft Computing*, *34*, 286–300. doi:10.1016/j.asoc.2015.04.061

Gropp, W., Lusk, E., Doss, N., & Skjellum, A. (1996). A high-performance, portable implementation of the MPI message passing interface standard. *Parallel Computing*, *22*(6), 789–828. doi:10.1016/0167-8191(96)00024-5

Gu, J., Liu, S., Zhou, Z., Chalov, S. R., & Zhuang, Q. (2022). A Stacking Ensemble Learning Model for Monthly Rainfall Prediction in the Taihu Basin, China. *Water (Basel)*, *14*(3), 492. doi:10.3390/w14030492

Haidar, A., & Verma, B. (2018). Monthly Rainfall Forecasting Using One-Dimensional Deep Convolutional Neural Network. *IEEE Access : Practical Innovations, Open Solutions*, *6*, 69053–69063. doi:10.1109/ACCESS.2018.2880044

Hung, P. D., Hanh, T. D., & Diep, V. T. (2018). Breast Cancer Prediction Using Spark MLlib and ML Packages. *Proceedings of the 2018 5th International Conference on Bioinformatics Research and Applications*, (pp. 52–59). ACM. 10.1145/3309129.3309133

Jain, H., & Jain, R. (2017). Big data in weather forecasting: Applications and challenges. *2017 International Conference on Big Data Analytics and Computational Intelligence (ICBDAC)*, (pp. 138–142). IEEE. 10.1109/ICBDACI.2017.8070824

Ji, G., & Ling, X. (n.d.). Ensemble Learning Based Distributed Clustering. In *Emerging Technologies in Knowledge Discovery and Data Mining* (pp. 312–321). Springer Berlin Heidelberg. doi:10.1007/978-3-540-77018-3_32

Kaelbling, L. P., Littman, M. L., & Moore, A. W. (1996). Reinforcement Learning: A Survey. *Journal of Artificial Intelligence Research*, *4*, 237–285. doi:10.1613/jair.301

Kwon, D., Kim, H., Kim, J., Suh, S. C., Kim, I., & Kim, K. J. (2019). A survey of deep learning-based network anomaly detection. *Cluster Computing*, *22*(S1), 949–961. doi:10.100710586-017-1117-8

Leu, J.-S., Su, K.-W., & Chen, C.-T. (2014). Ambient mesoscale weather forecasting system featuring mobile augmented reality. *Multimedia Tools and Applications*, *72*(2), 1585–1609. doi:10.100711042-013-1462-4

Levitin, G., & Dai, Y.-S. (2007). Service reliability and performance in grid system with star topology. *Reliability Engineering & System Safety*, *92*(1), 40–46. doi:10.1016/j.ress.2005.11.005

Lin, M.-S., Chang, M.-S., Chen, D.-J., & Ku, K.-L. (2001). The distributed program reliability analysis on ring-type topologies. *Computers & Operations Research*, *28*(7), 625–635. doi:10.1016/S0305-0548(99)00151-3

Mohindru, G., Mondal, K., & Banka, H. (2022). Performance Analysis of Software Enabled Accelerator Library for Intel Architecture (pp. 465–472). doi:10.1007/978-981-16-3690-5_40

N, R., S, S., & S, K. (2016). Comparison of Decision Tree Based Rainfall Prediction Model with Data Driven Model Considering Climatic Variables. *Irrigation & Drainage Systems Engineering, 05*(03). doi:10.4172/2168-9768.1000175

Neumeyer, L., Robbins, B., Nair, A., & Kesari, A. (2010). S4: Distributed Stream Computing Platform. *2010 IEEE International Conference on Data Mining Workshops*, (pp. 170–177). IEEE. 10.1109/ICDMW.2010.172

Opitz, D. W., & Maclin, R. F. (n.d.). An empirical evaluation of bagging and boosting for artificial neural networks. *Proceedings of International Conference on Neural Networks (ICNN'97)*, (pp. 1401–1405). IEEE. 10.1109/ICNN.1997.613999

Orriols-Puig, A., Casillas, J., & Bernado-Mansilla, E. (2009). Fuzzy-UCS: A Michigan-Style Learning Fuzzy-Classifier System for Supervised Learning. *IEEE Transactions on Evolutionary Computation*, *13*(2), 260–283. doi:10.1109/TEVC.2008.925144

Peteiro-Barral, D., & Guijarro-Berdiñas, B. (2013). A survey of methods for distributed machine learning. *Progress in Artificial Intelligence*, *2*(1), 1–11. doi:10.100713748-012-0035-5

Shahid, N., Rappon, T., & Berta, W. (2019). Applications of artificial neural networks in health care organizational decision-making: A scoping review. *PLoS One*, *14*(2), e0212356. doi:10.1371/journal.pone.0212356 PMID:30779785

Shin, J.-Y., Ro, Y., Cha, J.-W., Kim, K.-R., & Ha, J.-C. (2019). Assessing the Applicability of Random Forest, Stochastic Gradient Boosted Model, and Extreme Learning Machine Methods to the Quantitative Precipitation Estimation of the Radar Data: A Case Study to Gwangdeoksan Radar, South Korea, in 2018. *Advances in Meteorology*, *2019*, 1–17. doi:10.1155/2019/6542410

Simm, J., Arany, A., Zakeri, P., Haber, T., Wegner, J. K., Chupakhin, V., Ceulemans, H., & Moreau, Y. (2017). Macau: Scalable Bayesian factorization with high-dimensional side information using MCMC. *2017 IEEE 27th International Workshop on Machine Learning for Signal Processing (MLSP)*, (pp. 1–6). IEEE. 10.1109/MLSP.2017.8168143

Sonntag, D., & Profitlich, H.-J. (2019). An architecture of open-source tools to combine textual information extraction, faceted search and information visualisation. *Artificial Intelligence in Medicine*, *93*, 13–28. doi:10.1016/j.artmed.2018.08.003 PMID:30195983

Tavana, P., Akraminia, M., Koochari, A., & Bagherifard, A. (2023). An efficient ensemble method for detecting spinal curvature type using deep transfer learning and soft voting classifier. *Expert Systems with Applications*, *213*, 119290. doi:10.1016/j.eswa.2022.119290

Tejedor, E., Becerra, Y., Alomar, G., Queralt, A., Badia, R. M., Torres, J., Cortes, T., & Labarta, J. (2017). PyCOMPSs: Parallel computational workflows in Python. *International Journal of High Performance Computing Applications*, *31*(1), 66–82. doi:10.1177/1094342015594678

Thusoo, A., Sen Sarma, J., Jain, N., Shao, Z., Chakka, P., Zhang, N., Antony, S., Liu, H., & Murthy, R. (2010). Hive - a petabyte scale data warehouse using Hadoop. *2010 IEEE 26th International Conference on Data Engineering (ICDE 2010)*, (pp. 996–1005). IEEE. 10.1109/ICDE.2010.5447738

Verbraeken, J., Wolting, M., Katzy, J., Kloppenburg, J., Verbelen, T., & Rellermeyer, J. S. (2021). A Survey on Distributed Machine Learning. *ACM Computing Surveys*, *53*(2), 1–33. doi:10.1145/3377454

Wang, Y., Wu, H., Zhang, J., Gao, Z., Wang, J., Yu, P. S., & Long, M. (2021). *PredRNN: A Recurrent Neural Network for Spatiotemporal Predictive Learning*.

Wei, J., Dai, W., Qiao, A., Ho, Q., Cui, H., Ganger, G. R., Gibbons, P. B., Gibson, G. A., & Xing, E. P. (2015). Managed communication and consistency for fast data-parallel iterative analytics. *Proceedings of the Sixth ACM Symposium on Cloud Computing*, (pp. 381–394). ACM. 10.1145/2806777.2806778

Weiss, S. M., & Indurkhya, N. (1995). Rule-based Machine Learning Methods for Functional Prediction. *Journal of Artificial Intelligence Research*, *3*, 383–403. doi:10.1613/jair.199

Wilson, S. W. (1995). Classifier Fitness Based on Accuracy. *Evolutionary Computation*, *3*(2), 149–175. doi:10.1162/evco.1995.3.2.149

Xing, E. P., Ho, Q., Xie, P., & Wei, D. (2016). Strategies and Principles of Distributed Machine Learning on Big Data. *Engineering*, *2*(2), 179–195. doi:10.1016/J. ENG.2016.02.008

Yeo, C. S., Buyya, R., Pourreza, H., Eskicioglu, R., Graham, P., & Sommers, F. (n.d.). Cluster Computing: High-Performance, High-Availability, and High-Throughput Processing on a Network of Computers. In Handbook of Nature-Inspired and Innovative Computing (pp. 521–551). Kluwer Academic Publishers. doi:10.1007/0-387-27705-6_16

Zhang, F., & O'Donnell, L. J. (2020). Support vector regression. In *Machine Learning* (pp. 123–140). Elsevier. doi:10.1016/B978-0-12-815739-8.00007-9

Zhang, P., Jia, Y., Gao, J., Song, W., & Leung, H. (2020). Short-Term Rainfall Forecasting Using Multi-Layer Perceptron. *IEEE Transactions on Big Data*, *6*(1), 93–106. doi:10.1109/TBDATA.2018.2871151

Chapter 4

Distributed Deep Learning for Smart IoMT Challenges in the Healthcare Domain

Agila Harshini Thangavel
Vellore Institute of Technology, Chennai, India

ABSTRACT

The Internet of Medical Things (IoMT) collects and transfers healthcare data over the network using sensors, software applications, and Edge devices. A greater number of Healthcare devices are being manufactured and there are various challenges like Interoperability, Security, Scalability, and privacy. IoMT devices are used to monitor and deliver treatments to patients remotely. For IoMt devices to reach their full potential the challenges need to be addressed. Healthcare devices when compromised can harm patients by disrupting personal data.

INTRODUCTION

Digital healthcare products like fitness trackers, heart monitors, etc., which record real-time and biometric data are the clearest area of excitement now and in the future. Sustainable Digital healthcare shall transform society digitally by providing a faster response for emergency, and acute care and also reducing the amount of energy which in turn will reduce the carbon footprint of the server farm. Latency and Cyber security are the most dangerous challenges in IoMT devices. The classic security mechanisms in IoMT are provided by encryption, multifactor authentication, etc., which require more energy because of the longer bit length and are stored in a device that could be compromised. A lightweight technique that is both energy efficient and does not require the storing of encryption keys is ideally suited for a highly secure and energy efficient IoMT.

DOI: 10.4018/978-1-6684-9804-0.ch004

Figure 1. Outline of latency from healthcare devices to server

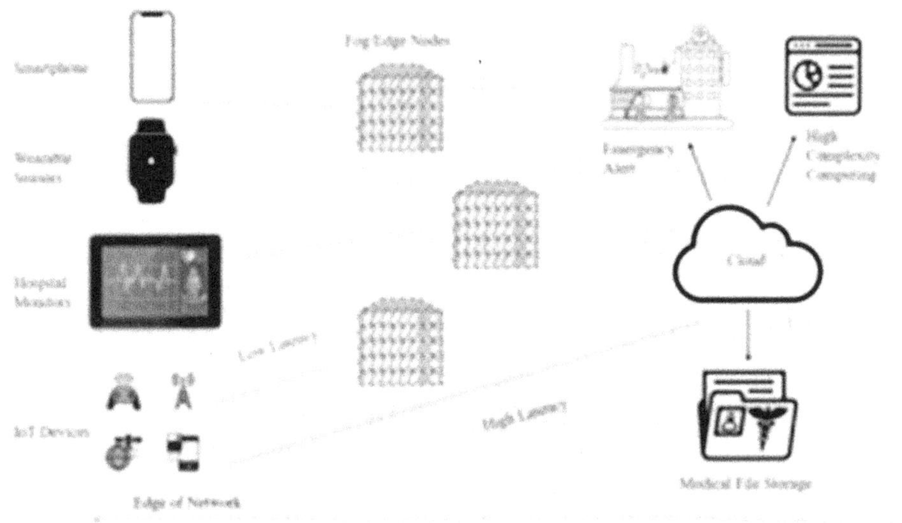

ADVANCEMENT IN HEALTHCARE COMPUTING

This segment examines the fundamentals of computing in the healthcare domain as well as the catalyst which took computing towards a distributed architecture from a centralized cloud, which paved the way for the foundation for edge computing and fog computing. The specific point of reference for pioneering digital healthcare regarding price, use of less energy, and quality of experience are also examined.

Healthcare Application Types

Healthcare applications can be classified into various types by the type of device, data, or unique use case. The following are the primary healthcare classifications based on use cases:

- Monitoring health in Real-Time
- Emergency Management Systems
- Information Dissemination in Healthcare
- Health-aware Edge Devices

Multiple platforms can be used for real-time health monitoring at the same time. Observation of the body's most basic functions like heartbeat, blood pressure, and temperature can be processed on Edge devices, and wearable sensors or can be combined and used. When a patient's health falls below a specific value a real-time monitoring system will activate an alarm as patients these days have diagnostic tools in their hands because of the technological advancements in modern mobile gadgets. Many websites give information about healthcare, employing mobile devices, and customized applications to provide additional health information and assistance to individuals, particularly those suffering from certain chronic conditions.

Examples of modern health care for people are Wearable Sensors like smart watches, Mobile phone-based Sensors like heart rate sensors, and Ambient Sensors for example pedometers. Abnormal heart rates, blood pressure, glucose levels, and body temperature can be identified by Wearable sensors faster than finger prick glucose meters which are older technology. Sensor data is sent across long distances to a server from an edge computing application. For digital health-related purposes, built-in sensors like microphones, gyroscopes, and temperature sensors in smartphones can be used. Ambient sensors are placed around a room or series of rooms to gather data on the user's position without the patient wearing them. They provide better convenience, and this configuration is widely utilized in applications involving fall detection or, in dementia instances, for geriatric location tracking. Ambient sensors can be either interior or outside location sensors or both in certain specialist sensors.

DEMAND FOR IoMT SECURITY-MOTIVES

The Sustainable Development Goals set by United Nations like "Ensure healthy lives and promote well-being for all at all ages", "Take urgent action to combat climate change and its impacts" etc., are yet to be achieved by 2030. In Connected medical devices, cyber security is among the most dangerous IoT challenges for the medical industry. The causes of Healthcare data breaches as of 2022 are 57% Hacking which mostly happens in the network layer, and 13% of unauthorized access, loss, and improper disposal. The capability of a system to add extra resources to manage work of increasing quantity remains a challenge. A huge number of IoT devices are emerging in the market with new technologies and it is assumed that by 2024 IoT connections may reach 83 billion

In traditional systems, security in many IoMT devices is provided by encryption, multifactor authentication, and signature-based intrusion detection systems which requires more energy. The classic security mechanisms use a lot of energy. The longer the bit length, especially for encryption, the more energy is consumed. Another problem of employing this traditional security mechanism is that the keys are stored in a device or storage that could be compromised. A lightweight technique that is both energy efficient and does not require the storing of encryption keys is ideally suited for highly secure and energy efficient IoT. This ensures storage servers and encrypting servers will be reduced and in turn, the carbon footprint for the security mechanism is also considerably reduced. There is an urgent need for extensive study in the service of healthcare management because certain medical needs require more immediate treatment than others. For prioritizing services within the distributed edge network a pre-defined protocol is required

CHALLENGES

- Security

Each device is a vulnerable endpoint. Small data centers like embedded devices are not designed with security measures and are not updated frequently

- Resource allocation

Edge nodes have limited resources when compared to the cloud so for classifying services that can be processed at the edge and which can be transferred to the cloud smart as well as quick decisions are needed

- Integrating heterogeneous entities

Connecting nodes and links of types remains a challenge

- Bandwidth

There is a higher bandwidth allocation at the central data center and a low at the endpoints where a large number of devices growing and the amount of data generated is huge the server may crash

ALARMING CONSEQUENCES OF HEALTHCARE DATA BREACH IN INDIA

There was a leak of CoWIN data via the telegram app and personal data were exposed, though it had "state-of-the-art security infrastructure" data like name, mobile number, Covid vaccination status, and Aadhar national IDs were stolen

The absence of proper security and data protection law leaves individuals vulnerable to scams. Increased Digitization of healthcare data is happening without adequate data protection and refusal to accept cyber attacks. The citizens are at risk of data being leaked since a large amount of data collection, processing, and exchange is happening

India is worst hit by the data breaches reported by a study by NordVPN, where some 600,000 people's data were stolen and sold

RELATED WORKS

- **Communication protocols and network**

To communicate between an edge device and a fog node communication protocols like Bluetooth, and LR-WPAN which have short ranges are used. Using a wireless medium the 802.11 protocol a part of IEEE 802 LAN is frequently used to link a sensor node to various cloud services and computing devices in the work of Rolim et al. (2010). For performing computations most of the applications in previous work of Al Hamid et al. (2017) and Wu et al. (2008) use IEEE 802.15.1 or Bluetooth where computation is performed on a mobile device. Data is being consigned to a medical specialist or another central server utilizing a service of mobile connection such as 4G or 5G. When adequate information that is required accumulates at the network edge which incorporates the sensors is sent to a far end for storage and processing. Tiny handheld devices like smartwatches or e-pills may not be able to provide the processing capacity of a fog node where a large amount can be processed and sent to the server for storage. Data activities such as categorization and compression are conducted at the network's edge in an edge computing architecture. Better than mobile devices edge nodes are frequently modest servers that provide faster data processing. Edge and fog nodes are devices that are placed at various distances and locations between the Cloud and the edge device of the user. This depends on the operational range of the devices

Previously published research for edge gateways used Raspberry Pi, by author Arduino Bhunia et al. (2014), Fratu et al. (2014), and Akrivopoulos et al. (2017) a field-programmable gate array (FPGA) platforms as commercially accessible devices. Because of their low cost and ease of use, they are popular options. In a research paper by Castro et al. (2015) uses a graphics processing unit the input data will be taken as images and computed. Cloud data centers offer services for additional data storage, processing, and retrieval of digital health data. Much research investigates the linkage between fog and cloud, progressing to a better cloud-fog architecture to balance the workloads between nodes for huge event streams.

- **Encryption and authentication**

Few encryption algorithms which are used on edge devices consume minimal energy than other algorithms. When the encryption system consumes low energy a better percentage of energy will be made available for computing the emergency medical data. Elliptic-curve cryptography is a popular encryption method for smart edge devices (ECC). As an example a work by Jia et al. (2018), using the Diffie-Hellman (DH) a key agreement is accomplished and on the edge device, a key is created using the ECC technique. Further in a paper, the scientists describe how they expand their work to incorporate a safe encryption technique by using mobile phones to adequately measure the body vitals like heart rate and blood pressure. ECC is mostly preferred because it requires a significantly smaller key size, which is best suited for a smartphone with limited storage and computational power.

Study by Al Hamid et al. (2017) explains to significantly lessen the cost per bit for a 256-bit security level by ECC form in conjunction with bilinear pairing IBE in a fog architecture when compared to an RSA form. Hardware-based encryption is another source work by Tao et al. (2019), FPGA (Field Programmable Gate Arrays) uses the KATAN ciphers which are lightweight. A comparative study of Tang et al. (2019), reveals that a larger key size is generated by RSA and Diffie-Hellman than ECC and Symmetric Encryption for a similar degree of security. As a result, the creator employs an ECC-based technique over the LR-WPAN for monitoring applications indoors. Many works employ Fully Homomorphic Encryption (FHE) because of its capacity to examine data in an encrypted form to understate the number of ciphertexts transmitted back to a receiver in their medical smart cities design, which is an efficient energy method in improvement of an existing approach employing FHE.

Another security problem for healthcare systems is achieving an efficient kind of privacy. Recent research has a high level of privacy in patient data concealing and has improved value substitution (EVS) in a paper by Elmisery et al. (2016). One of the publications reviewed offered a privacy approach dubbed Decoy Medical Big Data (DMBD). Unlike prior solutions, which only get files that are decoyed when an attacker tries to attack. By storage of digital health profiles on a fog node of a user, a privacy management system maintains the anonymity of patient files. According to Jia et al. (2018), authenticated key agreement (AKA) is a privacy guarantee for healthcare applications. For a wide range of attacks such as a stolen verifier, offline dictionary, and replay AKA offers complete forward privacy and resistance. Further work by Ramli et al. (2013), describes a particular method for working a message authentication code (MAC) by obtaining details of ECG signal from a patient and comparing it to previously saved details. The proposed SecHealth architecture by Giri et al. (2017), employs a very similar authentication method in which a key is equal and approved by either side party, and if not equal and it is refused. This eliminates the need for the device to produce a key and instead delivers the data of a patient, which is validated by the server or rejected depending on the attributes of the data. In this work node attacks like user impersonation, replay, and session key discloser attacks are resistant to authentication. The research employs an authentication protocol that is mutual and every participant (node) should authenticate the participant to assure security prior to any communication to be exchanged using a randomly generated mutual authentication key.

CONCLUSION

Distributed smart IoMT has the capacity to change healthcare digitally by providing real-time monitoring and analyses of data. However, the challenges discussed should be addressed. Despite challenges like heterogeneity, limited computational resources, data privacy, and security deep learning can revolutionize the healthcare sector and improve patient care. Healthcare applications that need a large data set require a promising approach like distributed deep learning. This technology can improve healthcare in many ways including Improved efficiency and patient outcomes by reducing complications, and better decision-making about patient care. The future of healthcare is likely to be shaped by distributed smart IoMT devices which will provide a healthier life for patients around the world.

REFERENCES

Ahila, Dahan, Alroobaea, Alghamdi, Mohammed, Hajjej, Alsekait, & Raahemifar. (2023). A smart IoMT based architecture for E-healthcare patient monitoring system using artificial intelligence algorithms. *Frontires-Sec. Computational Physiology and Medicine*.

Akarsh, Sahoo, & Raj. (n.d.). *Privacy preserving Federated Learning framework for IoMT based big data analysis using edge computing*. Academic Press.

Akrivopoulos, O., Amaxilatis, D., Antoniou, A., & Chatzigiannakis, I. (2017). Design and Evaluation of a Person-Centric Heart Monitoring System over Fog Computing Infrastructure. In *Proceedings of the First International Workshop on Human-centered Sensing, Networking, and SystemsHumanSys'17*. ACM. 10.1145/3144730.3144736

Al Hamid, Rahman, Hossain, Almogren, & Alamri. (2017). A Security Model for Preserving the Privacy of Medical Big Data in a Healthcare Cloud Using a Fog Computing Facility With Pairing-Based Cryptography. *IEEE Access, 5,* 22313-22328. doi:10.1109/ACCESS.2017.2757844

Bhunia, S. S., Dhar, S. K., & Mukherjee, N. (2014). iHealth: A fuzzy approach for provisioning intelligent health-care system in smart city. *2014 IEEE 10th International Conference on Wireless and Mobile Computing, Networking and Communications (WiMob),* 187-193.

Castro, D., Hickson, S., & Bettadapura, V. (2015). Predicting Daily Activities from Egocentric Images Using Deep Learning. In *Proceedings of the 2015 ACM International Symposium on Wearable ComputersISWC '15.* ACM. 10.1145/2802083.2808398

Correia, Alencar, & Assis. (2023). Stochastic modeling and analysis of the energy consumption of wireless sensor networks. *IEEE Xplore.*

Divya Gupta, Bhatia, & Kumar. (2021). *Resolving Data Overload and Latency Issues in Multivariate Time-Series IoMT Data for Mental Health Monitoring.* IEEE.

Elmisery, Rho, & Botvich. (2016). A Fog Based Middleware for Automated Compliance With OECD Privacy Principles in Internet of Healthcare Things. *IEEE Access, 4,* 8418-8441. doi:10.1109/ACCESS.2016.2631546

Fratu, O., Pena, C., Craciunescu, R., & Halunga, S. (2015). Fog computing system for monitoring Mild Dementia and COPD patients - Romanian case study. *2015 12th International Conference on Telecommunication in Modern Satellite, Cable and Broadcasting Services (TELSIKS),* 123-128.

Garcia-Martin, E., Rodrigues, C. F., Riley, G., & Grahn, H. (2019, December). Estimation of energy consumption I machine learning -. *Journal of Parallel and Distributed Computing, 134,* 75–88. doi:10.1016/j.jpdc.2019.07.007

Giri, D., Obaidat, M. S., & Maitra, T. (2017). SecHealth: An Efficient Fog Based Sender Initiated Secure Data Transmission of Healthcare Sensors for e-Medical System. *GLOBECOM 2017 - 2017 IEEE Global Communications Conference,* 1-6.

Hazratifard, Gebali, & Mamun. (2022). Using Machine Learning for Dynamic Authentication in Telehealth: A Tutorial. *Sensors, 22*(19).

Jamshidi, Moztarzadeh, Jamshid, Abdelgawad, & Hauer. (2023). Future of Drug Discovery: The Synergy of Edge Computing, Internet of Medical Things, and Deep Learning. *Internet of Things and Internet of Everything: Current Trends, Challenges, and New Perspectives.*

Jia, X., He, D., Kumar, N., & Choo, K. K. R. (2018). Authenticated key agreement scheme for fog-driven IoT healthcare system. *Wireless Networks.* Advance online publication. doi:10.100711276-018-1759-3

Jiang, Guo, Khan, Cui, & Lin. (2023). *Energy-saving Service Offloading for the Internet of Medical Things Using Deep Reinforcement Learning.* ACM.

Kebira Azbeg, Ouchetto, & Andaloussi. (2022). *BlockMedCare: A healthcare system based on IoT, Blockchain and IPFS for data management security.* Elsevier B.V.

Martinez, Monton, Vilajosana, & Prades. (2015). Modeling power consumption for IoT devices. *IEEE Xplore.*

Mudasir Khan, Shah, Khan, ul Islam, Ahmad, Khan, & Lee. (2023). IoMT-Enabled Computer-Aided Diagnosis of Pulmonary Embolism from Computed Tomography Scans Using Deep Learning. *Artificial Intelligence and Advances in Smart IoT.*

Natarajan, Lokesh, Flammini, Premkumar, Venkatesan, & Gupta. (2023). *A Novel Framework on Security and Energy Enhancement Based on Internet of Medical Things for Healthcare 5.0.* MDPI.

Nazli Tekin, Axar, Aris, Uluagac, & Gungor. (2023). *Energy consumption of on-device machine learning models for IoT intrusion detection.* Elsevier.

Qi, Chiaro, Giampaolo, & Piccialli. (2023). *A blockchain-based secure Internet of medical things framework for stress detection.* Elsevier.

Ramli, S. N., Ahmad, R., Abdollah, M. F., & Dutkiewicz, E. (2013). A biometric-based security for data authentication in Wireless Body Area Network (WBAN). *2013 15th International Conference on Advanced Communications Technology (ICACT),* 998-1001.

Rolim, C. O., Koch, F. L., Westphall, C. B., Werner, J., Fracalossi, A., & Salvador, G. S. (2010). A Cloud Computing Solution for Patient's Data Collection in Health Care Institutions. *2010 Second International Conference on eHealth, Telemedicine, and Social Medicin*e, 95-99. 10.1109/eTELEMED.2010.19

Saravanan, Sreelatha, Atyam, Madiajagan, Saravanan, Kumar, & Sultana. (2023). Design of a deep learning model for radio resources allocation in 5G for massive IoT device. In *Sustainable energy technologies, and assessments.* Elsevier.

Sun, X., Zhang, P., Sookhak, M., Yu, J., & Xie, W. (2017). Utilizing fully homomorphic encryption to implement secure medical computation in smart cities. *Personal and Ubiquitous Computing*, *21*(5), 831–839. doi:10.100700779-017-1056-7

Tang, W., Zhang, K., Zhang, D., Ren, J., Zhang, Y., & Shen, X. S. (2019). Fog-Enabled Smart Health: Toward Cooperative and Secure Healthcare Service Provision. *IEEE Communications Magazine*, *57*(5), 42–48. doi:10.1109/MCOM.2019.1800234

Tao, H., Bhuiyan, M. Z. A., Abdalla, A. N., Hassan, M. M., Zain, J. M., & Hayajneh, T. (2019). Secured Data Collection With Hardware-Based Ciphers for IoT-Based Healthcare. *IEEE Internet of Things Journal*, *6*(1), 410–420. doi:10.1109/JIOT.2018.2854714

Wagan, Koo, Siddiqui, Qureshi, Attique, & Shin. (2023). *A Fuzzy-Based Duo-Secure Multi-Modal Framework for IoT Anomaly Detection*. Elsevier.

Wu, W., Cao, J., Zheng, Y., & Zheng, Y. (2008). WAITER: A Wearable Personal Healthcare and Emergency Aid System. *2008 Sixth Annual IEEE International Conference on Pervasive Computing and Communications (PerCom)*, 680-685. 10.1109/PERCOM.2008.115

Yugank, Sharma, & Gupta. (2022). *An approach to analyse the energy consumption of an IoT system*. Springer.

Chapter 5
Smart Distributed Contactless Airport Baggage Management and Handling System

Ritik Agarwal
Vellore Institute of Technology, India

Azam Siddiqui
Vellore Institute of Technology, India

Shaunak Deshpande
Vellore Institute of Technology, India

Nikhil Chandrashekhar Chapre
Vellore Institute of Technology, India

Anmol Mishra
Vellore Institute of Technology, India

Ansh Khattar
Vellore Institute of Technology, India

Aswathy Ravikumar
iD https://orcid.org/0000-0003-0897-6991
Vellore Institute of Technology, India

Harini Sriraman
iD https://orcid.org/0000-0002-2192-8153
Vellore Institute of Technology, India

ABSTRACT

Smart contactless airport baggage management and handling system is a problem solver that fits in maximum aspects of airport luggage security and management system. Thus, ensuring contactless airport management would result in Covid safety. Current baggage handling management systems (BHMS) are highly error prone. The idea proposed here ensures Covid safety and enhances the current BHMS with the power of algorithms. With the use of this software, a revolutionary idea targets the elimination of the involvement of airport staff during the check-in of a passenger. The authors have developed a system that allows every passenger to validate the details of their luggage four times and maintains security by generating a unique QR at separate checkpoints. They also developed the luggage sorting knapsack algorithm to ensure that the goods are placed efficiently and optimized in the luggage compartment.

DOI: 10.4018/978-1-6684-9804-0.ch005

INTRODUCTION

This software is made to keep two essential goals in mind. First, the most important is ensuring luggage safety until the passenger leaves the airport (Baby, 2014; Khan & Efthymiou, 2021; Lin et al., 2015; S & Ravikumar, 2015). Second, to eliminate human contact from all possible points, thus ensuring the safety of health of everyone (Harini & Ravikumar, 2020; John et al., 2021; Li et al., 2021; Massaro & Rossetti, 2021). The software ensures that no passenger loses or exchanges their luggage. The main objectives are summarized as Providing efficient management for airports, increasing profits for the airline corporations, increasing profits for the management authority of airports, and providing a seamless operation platform. The software aims to improve the Airport experience for the masses. It also encounters the possibility of making the complete airport contactless with improved security measures and reliability. Even nowadays, bag mishandling occurs, resulting in a poor/awful experience for the passenger. Also, strive to eliminate maximum contact and provide a bio-bubble for each passenger.

Moreover, running an airline is not very profitable, so we even focus on managing cargo so that maximum space is utilized, which can, in turn, ripe better profitability. Creativity is one of the areas that airports have consistently exercised to ensure efficiency improvements, resource optimization, and production increases.

RELATED WORKS

The airport business has seen significant innovation in recent years. As airports strive to enhance safety and security, the emphasis on digitalization, efficiency, and productivity has grown (Baki et al., 2022)

Mismanaged passenger luggage is still a significant issue in the airline business. This project focuses on developing an RFID-based baggage handling system (BHS) for airport identification and monitoring of passenger luggage. The existing BHS system is comprised of identification hardware and cloud-based monitoring software. The BHS gadget is built using the UHF passive RFID system and Internet of Things technologies. The gadget may be utilized as a portable device at the check-in desk and in the arrivals area (Salman et al., 2021). The study (Alagiah & Joseph, 2020; Basjaruddin et al., 2019)investigated the applicability of Near Field Communication as just a non-contact data transfer in an aerodrome to improve passenger and baggage management. Passengers use their smartphones to perform frequent authorization in the airport and an NFC tag to hold the status and location of their baggage during the process. The experimental system was created utilizing several NFC scanners and Android-based smartphone apps. The notion of intelligent airports is now the future of major airports and has the potential to transform the sector in its adaptation to new technology fundamentally. In (Arora et al., 2021; Kováčiková et al., 2022), it focuses on the digital development of airports and the influence of Covid-19 on airports' digital transformation. The report presents a qualitative study in the form of an interview schedule with capable individuals holding executive positions in operation, safety, and repair at the airports studied. Airports in Slovakia and the Czech Republic are the topics of primary qualitative research. The information gathered via structured interviews provides a complete picture of the digital maturity of international airports in the Czech Republic and Slovakia and the influence of Covid-19 on the digitalization of the studied airports.

The proposed model has four main checkpoints that will provide real-time status and location of passenger luggage on their mobile device. It is an easy, user-friendly, and simple QR code-based system that will eliminate human contact and chances of error and decrease the risk of loss of luggage.

SMART CONTACTLESS AIRPORT BHMS

The software has mainly four checkpoints that ensure the proper handling and safety of the luggage.

Figure 1. Smart contactless airport BHMS

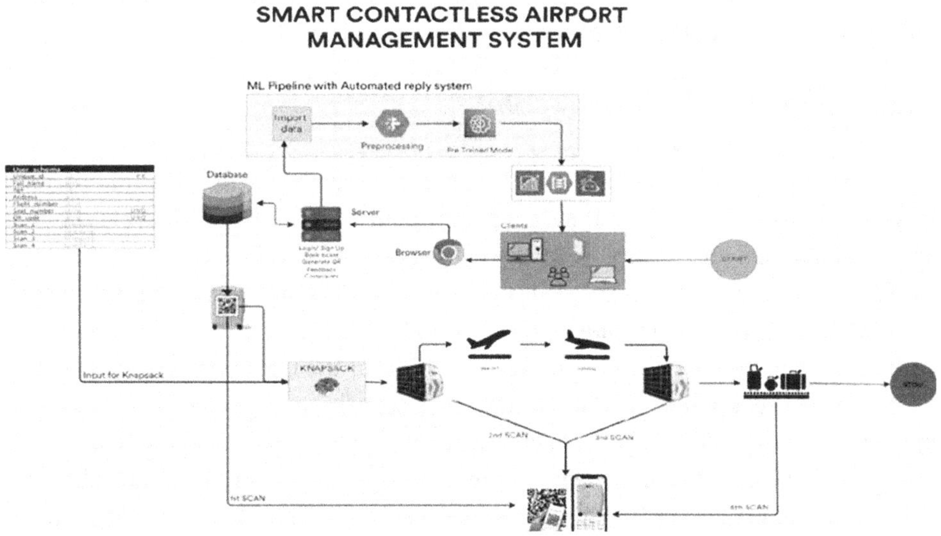

Checkpoint 1: Pre-journey requirements

The covid and RTPCR certificates will be already uploaded to the mobile app. The user will only be allowed inside the airport premises if the vitals are on a certain threshold. The passengers will submit their luggage at the check-in kiosk and get the physical measurements of their luggage. This is the first checkpoint where we will generate the first QR on their app. Post scanning, the passengers will know the status of their luggage linked to the QR.

Checkpoint 2: Application of Knapsack Algorithm

The dimensions and weight collected during the check-in will be used to determine the position of that luggage in the aircraft's luggage chamber, ensuring orderly management of luggage. The bounded Knapsack algorithm evenly distributes the weight between chambers. Given the masses and quantities of no objects, pack them into a knapsack with a total weight/mass W capacity to get the most outstanding total value. This helps free up some chambers or space in some chambers. This space can be used for other cargo shipments. It has been discussed in a research paper that Airlines profit more per kg of cargo shipped as compared to per kg of human passengers transported. Thus, this algorithm will add more profit to the airline's pocket. This will be regarded as the second checkpoint, and this information can be accessed via the application ensuring the user that their luggage is safely on board.

Checkpoint 3: Post-Landing Validation

Later, after the flight's landing, scanning the QR code will act as the third checkpoint; only then will the luggage be allowed on the conveyor belt.

Checkpoint 4: Final Checkpoint

Upon receiving the luggage, the passenger must scan it for the last time before leaving the airport to ensure they have their authentic luggage. This will be our application's final checkpoint to ensure the luggage is found.

The advantage of using QR codes over traditional barcodes is that QR codes store about ten times more data using only 30% of the paper. Also, QR codes can withstand up to 30% of information recoverability if the QR code gets damaged.

All these checkpoints ensure the luggage's security and reduce the chances of luggage exchange between passengers, which is a widespread anomaly. Thus, with this project, we plan to solve many problems by applying technology, and also, we make sure to reduce the risk of spreading diseases by eliminating human interaction.

Algorithm 1. Knapsack Algorithm

```
Declare W, w1, w2… wn, V1…. vn
A= [0, 0,0], V=0
Repeat n times:
    If W=0:
        Return (V, A)
    Select I with Wi> 0 and max vi/wi
    a=min(wi,W)
    V=V +a(vi/wi)
    wi= wi-a
  A[i]=A[i]+a
  W=W-a
Return (V, A)
```

IMPLEMENTATION DETAILS

To ensure proper security and safety of the luggage for each passenger, the airport authorities would assign a QR code to each bag which would be helpful to keep the bag in check at various checkpoints. An App in 'React Native' would be used by the passenger to fill in all the required details before the arrival and to scan his/her luggage at the time of arrival and departure. Software code languages, tools, and services used MongoDB Database **(Abbes & Gargouri, 2016; Ali et al., 2019)**, Android/iOS App.

There are 4 QR scans whose data would be stored in our MongoDB backend:

1. 1st Scan (By the Passenger at the time of departure)
2. 2nd Scan (By the Airport authorities at the time of loading the baggage into the cargo section)
3. 3rd Scan (By the Airport authorities at the time of unloading of the baggage into the airport at the time of arrival)
4. 4th Scan (By the passenger at the time of arrival to ensure the final collection of the bag).

The project focuses on providing a platform to passengers that would ease out the process of Air-Travel. Every year, 5% of the 1.2 billion mishandled bags are lost. This indicates that each year there really are 1,400,000 misplaced bags. In contrast, 18% are broken, and 77% are late, which amounts to 5,040,000 broken bags and 21,560,000 checked luggage that still need to be delivered to their owners on time.

Figure 2. Luggage collection management

Luggage collection:

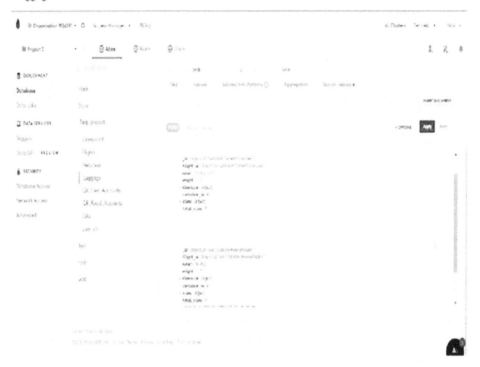

On a median, for every 1,000 travelers, 5.69 pieces of luggage are mishandled. As well as the number continues to increase by 2.2% this year, from 5.57 the prior year. These statistics are frightening; hence, the program benefits the BHMS's safety. It simplifies the process of certifying papers at the arrival time, saving passengers much time again and reducing airline labor expenses. In addition to enhancing the safety of passenger bags, software promotes the dependability of the entire airline. Our technology also improves the management of baggage and the usage of the luggage compartment, which increases the overall profitability of the airline.

The software can also be used in various domains, such as:

- Real world problem solving
- Algorithm development
- Web and App development (**Ravikumar & Sriraman, 2023a**)
- Machine Learning (**Ravikumar & Sriraman, 2023b**)
- Automation

Figure 3. Flight management

Flights collection:

Figure 4. App screenshots

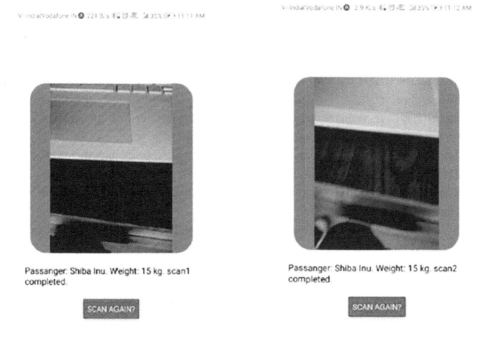

Passanger: Shiba Inu. Weight: 15 kg. scan1 completed.

SCAN AGAIN?

Passanger: Shiba Inu. Weight: 15 kg. scan2 completed.

SCAN AGAIN?

Figure 4. App screenshots

Passanger: Shiba Inu. Weight: 15 kg. scan1 completed.

SCAN AGAIN?

Passanger: Shiba Inu. Weight: 15 kg. scan2 completed.

SCAN AGAIN?

ETHICAL CONCERN

Smart contactless airport baggage systems may be unethical. Search results suggest the following ethical dilemmas:

Privacy issues: Smart baggage management systems use personal data and travel history to track and manage luggage.

Sharing passenger data with other service providers raises concerns about data security and privacy.

Smart baggage management technologies may put airport ground support personnel out of work, which might hurt their families.

Travelers with disabilities may struggle with smart luggage management systems. This might lead to bias towards traveler groups that struggle with luggage.

Safety and Reliability: Smart baggage management systems may be unsafe and unreliable if not routinely updated or maintained.

System malfunctions or faults might lead to mishandled or misplaced luggage, which could have major repercussions for travelers.

Use of intelligent baggage management systems may have an impact on the environment, particularly if those systems rely on energy-intensive technology.

This may exacerbate environmental problems like climate change.

Overall, the implementation of smart contactless airport baggage management and handling systems could raise ethical concerns related to privacy, job displacement, accessibility, reliability and safety, and environmental impact. It is important for airports and service providers to address these concerns and ensure that the systems are implemented in an ethical and responsible manner.

FUTURE SCOPE

Airport contactless luggage handling and management systems are promising. Integrating Smart Airport Solutions Airports are using automated luggage handling technologies. These methods reduce airport ground support staff workload and increase customer satisfaction. Smart airport technology help regional airports stay profitable and provide services. Enhanced Efficiency and Reliability: Smart contactless baggage management systems provide fast speeds, huge carrying capacity, and enhanced reliability. These gadgets can reduce delays by improving luggage handling. Better Customer Experience: Intelligent baggage management solutions improve travel experiences. By automating and streamlining baggage handling, airports can improve customer satisfaction. Technological Developments: Smart baggage management systems may use machine learning and mixed reality. Machine learning algorithms can allow people deposit baggage by taking pictures. Market Growth: The airport baggage handling systems market will increase considerably in the future years. By 2023, the market is expected to reach USD 2758.24 million, growing 12.84%. This indicates that airlines need more advanced baggage management systems. Smart contactless airport baggage management and handling technologies will improve efficiency, reliability, and customer experience.

CONCLUSION

For future improvements, the LSTM prediction model's robustness and the input factors' quality can be improved to improve accuracy. The given RNN Model can be transformed into a dynamic feedback control structure. The factor for the success of the biometrics entry-exit program is the cooperation of all parties involved, particularly airlines. CBP is now relying on airlines for the execution of the exit program at boarding gates due to human resources shortages and budgetary constraints. In the lack of Byzantine nodes, the PBFT algorithm may be enhanced to CSPBFT, which employs a more straightforward consistency protocol to minimize data transmission between nodes. With this carelessness, the aviation sector confronts an annual growth in flight travelers, and the number of lost bags likewise climbs annually. To handle smart luggage handling, RFID automation processes are used in areas where they drastically reduce the amount of mishandled luggage. There are various areas for development, such as making more comprehensive datasets accessible to the community. Data Surveys may be conducted on a larger population.

REFERENCE

Abbes, H., & Gargouri, F. (2016). Big Data Integration: A MongoDB Database and Modular Ontologies based Approach. *Knowledge-Based and Intelligent Information & Engineering Systems: Proceedings of the 20th International Conference KES-2016,* (pp. 446–455). Science Direct. 10.1016/j.procs.2016.08.099

Adek, R. T., & Ula, M. (2020). A Survey on The Accuracy of Machine Learning Techniques for Intrusion and Anomaly Detection on Public Data Sets. *2020 International Conference on Data Science, Artificial Intelligence, and Business Analytics (DATABIA).* IEEE. 10.1109/DATABIA50434.2020.9190436

Alagiah, M., & Joseph, B. (2020). Smart Airline Baggage Tracking and Theft Prevention with Blockchain Technology. *Test Engineering and Management, 83,* 3436–3440.

Ali, M., Sheikh, S., & Sohail, Y. (2019). Reduction of Food Wastage through Android Application. *Make You Smile, 10*(10).

Arora, M., Tuchen, S., Nazemi, M., & Blessing, L. (2021). Airport Pandemic Response: An Assessment of Impacts and Strategies after One Year with COVID-19. *Transportation Research Interdisciplinary Perspectives*, *100449*, 100449. doi:10.1016/j.trip.2021.100449 PMID:34458721

Baby, K. (2014). *Big Data: An Ultimate Solution in Health Care.*

Baki, T. A., Noordin, B., Mohamed, N., Idrus, S. M., & Rasid, S. Z. A. (2022). Digitalization of Airside Operations Process to Improve Airport Operations For The Case of Malaysia Airports. *2022 4th International Conference on Smart Sensors and Application (ICSSA),* (pp. 130–134). IEEE. 10.1109/ICSSA54161.2022.9870954

Basjaruddin, N. C., Ramadhan, S., Adinugraha, F., & Kuspriyanto, K. (2019). Baggage Tracing at Airports using Near Field Communication. *2019 International Conference on Advanced Mechatronics, Intelligent Manufacture and Industrial Automation (ICAMIMIA),* (pp. 109–113). IEEE. 10.1109/ICAMIMIA47173.2019.9223350

Harini, S., & Ravikumar, A. (2020). Effect of Parallel Workload on Dynamic Voltage Frequency Scaling for Dark Silicon Ameliorating. *2020 International Conference on Smart Electronics and Communication (ICOSEC)*, (pp. 1012–1017). IEEE. 10.1109/ICOSEC49089.2020.9215262

John, J., Ravikumar, A., & Abraham, B. (2021). Prostate cancer prediction from multiple pretrained computer vision model. *Health and Technology, 11*(5), 1003–1011. doi:10.100712553-021-00586-y

Khan, N., & Efthymiou, M. (2021). The use of biometric technology at airports: The case of customs and border protection (CBP). *International Journal of Information Management Data Insights, 1*(2), 100049. doi:10.1016/j.jjimei.2021.100049

Kováčiková, K., Remencová, T., Sedláčková, A. N., & Novák, A. (2022). The impact of Covid-19 on the digital transformation of the airports. *Transportation Research Procedia, 64*, 84–89. doi:10.1016/j.trpro.2022.09.011

Li, X., Yuen, K. F., Wang, X., & Wong, Y. D. (2021). Contactless technologies adoption during the coronavirus pandemic: A combined technology acceptance and health belief perspective. *Technology Analysis and Strategic Management*, 1–14. doi:10.1080/09537325.2021.1988919

Lin, J. T., Shih, P.-H., Huang, E., & Chiu, C.-C. (2015). Airport baggage handling system simulation modeling using SysML. *2015 International Conference on Industrial Engineering and Operations Management (IEOM)*, (pp. 1–10). IEEE. 10.1109/IEOM.2015.7093764

Massaro, A., & Rossetti, S. (2021). Comparing proximity for couples of close airports. Case studies on city-airports in the pre COVID-19 era. *Journal of Air Transport Management, 91*, 101977. doi:10.1016/j.jairtraman.2020.101977

Ravikumar, A., & Sriraman, H. (2023a). Computationally Efficient Neural Rendering for Generator Adversarial Networks Using a Multi-GPU Cluster in a Cloud Environment. *IEEE Access : Practical Innovations, Open Solutions, 11*, 1–1. doi:10.1109/ACCESS.2023.3274201

Ravikumar, A., & Sriraman, H. (2023b). Acceleration of Image Processing and Computer Vision Algorithms [Chapter]. Handbook of Research on Computer Vision and Image Processing in the Deep Learning Era. IGI Global. doi:10.4018/978-1-7998-8892-5.ch001

S, D., & Ravikumar, A. (2015). A Study from the Perspective of Nature-Inspired Metaheuristic Optimization Algorithms. *International Journal of Computer Applications, 113*(9), 53–56. doi:10.5120/19858-1810

Salman, A., Adiono, T., Abdurrahman, I., Aditya, Y., & Chandra, Z. (2021). *Aircraft Passenger Baggage Handling System with RFID Technology.*, doi:10.1109/ ISESD53023.2021.9501689

Chapter 6

On the Detection of Faces With Masks Using Tiny YOLOv7 Algorithm

Akhil Kumar
Vellore Institute of Technology, Chennai, India

Megha Singh
Vellore Institute of Technology, Chennai, India

ABSTRACT

Today every individual is expected to wear a mask, which poses a new challenge to security and surveillance of individuals for any governing body. Though notable work has been done in the area of face mask detection, there still exists a bottleneck of fast detection. Additionally, the complexity of features, size of frames, and inhomogeneity of data poses a challenge to achieve a model with high accuracy. And law offenders are quick to exploit this opportunity to their advantage. Through this work, the aim is to propose a system that combines Tiny YOLOv7 and Jestson Nano which is able to detect faces with or without mask based on the recently introduced Tiny YOLOv7 algorithm. The proposed system was able to achieve a mAP of 55.94% and an average IoU of 53.70%. The average precision achieved for people with masks was 83.80% and 79.67% for specific detection of the mask region. The model uses a total of 5.527 BFLOPs and was able to achieve an average FPS of 71.8, which ensures a higher throughput leading to a faster model both in terms of training and detection.

INTRODUCTION

With the rapid development and application of deep learning algorithms in the recent years, a number of research areas have achieved tremendous results, Computer

DOI: 10.4018/978-1-6684-9804-0.ch006

Vision being one of them (Zhou et al., 2017). Object detection, which deals with the problem of locating instances of objects in an image or a video, is one of the many subdomains of Computer Vision. Today in the age of COVID-19 pandemic, every individual is expected to wear a face mask to ensure their own safety. This is a necessary measure but it does impose a challenge to surveillance and security of people as it is hard to detect these faces because of the obstruction caused by the masks. Though, in the last couple of years significant work has been done in this field, most of the proposed methods struggle with the detection of face masks that are too small an object to detect and further achieve low detection accuracy (Kumar et al., 2022).

YOLO (You Only Look Once) is termed as a state-of-the-art object detection model that uses quite a different approach than most other object detectors. While the other models look at different parts of the image multiple times at multiple scales to detect objects, YOLO looks at the entire image only once. YOLO is a fast object detector with high efficiency, making it ideal for computer vision applications. YOLO learns generalizable representations of objects. When trained on natural images and tested on artwork, YOLO outperforms top detection methods like DPM and R-CNN by a wide margin (Redmon et al., 2016). The latest version of the YOLO algorithm which was released in July 2022 added a few new training routines to achieve faster detection with higher accuracy, which were: Extended Efficient Layer Aggregation (E-ELAN), Compound scaling for concatenation based-model, Re-parameterized planning and Coarse-to-fine auxiliary head.

Through this work, we aim to propose a system to detect faces with or without masks, which consists of a camera, a speaker, and a Jetson Nano-based processing unit and can be easily installed to conduct surveillance in real time. The camera provides us with visual input in real time, the feed is then processed by the processing unit which uses weights trained with the recently released Tiny TOLOv7 algorithm to detect faces and face masks. This processing unit generates a signal for the speakers to flag people with or without face masks. The FMD (Face Mask Detection) dataset (Kumar, Kalia, Verma et al, 2021) used to train these weights consists of 52,635 images annotated with 4 classes: with masks, without masks, mask worn incorrectly, and mask region. For each class label the dataset is richly annotated with more than 50,000 tight bounding boxes in total.

BACKGROUND

In the last couple of years, various machine learning and deep learning algorithms including a combination of CNN, R-CNN, ResNet-50, transfer learning, MobileNetv2 and different versions of YOLO have been proposed for the task of detecting faces with masks.

Kumar et al. (2022) proposed a new variant of the tiny YOLOv4 algorithm for face mask detection to achieve high precision and detection accuracy. This was possible by the addition of a dense SPP network to the feature extraction network and two additional YOLO detection layers to chosen convolutional layers. The proposed variant was able to achieve a 9.93% higher mAP (mean average precision) when compared to the original algorithm, also it attained an IoU (Intersection over union) value of 61.02% over the FMD (Face mask Detection) dataset. Kumar et al. (2021) collated a novel face masks detection dataset consisting of annotations for 4 classes namely, with masks, without masks, mask region, mask incorrectly, which consists of 52,635 diverse images. They also propose variants for tiny YOLOv1, tiny YOLOv2, tiny YOLOv3 and tiny YOLOv4 by adding additional convolutional layers to the original network architecture. Kumar et al. (2021) also proposed a variant for the tiny YOLOv4 algorithm which added a SPP (spatial pyramid pooling) module and additional YOLO detection layer to the network. The algorithm outperformed YOLOv1, tiny YOLOv1, YOLOv2, tiny YOLOv2, tiny YOLOv3 and tiny YOLOv4. It gives 6.6% higher mAP than the original tiny YOLOv4 model and 14.05% higher AP when detecting mask region on face. Loey et al. (2021) used ResNet-50 (Residual Neural Network), a kind of deep transfer learning based on residual learning, as a feature extractor and then replaced its last layer with SVM, decision tree and ensemble machine learning components. The SVM classifier was able to achieve a testing accuracy of 99.64% for RMFD (Real-World Masked Face Dataset), 99.49% for SMFD (Simulated Masked Face Dataset) and 100% for LFW (Labeled Faces in the Wild) dataset. Loey et al. (2021) combined ResNet-50 with YOLOv2, ResNet-50 is used as a deep learning model to extract features and YOLOv2 works as the detection network. The authors also generated a new face mask detection dataset by combining the MMD (Medical Mask Dataset) and FMD (Face Mask Detection), though it had no separate class label for mask region. The model achieved an average precision of 81%. Nagrath et al. (2021) proposed a model which used SSD (Single Shot Multibox Detector) as a face detector and MobileNet-v2 architecture as a framework for the classifier. The approach was able to attain an accuracy score of 0.9264 and F1 score of 0.93. Chowdary et al. (2020) fine-tuned the state-of-the-art deep learning model InceptionV3 for the task of face mask detection, the last layer was replaced by 5 additional layers. This was able to achieve an accuracy of 99.9% during training and 100% during testing for the given dataset.

Roy et al. (2020) compared the performance of YOLOv3, tiny YOLOv3, SSD and R-CNN on the proposed dataset for face mask detection, Moxa3k, which consists of 3000 images with class labels: 'mask' and 'nomask'. Maximum mAP of 66.84% was achieved by YOLOv3 608x608, however due to the increased input size and heavy processing overhead it fails to provide real time inference. Khandelwal et al. (2020) utilized pre-trained MobileNetv2 for the purpose of face mask detection. The proposed system was able to attain an accuracy of 97.8% for a small dataset of a total of 380 images. An original neural network of 8 layers was proposed by Inamdar et al. (2020). The model was trained on a small self-generated dataset of just 35 images and achieved a classification accuracy of 98.6%. Li et al. (2020) proposed a model to deal with head pose classification for faces with face mask on, which combines the H-channel of the HSV color channel with face portrait and grayscale image. It then used convolutional neural networks to extract features for classification. The proposed model was able to detect front view and side view with an accuracy of 93.64% and 87.17% respectively. Ramgopal et al. (2023) used the concept of transfer learning alongside the YOLO-v3 algorithm to tackle the problem of face mask detection. The proposed technique was able to achieve an accuracy of 92% and F1 score of 0.90 on the employed dataset. Putri et al. (2022) combined transfer learning with DenseNet169 to classify people into "with_mask" and "without_mask". The authors used DenseNet169 with fully connected layer architecture which used a ReLU activation function and Adam optimiser. The model was able to achieve an accuracy of 96% on the employed dataset of 8929 images. Abirami et al. (2022) utilized YOLOv3, YOLOv4 and the various variants of YOLOv5 algorithm to conduct real-time face mask detection. These models were tested on two varied datasets of 12,000 and 26,000 images and it was concluded that YOLOv5x1 gave the highest accuracy of 98%, though it also took the longest to train.

DATASET CHARACTERISTICS

The Face Mask Detection (FMD) dataset (Kumar, Kalia, Sharma et al, 2021) employed in this work consists of a total of 52,635 images with more than 50000 tight bounding boxes and was created by crawling the internet using Google and Bing APIs. Originally, 11,000 images for varying size and dimensions were collected from the internet and then resized to a size of 416x416. The images were then annotated

Figure 1. Sample images from FMD dataset

using the LabelImg annotation tool (Tzutalin, 2015) with 4 class labels: 'with mask', 'without mask', 'mask incorrectly' and 'mask region'. Lastly, data augmentation techniques such as rotation, shearing, flipping and HSV shift were applied to get an enhanced dataset of 52,635 images. The image samples of the employed dataset are presented in Figure 1.

Though many diverse datasets are available that contain the annotations for whether a person is wearing a mask or not in a given image, FMD dataset was the first one to include annotations for incorrect mask position and specific mask area on a person's face.

PROPOSED APPROACH

In this section, firstly we explain the architecture of the latest version of Tiny YOLO algorithm, Tiny YOLOv7, released in July of 2022. Then, we present a face mask detection system employing this algorithm which is able to detect faces with masks in real time.

Tiny YOLOv7 Algorithm

Object detection models can be classified into two types: one-stage detectors and two-stage detectors. YOLO adopts the one-stage detection principle where all the components of the object detection pipeline are unified into a single neural network. Meanwhile, a two-stage detector as presented in Figure 2 uses separate stages to detect regions of importance and classify whether an object is present in those detected regions, this makes it slower in comparison. Thus, using a one-stage detection model we are able to detect faces and face masks in real time. The network architecture of Tiny YOLOv7 algorithm provided by Figure 3 and Table 1.

Figure 2. Architecture for an object detection model

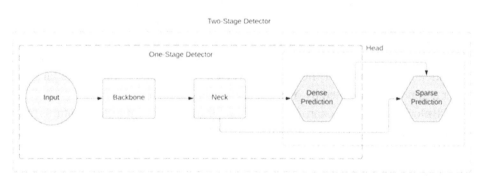

The model can be broken down into three sections namely, backbone, neck and head. Backbone is a deep learning network that works as the feature extractor for our model, neck aggregates all the feature maps generated at different stages in the backbone and the head conducts object detection.

Bag of freebies (BoF) refers to the set of methods that bring a change to the training strategy or increase the cost of training while keeping the cost of inference low. The YOLOv7 model also introduced a few new bag of freebies namely, Extended Efficient Layer Aggregation (E-ELAN), Compound scaling for concatenation based-model, Re-parameterised planning and Coarse-to-fine auxiliary head. On the other hand, bag of specials (BoS) refers to the set of methods which significantly improve the accuracy of the model while causing a small increase in inference cost. There are separate sets of methods assigned for the backbone and the detector. For example, for the backbone of YOLO the BoF features include data augmentation methods, DropBlock regularization, Class label smoothing, and for the detector/head it includes CIoU loss function, data augmentation methods, Cross-Iteration mini–Batch Normalization (CmBN), Self-Adversarial Training etc. The BoS for backbone includes Mish activation function, Cross-stage partial connections (CSP), Multi-input weighted residual connections (MiWRC), and for the detector it includes modified SPP block, SAM block, PANet block, Mish activation function and DIoU-NMS.

Feature Extraction Network

The backbone or the feature extraction network of tiny YOLOv7 is made up of CSPDarknet53, bag of freebies, and bag of specials. The CSPDarknet53 network was inspired by DenseNet which utilizes the concept of skipping connections between layers. But it's hard to train as it runs into the problem of having too many parameters. Thus, the concept of CSP (Cross Stage Partial) was adopted. The CSP architecture copies the base layer feature map, then sends one copy to the dense block and another copy straight to the next stage. This allows CSPDarknet53 to remove computational bottlenecks present in the DenseNet architecture. It also ensures better learning for the model because of the access to the unedited feature map.

Next, we have the neck which enriches the information given by the backbone to be then fed to the head. Neighboring feature maps from top-down stream and bottom-up stream are combined together and then fed to the head, this ensures spatially and semantically rich input for the object detection network. SPP and PANet are two major components adopted by YOLO for this very reason.

SPP block increases receptive field and is able to separate important features from the backbone. The convolutional neural networks generate feature maps using filters of different sizes, which leads to different sizes of feature maps. Spatial Pyramid Pooling layer allows us to generate fixed size features irrespective of the size of the

Table 1. Network architecture of Tiny YOLOv7

Type	Filters	Size/Stride	Output
Convolutional	32	3x3/2	208x208x32
Convolutional	64	3x3/2	104x104x64
Convolutional	32	3x3	104x104x32
Route			104x104x64
Convolutional	32	1x1	104x104x32
Convolutional	32	3x3	104x104x32
Convolutional	32	3x3	104x104x32
Route			104x104x128
Convolutional	64	1x1	104x104x64
Maxpool		2x2/2	52x52x64
Convolutional	64	1x1	52x52x64
Route			52x52x64
Convolutional	64	1x1	52x52x64
Convolutional	64	3x3	52x52x64
Convolutional	64	3x3	52x52x64
Route			52x52x256
Convolutional	128	1x1	52x52x128
Maxpool		2x2/2	26x26x128
Convolutional	128	1x1	26x26x128
Route			26x26x128
Convolutional	128	1x1	26x26x128
Convolutional	128	3x3	26x26x128
Convolutional	128	3x3	26x26x128
Route			26x26x512
Convolutional	256	1x1	26x26x256
Maxpool		2x2/2	13x13x256
Convolutional	256	1x1	13x13x256
Route			13x13x256
Convolutional	256	1x1	13x13x256
Convolutional	256	3x3	13x13x256
Convolutional	256	3x3	13x13x256
Route			13x13x1024
Convolutional	512	1x1	13x13x512
SPP-CSP			
Convolutional	256	1x1	13x13x256
Route			13x13x512
Convolutional	256	1x1	13x13x256

continued on following page

Table 1. Continued

Type	Filters	Size/Stride	Output
SPP			
Maxpool		1x1/5	13x13x256
Route			13x13x256
Maxpool		1x1/9	13x13x256
Route			13x13x256
Maxpool		1x1/13	13x13x256
Route			13x13x1024
End of SPP			
Convolutional	256	1x1	13x13x256
Route			13x13x512
Convolutional	256	1x1	13x13x256
End of SPP-CSP			
Convolutional	128	1x1	13x13x128
Unsample		2	26x26x128
Route			26x26x256
Convolutional	128	1x1	26x26x128
Route			26x26x256
Convolutional	64	1x1	26x26x64
Route			26x26x256
Convolutional	64	1x1	26x26x64
Convolutional	64	3x3	26x26x64
Convolutional	64	3x3	26x26x64
Route			26x26x256
Convolutional	128	1x1	26x26x128
Convolutional	64	1x1	26x26x64
Unsample		2	52x52x64
Route			52x52x128
Convolutional	64	1x1	52x52x64
Route			52x52x128
Convolutional	32	1x1	52x52x32
Route			52x52x128
Convolutional	32	1x1	52x52x32
Convolutional	32	3x3	52x52x32
Convolutional	32	3x3	52x52x32
Route			52x52x128
Convolutional	64	1x1	52x52x64
Convolutional	128	3x3/2	52x52x128
Route			52x52x256

continued on following page

Table 1. Continued

Type	Filters	Size/Stride	Output
Convolutional	64	1x1	26x26x64
Route			26x26x256
Convolutional	64	1x1	26x26x64
Convolutional	64	3x3	26x26x64
Convolutional	64	3x3	26x26x64
Route			26x26x256
Convolutional	128	1x1	26x26x128
Convolutional	256	3x3/2	13x13x256
Route			13x13x512
Convolutional	128	1x1	13x13x128
Route			13x13x512
Convolutional	128	1x1	13x13x128
Convolutional	128	3x3	13x13x128
Convolutional	128	3x3	13x13x128
Route			13x13x512
Convolutional	256	1x1	13x13x256
Route			13x13x256
Convolutional	128	3x3	13x13x128
Convolutional	27	1x1	13x13x27
YOLO			
Route			26x26x128
Convolutional	256	3x3	26x26x256
Convolutional	27	1x1	26x26x27
YOLO			
Route			
Convolutional	512	3x3	13x13x512
Convolutional	27	1x1	13x13x27
YOLO			

feature maps. It uses pooling layers such as Max Pooling and generates different representations of the feature maps while giving a fixed length output. Sliding window pooling uses a single window size whereas SPP which utilizes multi-level spatial-bins is able to work with object deformations. The YOLO network first divides the features along the depth dimension, then applies SPP separately to each part and later combines them together to generate the fixed length output feature map, while preserving the capital dimension.

PANet works as a feature aggregator in the YOLO network. It's a feature pyramid network which extracts important features from the backbone network. In case of a simple network, an input is passed through a number of layers, the output from the previous layer works as an input for the next layer. Early layers provide us with the localized texture and pattern information which is then needed by the later layers to build up semantic information. But the localized information may be lost by the network. Using the concept of PANet, YOLO concatenates the current layer with the information from the previous layer, this allows better propagation of layer information from bottom-up and top-down.

Detection Network

In case of one-stage detectors, the head is required to just provide dense prediction, whereas for two-stage detectors, it also gives sparse predictions. For YOLO, we have dense predictions which gives us a vector with coordinates of the predicted bounding box, the confidence score of prediction and the predicted class label.

The authors of YOLO tried and tested many different concepts to get the best possible combination of inference speed and mAP score. For anchor-based detection, they tested RPN (Region Proposal Network), SSD (Single Shot-Detector), RetinaNet and YOLO, and for anchor less detection CornerNet, CenterNet, MatrixNet and FCOS (Fully Convolutional One-Stage Object Detection). For anchor-based object detection, YOLO was termed as the most efficient detector.

Loss Function

Many of the object detection models use bounding boxes to determine the location of an object. When a model uses L2 loss for calculating the difference in position and size of the predicted bounding box and the real bounding box, it minimizes the errors on small objects. IoU loss tries to resolve this problem, instead of optimizing 4 coordinates individually, it considers the bounding box as a unit.

The Tiny YOLOv7 algorithm employs CIoU loss, which adds two additional features to the previously mentioned IoU loss, namely central point distance and aspect ratio. Central point distance, which is the distance between the actual bounding box center point and the predicted bounding box center point, is employed and aspect ratio of the actual bounding box and the predicted bounding box is compared as shown in equation (1).

$$L_{CIoU} = 1 - IoU + \frac{\rho^2(b, b^{gt})}{c^2} + \alpha v \tag{1}$$

where b and bgt denote the central points of the actual and predicted bounding boxes, ρ is the Euclidean distance, c is the diagonal length of the smallest enclosing box covering the two boxes, and v measures the consistency of the aspect ratio as shown in equation (2).

$$v = \frac{4}{\pi^2} \left(\frac{w^{gt}}{h^{gt}} - \frac{w}{h} \right)$$

(2)

where h is the height and w is the width of the bounding boxes.

Calculating Anchor Boxes

Anchor boxes refers to a set of predefined bounding boxes with specific height and weight, defined based on the object sizes in the training dataset. They are used to capture the scale and aspect ratio of the object classes and they allow us to evaluate all object predictions at the same time.

In the case of earlier versions of YOLO, the authors only used K-means clustering to calculate the anchor boxes, but 1-IoU (Intersection over Union) was utilized as a distance metric instead of Euclidean distance as with Euclidean distance larger

Figure 3. Tiny YOLOv7 network

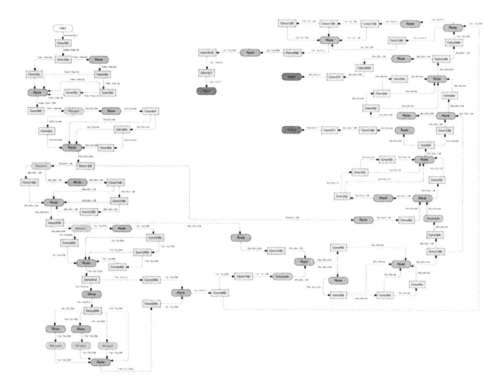

boxes generate more error than small metrics. However, for YOLOv5 and YOLOv7 a new approach was employed. K-means clustering with Euclidean distance was used to get the initial anchor boxes. Then the best anchor set, with respect to the chosen anchor fitness metric, is selected for use. The anchor set found by K-mean clustering is taken and changed slightly. Fitness metric for the new anchor set is calculated, if the results are better, then the next mutation is performed on the new anchor set, otherwise the old anchor set is used. The default number of anchor boxes was set to 9, and the same is used here. The final calculated anchor values for our dataset were: [(9 × 13), (17 × 27), (28 × 43), (37 × 69), (58 × 91), (75 × 148), (133 × 121), (131 × 229), (231 × 301)].

Face Mask Detection System

The face mask detection system we propose consists of a CCTV camera, a Jetson Nano based processing unit and speakers, to be used for the purpose of surveillance and warranting security. The CCTV camera provides us with a real time input for our system. The input is then fed to the processing unit which utilizes the weights we generated by training the Tiny YOLOv7 model on Face Mask Detection (FMD) dataset. The dataset is split into a train, test and validation set in a ratio of 80:10:10. Out of the total 52,635 images, 42,115 were part of the training set and both the test set and the validation set had 5,260 images each. The initial weights and configuration files used for training were provided by the authors of YOLO and can be acquired from the "darknet" repository on Github (Alexey, n.d.). After training the model, we tested it on random images and videos from the internet to check whether satisfactory results were obtained before moving ahead. Once it was confirmed that our model was able to detect faces and face masks with high accuracy, we took the final weights generated by this model for our processing unit. The processing unit implements a python script that utilizes the OpenCV library. The input is taken and processed using the configuration file for Tiny YOLOv7 and the weights generated by the trained model, after detection if we get a "Face with mask" class label, the system then produces an audio signal alerting the supervisors with presence of a person wearing a face mask. The system also generates a video output, which can be saved on the system or directly to the cloud, with all the predicted bounding boxes and class labels for later reference. The detailed architecture of the face mask detection system is presented in Figure 4.

Figure 4. Architecture of the face mask detection system

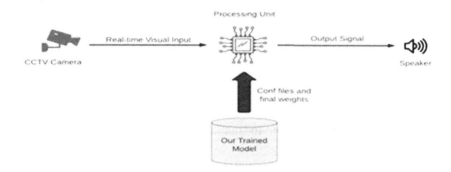

RESULTS

The proposed model was evaluated in comparison to several previously proposed face mask detection models utilizing different versions of Tiny YOLO algorithm. The metrics used for this purpose were average precision (AP) and mAP i.e., mean average precision. AP is calculated for each class and then mean average precision is calculated by averaging AP values achieved across all classes under consideration as presented in equation (3-4).

$$Average\ Precision = \int_{r=0}^{1} p(r)\ \mathrm{d}r \tag{3}$$

AP for any specific class is given by the area under the precision-recall curve of that class.

$$mAP = \frac{1}{n} \sum_{i=1}^{n} AP_i \tag{4}$$

where APi refers to the average precision of class i and n is the total number of classes in our dataset.

Our proposed system was able to achieve a mAP (mean average precision) value of 55.94% for the test set, where it has an AP (average precision) of 83.80% for faces with mask, 79.67% for mask region, 55.94% for faces without masks and 4.36% for masks worn incorrectly. The trained model had a F1-score of 0.64 with 0.58 recall and 0.70 precision. And average IoU (Intersection over Union) was found to be 53.70%. When this model was used to detect faces and face masks for a video input, it was able to do so with an average FPS (Frames-per-Second) of 71.8. Compared to a human eye which has an FPS between 30-60, the model is able to detect faces and face masks at a much higher detection rate, which allows it to be used conveniently in a real-time detection system. Alongside this, it also just uses a total of 5.527 BFLOPs, which is a much smaller value when compared to other face mask detection models. BFLOPs or Billion Floating-Point Operations is a measure of computer performance and refers to how many billion floating point operations are required to run a single instance of any given model in the domain of deep learning. Our model is able to train at a faster rate and hence can be used to develop an autonomous system.

The Table 2 highlighting the quantitative results concludes that when compared on the basis of mAP and BFLOPs our model is able to effectively balance precision with computation costs, which was proven by the accurate bounding boxes generated by the system for random test images taken from the internet. Though the model has lower mAP value when compared to Tiny YOLO v4 algorithm, it uses significantly lesser BFLOPs. Whereas, in comparison to earlier versions of Tiny YOLO algorithm it is able to provide much better mAP value leading to only a minor increase in computation cost. Also, the earlier versions of Tiny YOLO algorithm were able to achieve a detection speed of 45-60 FPS, making our model, with 71.8 FPS, much faster in comparison. Hence, the proposed system is able to achieve the best of both worlds. The qualitative detection results are presented in Figure 5.

DISCUSSION AND CONCLUSION

Through this work, we were able to propose a solution to the issue of surveillance that has risen with the increased usage of face masks in the age of COVID-19 pandemic. The system was able to provide real-time feedback with a mAP of 83.80% for people wearing masks and 79.67% for the mask region at a much faster detection rate than the human eye. The proposed model requires less time in training than its

Table 2. Comparative statistics of performance

Algorithm	mAP	BFLOPs
Tiny YOLOv1	30.75%	5.20
Tiny YOLOv2	33.78%	5.34
Tiny YOLOv3	49.03%	6.81
Tiny YOLOv4	57.71%	8.72
Tiny YOLOv7	55.94%	5.527

Figure 5. Results obtained by the trained face mask detection model

predecessors, allowing it to be used on mobile devices installed with Jetson Nano or Raspberry Pi with high efficiency.

Though the proposed system is the first to utilize the Tiny YOLOv7 algorithm for the task of detection of people with face masks and is much faster than the previously proposed works which use earlier versions of the Tiny YOLO algorithm, while the mAP and F1-score achieved by this model is comparable to them. The proposed work can be further extended by configuring the Tiny YOLOv7 network architecture for the specific purpose of detection of people with face masks to get even better results.

REFERENCES

Abirami, T., Priakanth, P., & Madhuvanthi, T. (2022). Effective Face Mask and Social Distance Detection with Alert System for Covid-19 Using YOLOv5 Model. In Advances in Parallel Computing Algorithms, Tools and Paradigms (pp. 80-85). IOS Press. doi:10.3233/APC220011

Alexey, A. B. (n.d.). *Darknet.* Github repository. https://github.com/AlexeyAB/darknet

InamdarM.MehendaleN.(2020).Real-timefacemaskidentificationusingfacemasknet deep learning network. Available at SSRN 3663305. doi:10.2139/ssrn.3663305

Jignesh Chowdary, G., Punn, N. S., Sonbhadra, S. K., & Agarwal, S. (2020, December). Face mask detection using transfer learning of inceptionv3. In *International Conference on Big Data Analytics* (pp. 81-90). Springer. 10.1007/978-3-030-66665-1_6

Khandelwal, P., Khandelwal, A., Agarwal, S., Thomas, D., Xavier, N., & Raghuraman, A. (2020). Using computer vision to enhance safety of workforce in manufacturing in a post covid world. arXiv preprint arXiv:2005.05287.

Kumar, A., Kalia, A., & Kalia, A. (2022). ETL-YOLO v4: A face mask detection algorithm in era of COVID-19 pandemic. *Optik (Stuttgart)*, *259*, 169051. doi:10.1016/j.ijleo.2022.169051 PMID:35411120

Kumar, A., Kalia, A., Sharma, A., & Kaushal, M. (2021). A hybrid tiny YOLO v4-SPP module based improved face mask detection vision system. *Journal of Ambient Intelligence and Humanized Computing*, 1–14. PMID:34691278

Kumar, A., Kalia, A., Verma, K., Sharma, A., & Kaushal, M. (2021). Scaling up face masks detection with YOLO on a novel dataset. *Optik (Stuttgart)*, *239*, 166744. doi:10.1016/j.ijleo.2021.166744

Li, S., Ning, X., Yu, L., Zhang, L., Dong, X., Shi, Y., & He, W. (2020, May). Multi-angle head pose classification when wearing the mask for face recognition under the COVID-19 coronavirus epidemic. In *2020 international conference on high performance big data and intelligent systems (HPBD&IS)*, (pp. 1-5). IEEE.

Loey, M., Manogaran, G., Taha, M. H. N., & Khalifa, N. E. M. (2021a). A hybrid deep transfer learning model with machine learning methods for face mask detection in the era of the COVID-19 pandemic. *Measurement*, *167*, 108288. doi:10.1016/j.measurement.2020.108288 PMID:32834324

Loey, M., Manogaran, G., Taha, M. H. N., & Khalifa, N. E. M. (2021b). Fighting against COVID-19: A novel deep learning model based on YOLO-v2 with ResNet-50 for medical face mask detection. *Sustainable Cities and Society*, *65*, 102600. doi:10.1016/j.scs.2020.102600 PMID:33200063

Nagrath, P., Jain, R., Madan, A., Arora, R., Kataria, P., & Hemanth, J. (2021). SSDMNV2: A real time DNN-based face mask detection system using single shot multibox detector and MobileNetV2. *Sustainable Cities and Society*, *66*, 102692. doi:10.1016/j.scs.2020.102692 PMID:33425664

Putri, L. F. O., Sudrajad, A. J., & Nastiti, V. R. S. (2022). Classification of Face Mask Detection Using Transfer Learning Model DenseNet169. *Jurnal RESTI*, *6*(5), 790–796.

Ramgopal, M., Roopesh, M. S., Chowdary, M. V., Madhav, M., & Shanmuga, K. (2023). Masked Facial Recognition in Security Systems Using Transfer Learning. *SN Computer Science*, *4*(1), 1–7. PMID:36311350

Redmon, J., Divvala, S., Girshick, R., & Farhadi, A. (2016). You only look once: Unified, real-time object detection. In *Proceedings of the IEEE conference on computer vision and pattern recognition* (pp. 779-788). IEEE. 10.1109/CVPR.2016.91

Roy, B., Nandy, S., Ghosh, D., Dutta, D., Biswas, P., & Das, T. (2020). MOXA: A deep learning based unmanned approach for real-time monitoring of people wearing medical masks. *Transactions of the Indian National Academy of Engineering*, 5(3), 509–518. doi:10.100741403-020-00157-z

Tzutalin. (2015). *LabelImg*. Github. https://github.com/heartexlabs/labelImg

Zhou, X., Gong, W., Fu, W., & Du, F. (2017, May). Application of deep learning in object detection. In *2017 IEEE/ACIS 16th International Conference on Computer and Information Science (ICIS)* (pp. 631-634). IEEE. 10.1109/ICIS.2017.7960069

Chapter 7

Stock Market Analysis and Prediction Using ARIMA, Facebook Prophet, and Stacked Long Short-Term Memory Recurrent Neural Network

Parvathi R
Vellore Institute of Technology, Chennai, India

Xiaohui Yuan
University of North Texas, USA

ABSTRACT

Stock analysis involves comparing a company's current financial statement to its financial statements in previous years to give an investor a sense of whether the company is growing, stable, or deteriorating. Stock market analysis helps in getting insights into a company's stock and to make better decisions in buying or selling shares in the stock market. This chapter proposes a method to analyze and predict stock market prices based on historical data of 4 MNCs namely, Amazon, Apple, Google, and Microsoft. The prediction is implemented using three models; namely, ARIMA model, Facebook's Prophet model, and lastly a self-constructed, stacked LSTM model. The results of the three models are compared and analyzed. Mean absolute error is used to analyze the performance of the models on real-time test data. The minimum loss achieved by Facebook Prophet Model is 2.445, by ARIMA Model is 10.782, and the Stacked LSTM Model achieved a minimum loss of 6.552.

DOI: 10.4018/978-1-6684-9804-0.ch007

INTRODUCTION

Forecasting is the process of predicting a future event with the help of historical data. It is widely used in many applications such as business, industries, finance, etc. Forecasting problems involves analysis of time, and are classified into three types,

- Short term forecasting, where the prediction is done for the duration of few seconds, minutes, days, weeks or months.
- Medium term forecasting, where the duration of prediction ranges from one to two years.
- Long term forecasting, where the duration of prediction is beyond two years.

A time series data consists of sequential observations or information for a particular variable. For our research paper, the variable taken into consideration is the stock price which is either univariate or multivariate. Univariate data comprises of information about a single stock, whereas multivariate data includes stock prices of multiple companies at various time instances. Time series data analysis aids in identifying different trends, patterns, and cycles or periods that is present in the data. Knowledge about the bullish or bearish mode in case of stock market data, helps in wise investment of money. Additionally, analyzing the patterns helps in determining the good performing companies for a certain time period. As a result, time series analysis and forecasting are extremely important areas of research. The existing approaches for predicting stock prices are classified as technical analysis, fundamental analysis, and time series forecasting (Devadoss & Ligori, 2013).

Fundamental analysis is defined as a type of investment analysis specifically used for long-term forecasting, helps in determining the company's share value by assessing the profits, sales, earnings, and other economic factors. In technical analysis, the historical stock data is used for prediction of future prices. One of the popular technical analysis methods is the moving average which is defined as the unweighted mean of the last n data points. and is best suitable for short term predictions. It can be considered as the unweighted mean of past n data points. This method is suitable for short term predictions. The third method is the analysis of time series data and involves two classes of algorithms, namely linear model and non-linear models.

The different linear models are AR, ARMA, ARIMA and using predefined equations to fit a mathematical model to a univariate time series. The main disadvantage is that the model cannot identify inter dependencies as they consider only univariate time series data, and also does not account for the latent dynamics existing in the data. Hence resulting in a model, that is not capable of identifying dynamics or patterns in the whole data. Non-linear models involve methods like

ARCH, GARCH,(Menon et al., 2016) TAR, Deep learning algorithms (Batres-Estrada, 2015). In (Abinaya et al., 2016), an analysis is performed regarding the inter dependency between stock price and stock volume for 29 selected companies listed in NIFTY 50. The proposed methodology focuses on the application of deep learning algorithms for stock price prediction (Heaton et al., 2016) (Jia, 2016). Deep neural networks are considered as non-linear functions that are capable of non-linear functional mappings. Various deep neural network models like Convolutional Neural Network, Long Short-Term memory, multi-layer perceptron is employed depending on its application like image processing, time series analysis, natural language processing, etc. (Goodfellow et al., 2016).

The stock market is an area which goes through variations every single day, and needs constant refinements. Forecasting of stock market data is based on an assumption that the future data can be predicted with the data available at present. Hence this can help the investors to plan intensively and to make profit. Stock trend forecasting is one of the most difficult tasks to achieve in finance market because of the difficulty in the highly intricate world of stock market. Investors in the stock market are always looking for a methodology that may assure simple profit by anticipating stock movements and minimizing investment risk. This encourages domain researchers to develop new forecasting models. Stock prices cannot be randomly generated, rather the data has to be generated based upon historical data obtained at regular time periods. As it is essential to design a model to study and predict stock prices with appropriate information for decision making, it is suggested that the transformation of time series is done using ARIMA model (Batres-Estrada, 2015). Another common model named Prophet (Mondal et al., 2014) by Facebook can also be used, as it works well on seasonal time series data. This model provides several alternatives to handle the seasonality of the dataset. With available seasonality options like yearly, weekly and daily, a data analyst can choose a desired time granularity for model forecasting on the dataset (Menon et al., 2016). The proposed method uses ARIMA model, Facebook Prophet, and lastly a self-constructed, stacked LSTM model for prediction of stock market prices.

RELATED WORK

This paper presented by (Ariyo et al., 2014) describes a detailed process of building stock price predictive model using the ARIMA model. The stock data from New York Stock Exchange (NYSE) and Nigeria Stock Exchange (NSE) are applied to the generated forecasting model. The results obtained by applying the model to Nokia Stock data and Zenith bank data revealed that the ARIMA model has a high potential for short-term prediction and can compete well with existing stock price prediction strategies. In this work proposed by (Roondiwala et al., 2017), they have used one of the most precise forecasting technologies using Recurrent Neural Network and Long Short-Term Memory unit which helps investors, analysts or any person interested in investing in the stock market by providing them a good knowledge of the future situation of the stock market. After performing various simulations with a different number of parameters and epochs, and by considering 4 features set such as High, Low, Open, Close with 500 epochs, the model achieved results with training and testing RMSE values of 0.00983 and 0.00859 respectively.

In this paper proposed by (Mondal et al., 2014), a study has been conducted on the effectiveness of Autoregressive Integrated Moving Average (ARIMA)model, on fifty-six Indian stocks belonging to different sectors. ARIMA model is chosen because of its wide acceptability and simplicity. The comparison and parameterization of the ARIMA model have been done using Akaike information criterion (AIC). For all the sectors, the ARIMA model achieved an accuracy above 85% in predicting stock prices indicating that the model gives good accuracy for prediction. For Information Technology sector, the standard deviation is not too low or not too high, and the accuracy is above 90% in prediction for this sector. In this work, (Nelson et al., 2017) studies the usage of LSTM networks on a scenario to predict future trends of stock prices based on the historical prices, along with technical analysis indicators. For that goal, a prediction model was built, and a series of experiments were executed and theirs results analyzed against a number of metrics to assess if this type of algorithm presents and improvements when compared to other Machine Learning methods and investment strategies. The results that were obtained achieved an average of 55.9% of accuracy when predicting if the price of a particular stock price will rise or decrease in the future.

(Zunic et al., 2020) presents a framework that is capable of effectively estimating future sales values in the retail industry and categorizing the product portfolio according to the expected level of forecasting reliability. The proposed framework, which would be extremely useful for any retail organization, is based on Facebook's Prophet algorithm and backtesting technique. The framework is evaluated with the real-world sales forecasting data obtained from biggest retail companies in Bosnia and Herzegovina, and the model's capabilities are demonstrated in a real-world use case scenario. The methodology proposed by (Selvin et al., 2017) is model independent. Rather than fitting the data to a predefined model, we use deep learning architectures to uncover the underlying dynamics in the data. In this paper, they examine the performance of three alternative deep learning architectures for price prediction of NSE companies. Finally, they are using a sliding window methodology to forecast future values on a short-term basis. The performance of the models was quantified using percentage error.

PREDICTION MODELS

Facebook Prophet

Facebook Prophet is a procedure that makes use of an additive model for forecasting time series data by fitting non-linear trends with daily, weekly, yearly seasonality, and also holiday effects. It is known to work efficiently with time series data having strong seasonal effects, and also several seasons of historical data. It is robust to factors like missing data and shifts in the trend, and handles outliers well. The model is similar to the decomposable time series model with three main model components such as holidays, trend, seasonality which is given in the equation (1)

$$y(t) = g(t) + h(t) + \varepsilon(t) \tag{1}$$

The g(t) denotes the trend function which models the non-periodic changes in time series values. The s(t) represents periodic changes such as weekly or yearly seasonality. The h(t) denotes the holidays effects that occur on irregular schedules over one or more days, and lastly εt represents the error term.

ARIMA Model

ARIMA is known as "Autoregressive Integrated Moving Average". Here, AR stands for "Autoregression" which represents a model that makes use of the dependent relationship between observations and their lagged ones. The I stand for "Integrated", that involves in making the time series data stationary. Lastly, MA stand for "Moving Average" that makes use of dependency between an observation and residual error from the model to the lagged observations.

An ARIMA model can forecast future values based on its own past data comprising of lags of its own and forecast errors. It is mainly denoted by 3 terms, namely p, d, q where p is the order of the "Autoregression" term, q is the order of the "Moving Average" term, and d is the number of differencing required to make the time series stationary. ARIMA models can be used to represent all kinds of 'non-seasonal' time series data that has patterns and not random white noise. The prediction is done based on the lags from the linear regression model, and gives the best results when the predictors, that is the lags are independent of each other.

Long Short-Term Memory

A Recurrent Neural Network (RNN) is a feedforward neural network with an internal memory. RNN is recurrent in nature as it executes the same function for each and every input data as the outcome of the current input is dependent on the past data. After generation of the output, it is replicated and returned to the recurrent network. For making a decision, it considers both the input and the output that it has learned from the previous input. RNNs, unlike feedforward neural networks, can handle input sequences using their internal memory. As a result, they may be used for tasks like handwriting recognition or speech recognition. The inputs are independent of each other in other neural networks, whereas in case of RNN, all inputs are dependent on each other.

Initially, it takes X(0) from the sequence of input and then outputs h(0) which together with X(1) is the input for the next step. So, the h(0) and X(1) together is the input for the next step. Similarly, h(1) from the next is the input with X(2) for the next step and it goes on.

The formula for the current state is given in equation (2),

$$\mathbf{h}_t = f(\mathbf{h}_{t-1}, \mathbf{x}_t) \tag{2}$$

Applying Activation Function as in equation (3),

$$\mathbf{h}_t = \tanh(W_{hh}\mathbf{h}_{t-1} + W_{xh}\mathbf{x}_t) \tag{3}$$

W is weight, **h** is the single hidden vector, W_{hh} is the weight at previous hidden state, W_{xh} is the weight at current input state, **tanh** is the Activation function, that implements a non-linearity that squashes the activations to the range [-1.1]

Long Short-Term Memory (LSTM) model is a type of RNN that can remember and maintain long term dependencies from the data. This is because of the basic architecture and principle followed by the RNN. In order to learn new information by the model, it alters the current information that is stored by applying a function. This model further tries to remove all irrelevant information too. As a result, the entire information is modified accordingly.

PROPOSED METHODOLOGY

The proposed methodology can be divided into two modules, namely the visualization module, and the prediction module. The visualization module is all about the visualization of the stock market data of four companies namely Amazon, Apple, Google and Microsoft obtained from Yahoo Finance. Visualization is implemented using the Matplotlib library, and respective inferences are obtained. The second module deals with the prediction, which will help in predicting stock market data using historical data. The module deals with three types of implementations such as ARIMA model, Facebook's Prophet model and lastly a self-constructed LSTM model. The results of the predicted prices are plotted in the graph, and compared with the original prices. Figure 1 depicts the architecture diagram of the proposed model.

Visualization

The visualization of the stock data is important, as it helps the investors to extract inferences that could help them in making decision regarding investments. Graphs can be plotted to understand the trend, and to identify hidden patterns. Moreover, this can also be used for risk analysis.

Dataset Description

The dataset used for visualization is retrieved in real-time from Yahoo Finance. Figure 2 shows the sample dataset. The dataset consists of the columns High, Low, Open, Close, Volume, and lastly Adjusted Close values of the particular stock. The open values denote the price at which the stock starts trading. Similarly, the close values denote the stock's price at the end of the day. The high and low value are the highest price and the lowest price of the period. The adjusted close value includes factors like dividends, stock splits, and new stock offerings. The following is implemented for all the four company's stock market data visualization.

Figure 1. System architecture

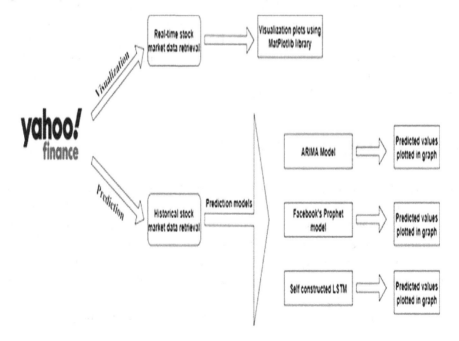

Figure 2. Sample dataset

Date	High	Low	Open	Close	Volume	Adj Close
2020-06-05	82.937500	80.807503	80.837502	82.875000	137250400.0	82.320328
2020-06-08	83.400002	81.830002	82.562500	83.364998	95654400.0	82.807037
2020-06-09	86.402496	83.002502	83.035004	85.997498	147712400.0	85.421921
2020-06-10	88.692497	86.522499	86.974998	88.209999	166651600.0	87.619614
2020-06-11	87.764999	83.870003	87.327499	83.974998	201662400.0	83.412964

Visualization

The 'Close' values are plotted from Amazon, Apple, Google and Microsoft stock market data in Figure 3.

The 'Volume' values are plotted from Amazon, Apple, Google and Microsoft stock market data in Figure 4.

The 'Moving Average' values is calculated from the Amazon, Apple, Google and Microsoft stock market data, and are plotted in Figure 5.

The Percent change value for each day is calculated and is plotted from Amazon, Apple, Google and Microsoft stock market data in Figure 6.

The Daily return for each day is calculated and is plotted from Amazon, Apple, Google and Microsoft stock market data in form of histograms, and additionally density plots are also plotted in Figure 7.

The Monte Carlo plots are plotted for Amazon, Apple, Google and Microsoft stock market data, which is done for risk analysis in Figure 8.

Analysis and Inferences

From the Figure 3, we can infer that the close values of the MNCs such as Apple, Amazon, Microsoft, Google are in an increasing trend with dips at few instances.

Figure 3. Plots of closing values

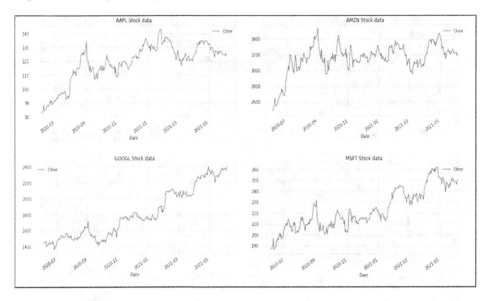

Figure 4. Plots of volume values

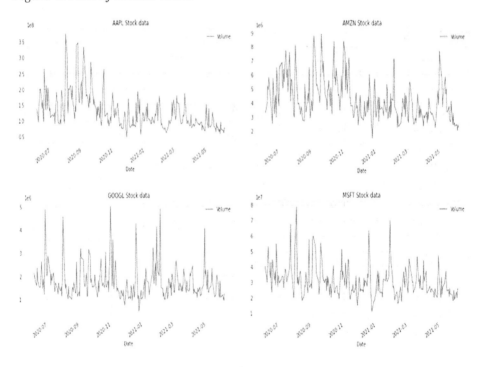

Figure 5. Plots of moving average values

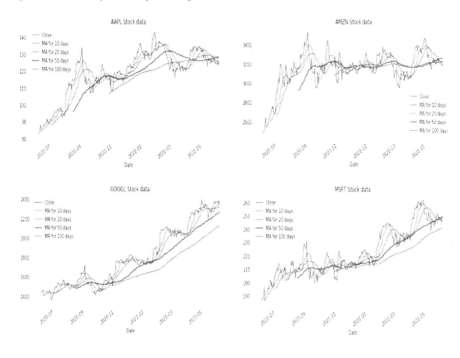

Figure 6. Plots of percent change of each company

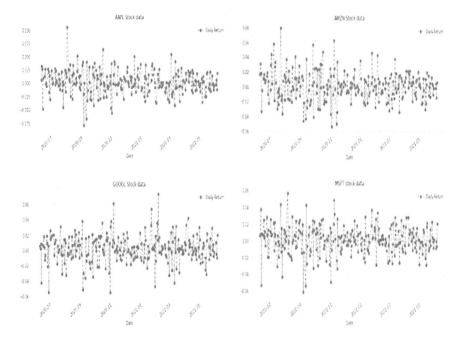

Figure 7. Histogram plots of daily returns, and the density plots of the same

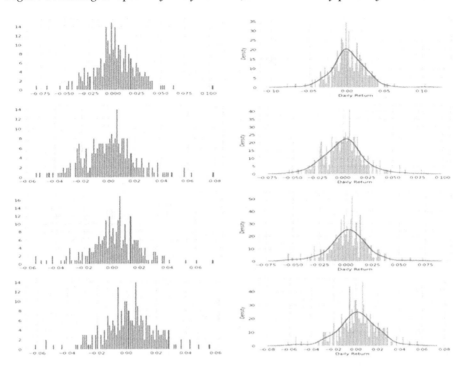

Figure 4 depicts the volume trend values of all the MNCs we have considered where companies such as Amazon, Google, Microsoft have periodic increase and dips in the volume values. But in the Amazon stock data, the volume value had a steep increase, but kept gradually decreasing after that. Figure 5 plots the moving average values in the range of 10, 20, 50 and 100 days of the close values. All the companies except Amazon have an increasing trend, whereas in Amazon, we can notice a stagnant trend. Figure 6 plots the percent change values for each day for each of the company to understand the trend change with respective to each company. Figure 7 depicts the histogram for the daily return value for each of the company, and a density plot is plotted for the same. Figure 8 depicts the Monte Carlo plot for risk analysis with respective to each of the company such as Amazon, Apple, Apple, Microsoft.

Prediction

Dataset Description

Figure 9 shows the sample historical dataset used for prediction. For prediction, we make use of historical data from the year 2016 up to 2021. Here, we have an

Figure 8. Monte Carlo analysis

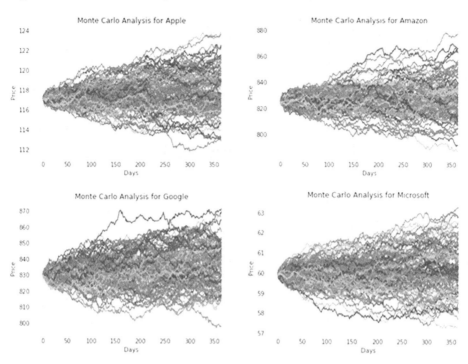

Figure 9. Sample historical dataset

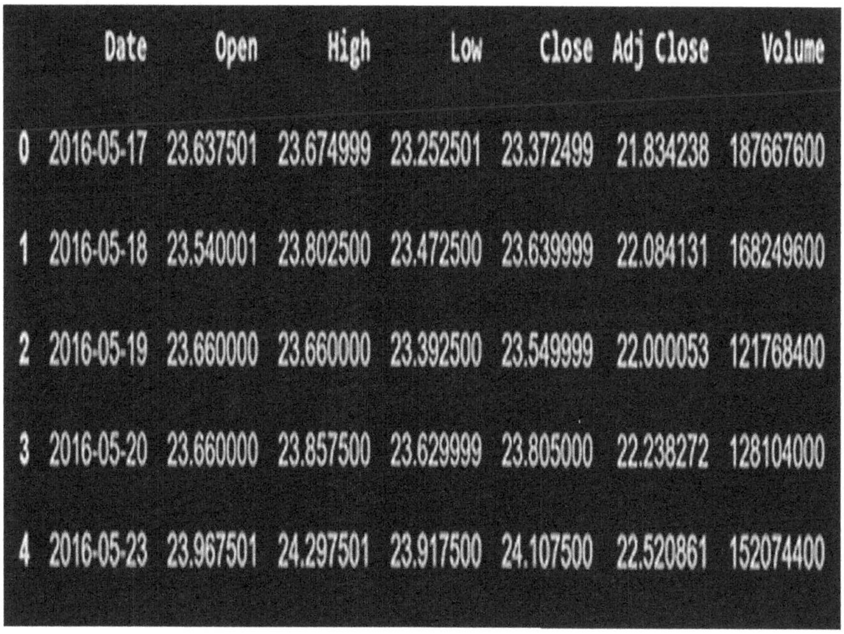

	Date	Open	High	Low	Close	Adj Close	Volume
0	2016-05-17	23.637501	23.674999	23.252501	23.372499	21.834238	187667600
1	2016-05-18	23.540001	23.802500	23.472500	23.639999	22.084131	168249600
2	2016-05-19	23.660000	23.660000	23.392500	23.549999	22.000053	121768400
3	2016-05-20	23.660000	23.857500	23.629999	23.805000	22.238272	128104000
4	2016-05-23	23.967501	24.297501	23.917500	24.107500	22.520861	152074400

additional column named Date which depicts the values of Open, High, Low, Close, Adjusted Close for each date value. The prediction model gets trained with respect to this data. Now let's look into the implementation of the three models.

ARIMA Model

The ARIMA model is trained using the historical data and the predicted values are plotted along with the real values.

In the Figure 10, the blue line indicates the predicted values and the red line indicates the real values. From the plotted graph, we can see that both the predicted and actual values are almost near.

Facebook Prophet

Using the Facebook's Prophet model, the predicted values are obtained, along with the confidence interval. In the Figure 11, the black dots are the real values, whereas the blue color line is the predicted line, along with the light blue region which is the

Figure 10. ARIMA model graphs

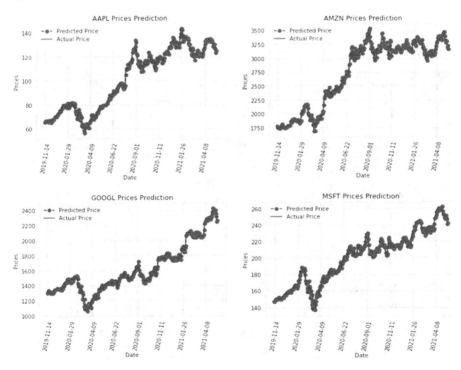

Figure 11. Prediction using prophet model

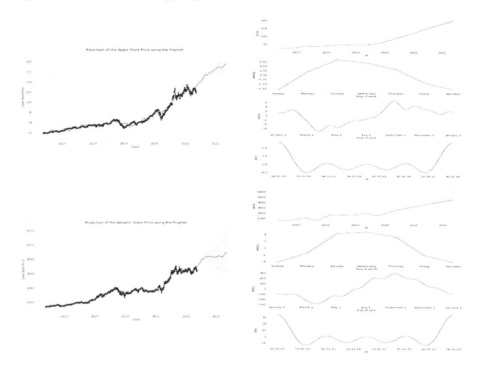

confidence interval range. Along with this, the seasonal components of the data are also plotted which depicts the trend, the weekly, daily, and yearly trend.

Self-Constructed, Stacked LSTM

The LSTM model is given in the Figure 12. The model is trained separately for each historical data belonging to each of the company such as Apple, Amazon, Microsoft, Google. The model predicts the future values, and the values are plotted in the graph in Figure 13 along with the real values.

RESULTS

The three models used for predicting stock prices such as ARIMA model, LSTM model, and lastly Facebook's Prophet model has been validated using the mean absolute error values, and the results are as follows.

Table 1 shows the mean absolute error value for four companies Amazon, Apple, Microsoft, Google with respect to the ARIMA model for prediction. The model

Figure 12. Constructed LSTM model for prediction

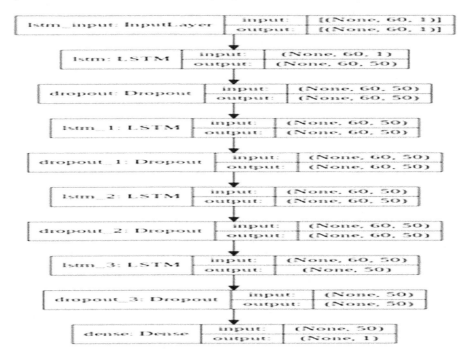

Figure 13. LSTM model results

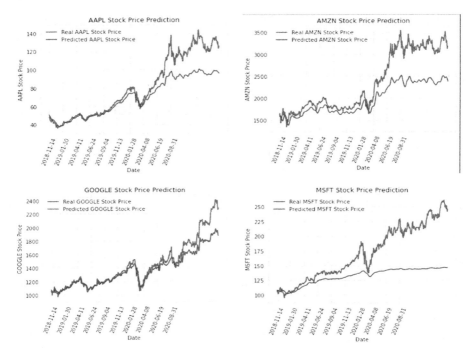

Table 1. Mean absolute error for ARIMA model

Stock Name	Mean Absolute Error
Amazon	42.829
Apple	10.782
Microsoft	43.042
Google	23.121

achieved the least error value for Apple data, whilst all the other companies' error value are in the range of 40.

Figure 14 depicts the training loss of the LSTM model with respective to four companies such as Apple, Amazon, Microsoft, Google. The training loss has gradually decreased as the number of epochs increases. From the plots, we can infer that the model achieved the most minimum loss with all the companies. Table 2 depicts the mean absolute error values on the testing data and achieved the least error value with Apple data. When compared with the error values obtained with the ARIMA model, the model achieved better results with the LSTM model.

Figure 14. Training loss of LSTM model

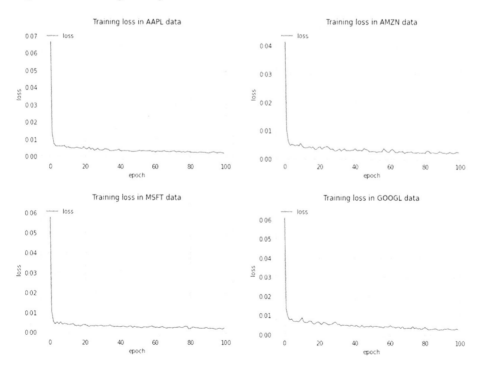

Table 3 shows the results obtained with Facebook Prophet model. The table depicts the mean absolute error values obtained on the testing data with the Facebook Prophet model.

From the above prediction graphs and also the mean absolute error values, we can conclude that the Facebook Prophet model, and the LSTM performed better in terms of prediction. But in the LSTM, few differences were observed as the stock prices sky rocketed than the normal trend. This could be because of the unusual trend observed in all the stock data because of the pandemic. The model was not able to consider these factors in predicting the stock data, but Facebook's Prophet can be considered as the best model. This is because of the confidence interval predicted by it. With the help of the confidence interval, we will have a specific safe range in which the investors can invest and preventing losses to an extent. This will give an idea about the range in which the future stock prices may range, and the investors can invest accordingly.

CONCLUSION

The popularity of stock market trading is growing rapidly and is encouraging researchers to find out new methods for the prediction using new techniques. The forecasting technique is not only helping the researchers but it also helps investors and any person dealing with the stock market. In order to help predict the stock

Table 2. Mean absolute error for LSTM model

Company Name	Mean Absolute Error
Amazon	11.228
Apple	6.552
Microsoft	12.556
Google	13.084

Table 3. Mean absolute error for Facebook Prophet model

Company Name	Mean Absolute Error
Amazon	5.901
Apple	2.445
Microsoft	3.695
Google	13.137

indices, a forecasting model with good accuracy is required. In this work, we have used one of the most precise forecasting technologies using Long Short-Term Memory unit, ARIMA model, and Facebook Prophet model which helps investors, analysts or any person interested in investing in the stock market by providing them a good knowledge of the future situation of the stock market.

REFERENCES

Abinaya, P., Kumar, V. S., Balasubramanian, P., & Menon, V. K. (2016). Measuring stock price and trading volume causality among Nifty50 stocks: The Toda Yamamoto method. In *2016 International Conference on Advances in Computing, Communications and Informatics (ICACCI)* (pp. 1886-1890). IEEE. 10.1109/ICACCI.2016.7732325

Ariyo, A. A., Adewumi, A. O., & Ayo, C. K. (2014). Stock price prediction using the ARIMA model. In *2014 UKSim-AMSS 16th International Conference on Computer Modelling and Simulation* (pp. 106-112). IEEE. 10.1109/UKSim.2014.67

Batres-Estrada, B. (2015). *Deep learning for multivariate financial time series.* Academic Press.

Box, G. E., Jenkins, G. M., Reinsel, G. C., & Ljung, G. M. (2015). Time series analysis, control, and forecasting. Academic Press.

De Gooijer, J. G., & Hyndman, R. J. (2006). 25 years of time series forecasting. *International Journal of Forecasting*, *22*(3), 443–473. doi:10.1016/j.ijforecast.2006.01.001

Devadoss, A.V. & Ligori, T.A.A. (2013). Forecasting of stock prices using multi-layer perceptron. *International Journal of Computing Algorithm, 2*, 440-449.

Goodfellow, I., Bengio, Y., Courville, A., & Bengio, Y. (2016). Deep learning: Vol. 1. *No. 2*. MIT Press.

Heaton, J. B., Polson, N. G., & Witte, J. H. (2016). Deep learning in finance. *arXiv preprint arXiv:1602.06561.*

Jia, H. (2016). Investigation into the effectiveness of long short-term memory networks for stock price prediction. *arXiv preprint arXiv:1603.07893.*

Menon, V. K., Vasireddy, N. C., Jami, S. A., Pedamallu, V. T. N., Sureshkumar, V., & Soman, K. P. (2016, June). Bulk price forecasting using spark over nse data set. In *International Conference on Data Mining and Big Data* (pp. 137-146). Springer. 10.1007/978-3-319-40973-3_13

Mondal, P., Shit, L., & Goswami, S. (2014). Study of effectiveness of time series modeling (ARIMA) in forecasting stock prices. *International Journal of Computer Science. Engineering and Applications*, *4*(2), 13.

Nelson, D. M., Pereira, A. C., & de Oliveira, R. A. (2017, May). Stock market's price movement prediction with LSTM neural networks. In *2017 International joint conference on neural networks (IJCNN)* (pp. 1419-1426). IEEE. 10.1109/IJCNN.2017.7966019

Roondiwala, M., Patel, H., & Varma, S. (2017). Predicting stock prices using LSTM. *International Journal of Scientific Research*, *6*(4), 1754–1756.

Selvin, S., Vinayakumar, R., Gopalakrishnan, E. A., Menon, V. K., & Soman, K. P. (2017, September). *Stock price prediction using LSTM, RNN and CNN-sliding window model. In 2017 international conference on advances in computing, communications and informatics (icacci)*. IEEE.

Zunic, E., Korjenic, K., Hodzic, K., & Donko, D. (2020). Application of Facebook's Prophet Algorithm for Successful Sales Forecasting Based on Real-world Data. *arXiv preprint arXiv:2005.07575*.

Chapter 8
Convolution Neural Network:
Architecture, Applications, and Recent Trends

Kalyani N. Satone
Datta Meghe Institute of Higher Education and Research, India

Chitra A. Dhawale
Datta Meghe Institute of Higher Education and Research, India

Pranjali B. Ulhe
(iD) https://orcid.org/0000-0002-6557-4334
Datta Meghe Institute of Higher Education and Research, India

ABSTRACT

Convolutional neural network (CNN) carries spatial information—not all nodes in one layer are fully connected to nodes in the next layer; weights are shared. The main goal of CNN is to process large image pixel matrix and try to reduce high matrix dimensions without losing information, and to simplify the network architecture with weight sharing, reducing the number of trainable parameters in the network, which helped the model to avoid overfitting and as well as to improved generalization and still to give high performance with desired accuracy. So, CNN has become dominant in various computer vision tasks and is attracting interest across a variety of domains involving image processing. This chapter focuses on the foundation of CNN, followed by architecture of CNN, activation functions, applications, and recent trends in CNN.

1. MOTIVATION

Feed Forward Network (FFN) is a class of Artificial Neural Network where the data passes from input layer and processed through multiple hidden layer which

DOI: 10.4018/978-1-6684-9804-0.ch008

eventually connected with output layer. Each node in one layer is connected to every other node in subsequent layers. But it does not carry any spatial information if input is images/video. Convolutional neural network (CNN), unlike FFN carries spatial information, not all nodes in one layer are fully connected to nodes in the next layer, weights are shared. (Albawi et al., 2017).

CNN is best suited for image/video data involving large pixel matrix. The main goal of CNN is to process large image pixel matrix and try to reduce high matrix dimensions without losing information, simplify the network architecture with weight sharing which reduces the number of trainable parameters in the network, which helped the model to avoid overfitting and as well as to improved generalization and still to give high performance with desired accuracy. So, CNN has become dominant in various computer vision tasks and is attracting interest across a variety of domains involving image processing. CNN is designed to automatically and adaptively learn spatial hierarchies of features through backpropagation by using multiple building blocks, such as convolution layers, pooling layers, and fully connected layers.

2. FOUNDATIONS OF CONVOLUTION NEURAL NETWORK

In 1959, neurophysiologists David Hubel and Torsten Wiesel worked intensively on cat's cortex structure, performed lots of experiment and then published their research work in paper, entitled "Receptive fields of single neurons in cat's striate cor- tex"(Hubel & Wiesel, 1968), described that the neurons inside the brain of a cat are organized in layered form. These layers learn how to recognize visual patterns by first extracting the local features and then combining the extracted features for higher level representation. Later on, this concept is essentially become one of the core principle of Deep Learning.

In 1980 Kunihiko Fukushima proposed Neocognitron (Fukushima, 1980), a self-organizing Neural Network, with multiple layers for recognizing visual patterns in hierarchical manner through learning and this architecture became the first theoretical model of CNN as in the Figure 1.

A further major improvement over the architecture of Neocognitron was done by LeCun et. in 1989 by developing a modern framework of CNN, called LeNet-5, a digit recognizer for MNIST handwritten digits dataset. LeNet-5 recognized visual patterns directly from raw input images without separated feature extraction. It was trained using error back-propagation algorithm.

After discovering LeNet-5, because of several limitation like lack of large training data, lack of innovation in algorithm and inadequate computing power, CNN did not perform well in various complex problems. But nowadays, in the era of Big Data we have large labeled datasets, more innovative algorithms and especially powerful GPU machines. With these type of upgradation, in 2012, Krizhevsky et al. designed AexNet, which achieved a fantastic accuracy on the ImageNet Large Scale Visual Recognition Challenge (ILSVRC(Russakovsky et al., 2015)). The achievement of AlexNet guided the way to invent several CNN models (Alzubaidi et al., 2021) as well as to apply those models in different field of computer vision and natural language processing.

3. FUNDAMENTALS OF CONVOLUTION NEURAL NETWORK

Convolutional Neural Network (CNN), also called ConvNet, is a type of Artificial Neural Net- work(ANN), with deep feed-forward architecture. It is trained to learn highly abstracted features of objects especially for spatial data.

A deep CNN model have a finite set of hidden processing layers that can learn various features of input data (e.g. image). The initiatory layers learn and extract the high level features (with lower abstraction), and the deeper layers learns and extracts the low level features (with higher abstraction). The basic CNN model is shown in Figure 2.

Convolutional neural network (CNN), a class of artificial neural networks that has become dominant in various computer vision tasks, is attracting interest across

Figure 1. Schematic diagram illustrating the interconnections between layers in the neocognitron, Kunihiko Fukushima (1980)

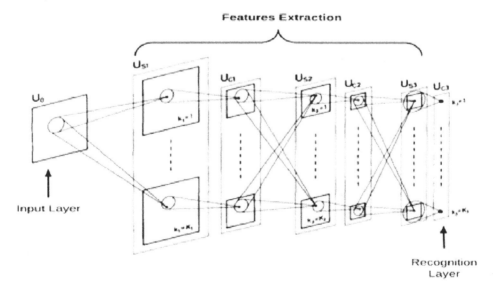

Figure 2. Basic CNN model

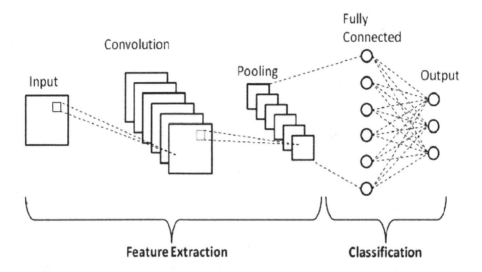

a variety of domains. CNN is designed to automatically and adaptively learn spatial hierarchies of features (Lecun et al., 1998) .

Basic CNN model composed of various layers like Convolution layer followed by Pooling Layer followed by:

3.1 Convolutional Layer

Convolutional layer is at heart of CNN architecture which plays an important role in working of CNN. It contains a set of convolutional filters (also called kernels), which gets convolved with the input image (N-dimensional metrics) to generate an output feature map.

3.1.1 Kernel

In Convolutional neural network, the kernel is nothing but a filter that is used to extract the features from the images. The kernel /filter is a matrix that moves over the input image metrics, performs the dot product with the sub-region of input data, and gets the output as the matrix of dot products. Kernel moves on the input data by the stride value. If the stride value is 2, then kernel moves by 2 columns of pixels in the input matrix. In short, the kernel is used to extract high-level features like edges from the image.

In the beginning of training process of an CNN model, generally all the weights of a kernel are initialized randomly. Then, with each training epoch, the weights are tuned and the kernel learned to extract meaningful features. In Fig.3, we have shown a 2D filter (Teuwen, 2020).

3.1.2 Convolution Operation

If we take a gray- scale image of 4 X 4 diamension, shown in Figure 4 and 2X2 kernel with randomly initialized weights as in Figure 5.

Now, in convolution operation, we take the 2 X 2 kernel and slide it over all the complete 1 X 4 image horizontally as well as vertically and along the way we take the dot product between kernel and input image by multiplying the corresponding values of them and sum up all values to generate one scaler value in the output feature map. This process continues until the kernel can no longer slide further.

Figure 6, shows few initial computations, in which the 2 X2 kernel (shown in light blue color) is multiplied with the same sized region (yellow color) within the 4 X 4 input image and the resulting values are summed up to obtain a corresponding entry (shown in deep blue) in the output feature map at each convolution step.

Figure 3. 2 X 2 convolution matrix

0	1
-1	2

Figure 4. An 4 × 4 gray-scale image

1	0	-2	1
-1	0	1	2
0	2	1	0
1	0	0	1

Figure 5. A kernel of size 2 × 2

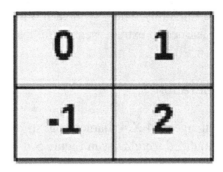

Figure 6. Few steps in convolution operation

Step-1

1	0	-2	1
-1	0	1	2
0	2	1	0
1	0	0	1

⊗

0	1
-1	2

→

1		

Step-2

1	0	-2	1
-1	0	1	2
0	2	1	0
1	0	0	1

⊗

0	1
-1	2

→

1	0	

Step-3

1	0	-2	1
-1	0	1	2
0	2	1	0
1	0	0	1

⊗

0	1
-1	2

→

1	0	4

Step-4

1	0	-2	1
-1	0	1	2
0	2	1	0
1	0	0	1

⊗

0	1
-1	2

→

1	0	4
4		

Step-5

1	0	-2	1
-1	0	1	2
0	2	1	0
1	0	0	1

⊗

0	1
-1	2

→

1	0	4
4	1	

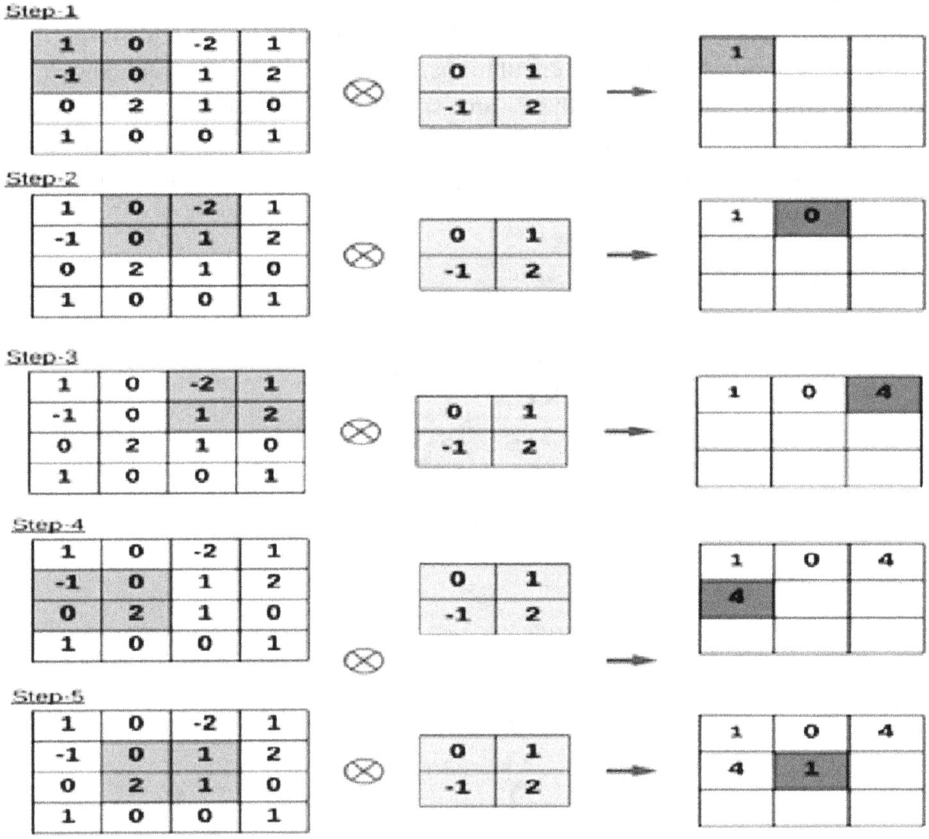

After performing the complete convolution operation, the final output feature map is shown in Figure 7 as follows.

Figure 7. The final feature map after the complete convolution operation

1	0	4
4	1	1
1	1	2

If the stride is increased from 1 to 2 or 3, resultant feature map get reduced and border side features get lost. In order to increase the input image size, and a resultant feature map, zero padding is used on the border side of input image matrix (Teuwen, 2020).

From the above discussion, it is clear that in a fully connected neural network every neuron in one layer connects with every neuron of in the subsequent layer but as it is image pixel matrix, a small number of weights are present between two layers as a result the amount of memory to store those weights is also small, so it is memory efficient. Also, the convolution dot(.) operation is computationally cheaper than matrix multiplication. Other thing is the weight sharing among multiple nodes which eventually reduces the training time as well as the other costs.

3.1.3 Pooling Layer

The purpose of Pooling Layer is to take larger size feature map obtained from the convolution layer and sub sampled it to shrinks it to lower sized feature maps by considering the most dominant featuresin each pool steps. The pooling operation is performed by specifying the pooled region size and the stride of the operation, similar to convolution operation. There are different types of pooling techniques are used in different pooling layers such as max pooling, min pooling, average pooling, gated pooling, tree pooling, etc. Max Pooling is the most popular and mostlyused pooling technique (Rodriguez-Martinez et al., 2022).

The main drawback of pooling layer is that it sometimes decreases the overall performance of CNN. The reason behind this is that pooling layer helps CNN to find whether a specific feature is present in the given input image or not without caring about the correct position of that feature.

Figure 8. Illustration of pooling layer

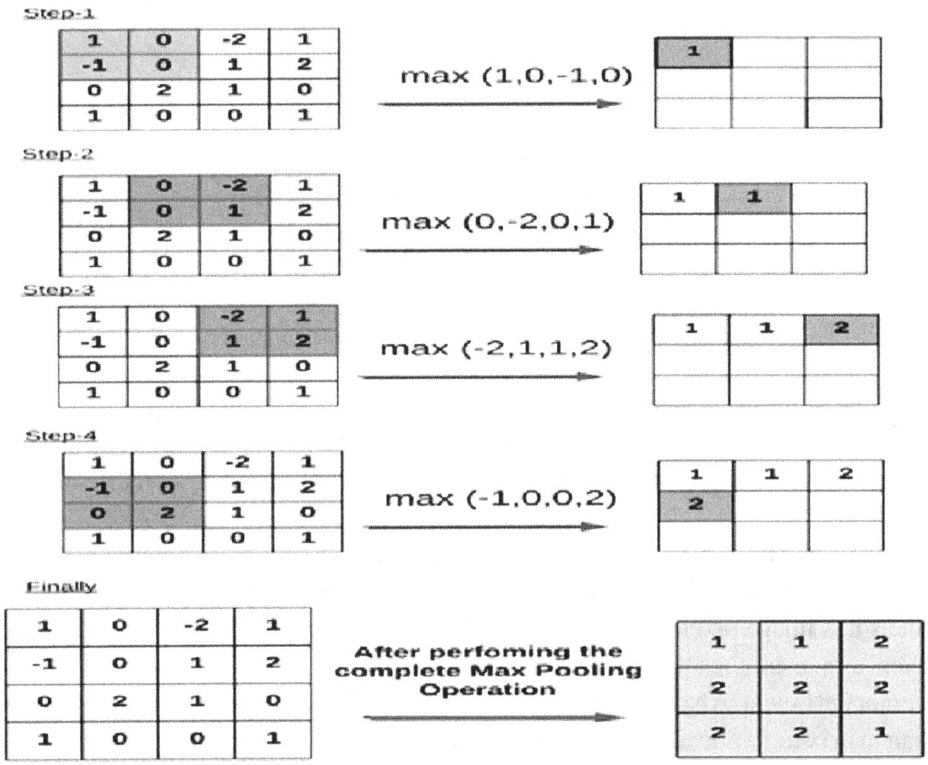

Step-1

1	0	-2	1
-1	0	1	2
0	2	1	0
1	0	0	1

max (1,0,-1,0) →

1		

Step-2

1	0	-2	1
-1	0	1	2
0	2	1	0
1	0	0	1

max (0,-2,0,1) →

1	1	

Step-3

1	0	-2	1
-1	0	1	2
0	2	1	0
1	0	0	1

max (-2,1,1,2) →

1	1	2

Step-4

1	0	-2	1
-1	0	1	2
0	2	1	0
1	0	0	1

max (-1,0,0,2) →

1	1	2
2		

Finally

1	0	-2	1
-1	0	1	2
0	2	1	0
1	0	0	1

After performing the complete Max Pooling Operation →

1	1	2
2	2	2
2	2	1

3.1.4 Activation Functions (Non-Linearty)

The key task of activation function in CNN model is to activate the output out of multiple inputs. Depending on the type of function, it maps the output values in the range between 0 to 1 or -1. In CNN architecture, after each learnable layers (layers with weights, i.e. convolutional and FC layers) non-linear activation layers are used. The most commonly used activation functions in CNN are briefly described below (Dubey et al., 2022).

3.1.4.1 Sigmoid

The sigmoid activation function which transforms any value in the domain (−¥,¥) to a number between 0 and 1. The curve of the sigmoid function is of 'S' shaped. The mathematical representation of sigmoid is:

It is especially used for models where we have to predict the probability as an output. Since probability of anything exists only between the range of 0 and 1, sigmoid is the right choice. Sigmoid function is monotonic & differentiable, means function represents slope of curve.

Figure 9. Sigmoid curve

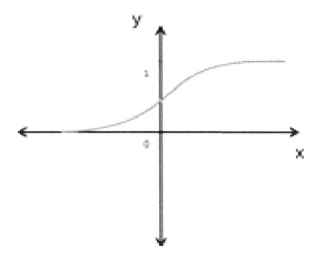

3.1.4.2 Tanh

The *Tanh* activation function is used to bind the input values (real numbers) within the range of [-1, 1].

The negative inputs will be mapped strongly negative and the zero inputs will be mapped near zero in the tanh graph. Tanh function is monotic and differentiable and mainly used in classification.

3.1.4.3 ReLU

The Rectifier Linear Unit (ReLU) is a non-linear function or piecewise linear function, that will output the input directly if it is positive, otherwise, it will output zero. The advantage of ReLU is that it requires very minimal computation load compared to others.

It is the most commonly used activation function in neural networks, especially in Convolutional Neural Networks (CNNs).

The mathematical representation of ReLU is:

$$f(x)_{ReLU} = \max(0, x)$$

3.1.4.4 Leaky ReLU

Unlike ReLU, a Leaky ReLU activation function does not ignore the negative inputs completely, rather than it down-scaled those negative inputs. Leaky ReLU is used to solve Dying ReLU problem.

Figure 10. Tanh function

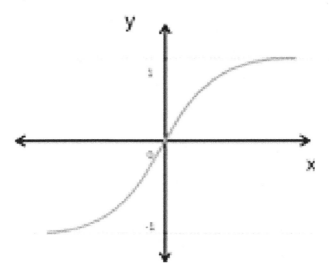

Figure 11. ReLu Curve

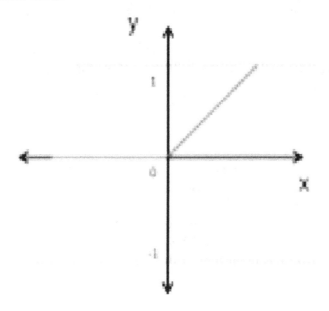

3.1.5 Fully Connected (FC) Layer

In Fully-Connected layers, every node in one layer is connected with each node in subsequent layer. The last layer of Fully-Connected layers is used as the output layer (classifier) of the CNN architecture.

Figure 12. Leaky ReLu curve

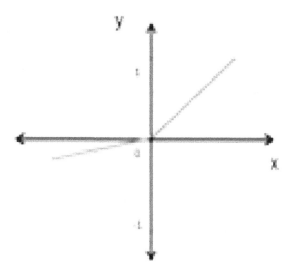

The Fully-Connected Layers are type of feed-forward artificial neural network (ANN). The FC layers take input from the final convolutional or pooling layer, which is in the form of a set of metrics (feature maps) and those metrics are flattened to create a vector and this vector is then fed into the FC layer to generate the final output of CNN as shown in Figure 13 (Wu, 2016).

Figure 13. The architecture of fully connected layers

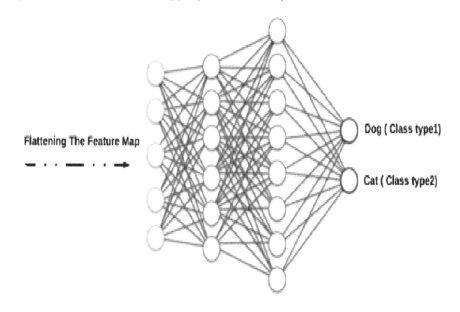

4. TRAINING PROCESS OF CONVOLUTIONAL NEURAL NETWORK

In the previous section, we have mentioned the basic concepts of convolutional neural network (CNN) as well as the different key components of CNN architecture. Now here we try to discuss the training or learning process of a CNN model with certain strategies in order to lessen the required training time and to improve model accuracy. The training process mainly includes the following steps (Yadan et al., 2013):

a.   Data pre-processing and Data augmentation.
b.   Parameter initialization.
c.   Regularization of CNN.
d.   Optimizer selection.

5. RECENT TRENDS IN CNN

In this section we try to explain some example of successful CNN architecture that shows the recent major advancements in CNN architecture in the computer vision field. Computer vision has three major sub-domain where several CNN architectures (models) contribute a vital role to achieve excellent result, let's discuss sub-domains with related CNN models as follows.

5.1 Image Classification

In image classification, we assume that the input image contains a single object and then we have to classify the image into one of the preselected target classes by using CNN models. Some of the major CNN models designed for image classification are as follows:

5.1.1 LeNet-5

The LeNet-5 (Ma et al., 2019) is one of the earliest CNN architecture introduced by LeCun et.al in 1998 which was designed for classifying the handwritten digits. The LeNet-5 has 5 weighted (trainable) layers, that is, three convolutional layer and two FC layers. Among them, each of first two convolution layer is followed by a max-pooling layer the last convolution layer is followed by two fully connected layers. The last layer of those fully connected layers is used as the classifier, which can classify 10 digits. The architecture of LeNet-5 is shown in Figure 14.

Figure 14. The architecture of LeNet-5

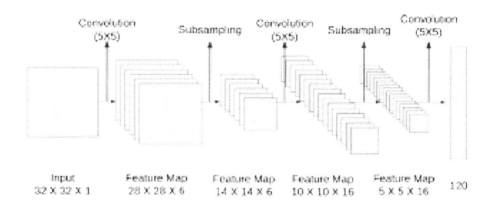

5.1.2 AlexNet

Inspired from LeNet, Krizhevky et al. designed first large-scale CNN model, called AlexNet (Thalagala & Walgampaya, 2021) in 2012, is designed to classify ImageNet data. It consists of eight weighted (learnable) layers among which the first five layers are convolutional layers, and afterward, the last three layers are fully connected layers. Since it was designed for ImageNet data, so the last output layer classify the input images into one of the thousand classes of the ImageNet dataset with the help of 1,000 units (Thalagala & Walgampaya, 2021) . The architecture of AlexNet is shown in Figure 15.

5.1.3 ZFNet

ZFNet (Zeiler & Fergus, 2014) was presented by Zeiler and Fergus in ECCV-2014, here they used 7 filter with stride 2 in 1'st convolutional layer. As a result ZFNet becomes more efficient than AlexNet and become the winner of ILSVRC-2013. The architecture of ZFNet is shown in Figure 16.

5.1.4 VGGNet

VGGNet (Simonyan & Zisserman, 2014) is one of the most popular CNN architecture, which is introduced by Simonyan and Zisserman in 2014. The authors introduced a total 6 different CNN configurations, among them the VGGNet-16 (configuration D) and VGGNet-19 (configuration E) are the most successful ones. The architecture of VGGNet-16 is shown in Figure 17.

Figure 15. The architecture of AlexNet (Szegedy et al., 2015)

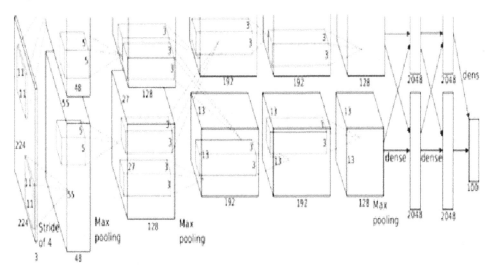

Figure 16. The architecture of ZFNet

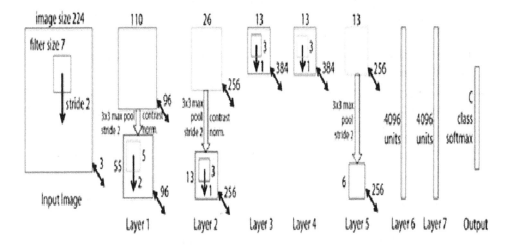

5.1.5 GoogLeNet

The GoogleNet (Szegedy et al., 2015) architecture uses network branches instead of using single line sequential architecture. The GoogleNet was proposed by Szegedy et al. in 2014. The GoogleNet has 22 weighted (learn- able) layers, it used "Inception Module" as the basic building block of the network.

Figure 17. The architecture of VGGNet (Sufian et al., 2019) (VGGNet-16)

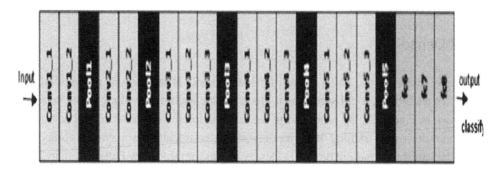

The processing of this module happens in parallel in the network, and each (a simple basic) module consist of 1 1, 3 3 and 5 5 filtered convolution layers in parallel and then it combines their output feature maps, that can resulted in very high-dimensional feature output.

5.1.6 ResNet

Since a deep CNN model suffers from vanishing gradient problems as we discussed earlier, He et al. from Microsoft, introduced the idea of "identity skip connection" to solve vanishing gradient problem by proposing the ResNet (He et al., 2016) model. The ResNet's architecture use residual mapping ($H(x) = F(x) + x$) instead of learning a direct mapping ($H(x) = F(x)$) and these blocks are called residual bocks. The complete ResNet architecture is consist of many residual bocks with 3 3 convolution layers.

Figure 18. (1) Simple inception module; (2) inception module with dimensionality reduction (Chen et al., 2019)

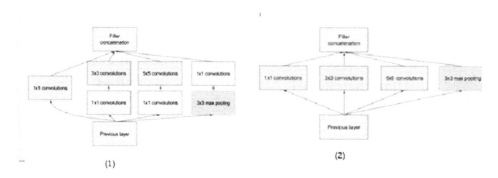

Figure 19 illustrates the difference between the direct mapping and the residual mapping.

5.1.7 DenseNet

DenseNet (Sufian et al., 2019) extends the idea of residual mapping by propagating the output of each block to all subsequent blocks inside each dense block in the network as shown in Figure 22. By propagating the information in both forward and backward directions during the training of the model it strengthens feature propagation ability and solve the vanishing gradient problem. DenseNet was introduced by Huang et al. in 2016 and it becomes the winner of ILSVRC-2016. Figure 20 shows a DenseNet based model.

5.2 Object Detection

An input image can contain more than one object. So here we try to detect those objects inside the input image with proper identification along with their correct

Figure 19. (a) Mapping inside residual block; (b) simple direct mappings

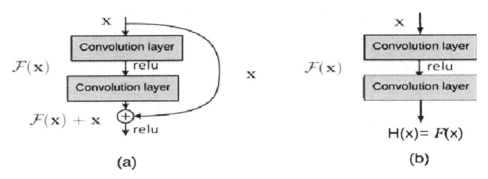

Figure 20. A DenseNet-based model with three dense blocks (Sufian et al., 2019)

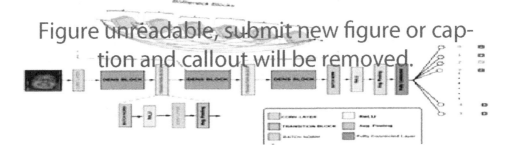

location inside that image. Some of the major CNN architectures(models) designed for object detection are as follows:

1. R-CNN: The first CNN model designed for object detection is Region-based CNN (R-CNN [Wu, 2016]), which uses sliding window based approaches for successfully detect the objects. It will extracts the region from each input images and warping to make all the extracted region of fixed sized and then the objects are classified from each region (Mahenge et al., 2022).
2. SPP-Net: SPP-Net removes the constraint of fixed sized input images from R-CNN and make itself more effective (Maggiori, Tarabalka, Charpiat, & Alliez, 2017).
3. Fast R-CNN: This architecture provides identification of each object along with their correct location Fast R-CNN uses region of interests (Roi) pooling layer for reshape the variable length region (window) proposals into fixed sized output before feeding them to the fully connected layers (Mahenge et al., 2022).
4. Faster R-CNN: Faster R-CNN achieves further speed-up in order to detect the objects inside the input image (Mahenge et al., 2022).
5. Mask R-CNN: Mask R-CNN (Ma et al., 2019) extend the concept of Faster R-CNN by locating exact pixels of each object (combinedly called object's mask), whereas Faster R-CNN just predicts the bounding boxes of each object (Mahenge et al., 2022).
6. YOLO: YOLO (You Only Look Once) is a single pipeline based detection model, that can directly detect the objects as well as their location using an end-to-end trained CNN model.

5.3 Image Segmentation

CNN has shown excellence in the segmentation task also. After the record-breaking performance of AlexNet in 2012, we have got many state-of-the-art models of semantic segmentation and instance segmentation. Some of them are highlighted below.

5.3.1. Semantic Segmentation

Unlike Classification and object detection, semantic segmentation is a low level vision task. It is the process of associating each pixel of an image with a class label i. e. It detects all the objects present in an image (Chen et al., 2019). This semantic segmentation consist of following network

1. Fully Convolutional Network (FCN): A fully connected layer refers to a neural network in which each neuron applies a linear transformation to the input vector through a weights matrix. As a result, all possible connections layer-to-layer are present, meaning every input of the input vector influences every output of the output vector.

2. DeepLab: DeepLab is a state-of-the-art semantic segmentation model designed and open-sourced by Google. The dense prediction is achieved by simply up-sampling the output of the last convolution layer and computing pixel-wise loss.

3. SegNet: SegNet is a semantic segmentation model. This core trainable segmentation architecture consists of an encoder network, a corresponding decoder network followed by a pixel-wise classification layer. The architecture of the encoder network is topologically identical to the 13 convolutional layers in the VGG16 network.

4. Deconvnet: The DeConvNet places the reconstructions from the layer above into appropriate locations based on the maxima found.

5. UNet: UNet, evolved from the traditional convolutional neural network, was first designed and applied in 2015 to process biomedical images.

5.3.2 Instance Segmentation

Instance segmentation takes the semantic segmentation one step ahead. It detects as well as distinguishes all the instances of an object present in an image.

This segmentation consist of following architecture like

1. DeepMask: DeepMask is applied closely to an image and generates a set of object masks, each with a corresponding object-ness score. These masks densely cover the objects in an image and can be used as a first step for object detection and other tasks in computer vision.

2. SharpMask: SharpMask is an extension of DeepMask architecture, which uses a top-down refinement module to compute more precise object mask proposal.

3. PANet: Path Aggregation Network, or PANet, aims to boost information flow in a proposal-based instance segmentation framework. A complementary branch capturing different views for each proposal is created to further improve mask prediction.

4. TensorMask: The main concept of TensorMask architecture is the use of structured high-dimensional tensors to present image content such as masks in a set of densely sliding windows.

6. APPLICATIONS AREAS OF CNNs

In this section, let's take a look on an important application areas that apply CNN to achieve state- of-the-art performance covers image classification, text recognition, action recognition, object detection, human pose estimation, image captioning, automatic colorization if image, security and surveillance, medical image analysis etc.

6.1 Image Classification

Especially in large scale datasets, CNN have been provided the better classification accuracy as compare to other architecture as CNN has significant features like weight sharing, feature extraction, classifier etc. With the first invention of AlexNet in the domain of image classification, it achieved lot of developments. After that, several advances in CNN model have been made by the researchers over the times, and makes CNN as the first choice for image classification problem (Kim et al., 2015).

6.2 Text Recognition

It has been very essential demand for text detection and text recognition within the image so that image can be easily classified along with the text, and it required a lot of research. The first innovative contribution of CNN in this field begins with LeNet-5, which recognized the data in MNIST (Liu et al., 2018) dataset with a good accuracy (Zhu et al., 2016). In recent years, with several changes, CNN contributes a dynamic role to recognize the text like digits, alphabets and symbols which may relate to different languages inside the image.

6.3 Action Recognition

Different effective CNN methods are helpful to predict the action or behavior of human aspect with a very precise accuracy. This methods works on the visual appearance and motion dynamics of any human body, due to this it brings the CNN to the next level in the context of Artificail Intelligence. It includes recognition of action or behaviour from a video sequence(frames) or from the still images (Zhao et al., 2020).

6.4 Image Caption Generation

It will obtain the detailed description about the target image, which might involves the detection and recognition of different objects inside the image. It also tells about the image and the status description (Sasibhooshan et al., 2023). CNN allows to recognize the image and also uses several Natural Language Processing (NLP) techniques using different datasets for a textual status description of images.

6.5 Medical Image Analysis

With the advancement in CNN-based image analysis, CNN is rapidly proved to be a state- of-the-art foundation, by achieving enhanced performances in the diagnosis of diseases of medical images (Wang et al., 2021) like MRI, X-rays, etc. Nowadays, CNN based models can effectively diagnose the various health problems like breast cancer, pneumonia, brain tumour, diabetes, Parkinson's diseases and many others.

6.6 Security and Investigation

Nowadays, Security system with Computer Vision capabilities provides constant surveillance to houses, metro stations, roads, universities, offices, schools, hospitals and many other places, that gives the ability to search or trace the criminals even in crowded areas (Jin, 2022).

6.7 Automatic Colorization of Image and Style Transfer

With the deep learning rebellion, some popular CNN models give an automation way to convert black and white images or gray images to an equivalent colorful RGB images (Chen et al., 2018). As a result we can see the old black and white movies in color format. In the USA, Legend movies used its automated technology to color old classics. In 1960, the movie Mughal-E-Azam was famous in India, was colorized in 2004. for example Mughal-E-Azam. On the other hand image style transfer is a concepts of representing an image in the style of other image, for that a new artificial image could be generated. This style transfer could be efficiently done using convolutional neural networks.

7. CONCLUSION

Convolutional Neural Networks (CNN) has become advanced algorithm for computer vision, natural language processing, and pattern recognition problems. This CNN is used to build many use cases models from simply digit recognition to complex medical image anal ysis. This chapter tried to clarify each component of a CNN, by what means it works to image analysis, and other relevant things. This chapter also gives a review from foundation of CNN to latest models and mentioned some applications areas.

REFERENCES

Albawi, S., Mohammed, T. A., & Al-Zawi, S. (2017). Understanding of a convolutional neural network. *2017 International Conference on Engineering and Technology (ICET)*, Antalya, Turkey. 10.1109/ICEngTechnol.2017.8308186

Alzubaidi, L., Zhang, J., Humaidi, A. J., Al-Dujaili, A., Duan, Y., Al-Shamma, O., Santamaría, J., Fadhel, M. A., Al-Amidie, M., & Farhan, L. (2021). Review of deep learning: Concepts, CNN architectures, challenges, applications, future directions. *Journal of Big Data*, *8*(1), 53. doi:10.118640537-021-00444-8 PMID:33816053

Anwar, S. M., Majid, M., Qayyum, A., Awais, M., Alnowami, M., & Khan, M. K. (2018, November). Medical image analysis using convolutional neural networks: A review. *Journal of Medical Systems*, *42*(11), 1–13. doi:10.100710916-018-1088-1 PMID:30298337

Chen, X., Girshick, R. B., He, K., & Doll, P. (2019). Tensormask: A foundation for dense object segmentation. *CoRR*, abs/1903.12174.

Chen, Y., Luo, Y., Ding, Y., & Yu, B. (2018). *Automatic Colorization of Images from Chinese Black and White Films Based on CNN*. *2018 International Conference on Audio, Language and Image Processing (ICALIP)*, Shanghai, China. 10.1109/ICALIP.2018.8455654

Dubey, S. R., Singh, S. K., & Chaudhuri, B. B. (2022, September). Activation functions in deep learning: A comprehensive survey and benchmark. *Neurocomput.*, *503*(C), 92–108. doi:10.1016/j.neucom.2022.06.111

Fukushima, K. (1980, April). Neocognitron: A self-organizing neural network model for a mechanism of pattern recognition unaffected by shift in position. *Biological Cybernetics*, *36*(4), 193–202. doi:10.1007/BF00344251 PMID:7370364

He, K., Zhang, X., Ren, S., & Sun, J. (2016). Deep residual learning for image recognition. In *The IEEE Conference on Computer Vision and Pattern Recognition (CVPR)*.

Hubel, D. H., & Wiesel, T. N. (1968). Receptive fields and functional architecture of monkey striate cortex. *The Journal of Physiology*, *195*(1), 215–243. doi:10.1113/jphysiol.1968.sp008455 PMID:4966457

Jin, Y. (2022, January 19). Surveillance, security, and AI as technological acceptance. *AI & Society*. doi:10.100700146-021-01331-9

Krizhevsky, A., Sutskever, I., & Hinton, G. E. (2012). Imagenet classification with deep convolu- tional neural networks. In F. Pereira, C. J. C. Burges, L. Bottou, & K. Q. Weinberger (Eds.), Advances in Neural Information Processing Systems (Vol. 25, pp. 1097–1105). Curran Associates, Inc.

Lecun, Y., Bottou, L., Bengio, Y., & Haffner, P. (1998, November). Gradient-based learning applied to document recognition. *Proceedings of the IEEE*, *86*(11), 2278–2324. doi:10.1109/5.726791

Liu, S., Qi, L., Qin, H., Shi, J., & Jia, J. (2018). Path aggregation network for instance segmenta- tion. *CoRR*, abs/1803.01534.

Ma, X., Yao, T., Hu, M., Dong, Y., Liu, W., Wang, F., & Liu, J. (2019). A Survey on Deep Learning Empowered IoT Applications. *IEEE Access : Practical Innovations, Open Solutions*, *7*, 181721–181732. doi:10.1109/ACCESS.2019.2958962

Maggiori, E., Tarabalka, Y., Charpiat, G., & Alliez, P. (2017, February). Convolutional neural networks for large-scale remote-sensing image classification. *IEEE Transactions on Geoscience and Remote Sensing*, *55*(2), 645–657. doi:10.1109/TGRS.2016.2612821

Maggiori, E., Tarabalka, Y., Charpiat, G., & Alliez, P. (2017, February). Convolutional neural networks for large-scale remote-sensing image classification. *IEEE Transactions on Geoscience and Remote Sensing*, *55*(2), 645–657. doi:10.1109/TGRS.2016.2612821

Mahenge, S. F., Wambura, S., & Jiao, L. (2022). *RCNN-GAN: An Enhanced Deep Learning Approach Towards Detection of Road Cracks*. In 2022 The 6th International Conference on Compute and Data Analysis (ICCDA 2022). Association for Computing Machinery, New York, NY, USA. 10.1145/3523089.3523104

Noh, H., Hong, S., & Han, B. (2015). Learning deconvolution network for semantic segmentation. *CoRR*. abs/1505.04366.

Rodriguez-Martinez, I., Lafuente, J., Santiago, R. H. N., Dimuro, G. P., Herrera, F., & Bustince, H. (2022, August). Replacing pooling functions in Convolutional Neural Networks by linear combinations of increasing functions. *Neural Networks*, *152*, 380–393. doi:10.1016/j.neunet.2022.04.028 PMID:35605303

Russakovsky, O., Deng, J., Su, H., Krause, J., Satheesh, S., Ma, S., Huang, Z., Karpathy, A., Khosla, A., Bernstein, M., Berg, A. C., & Fei-Fei, L. (2015). ImageNet Large Scale Visual Recogni- tion Challenge. *International Journal of Computer Vision*, *115*(3), 211–252. doi:10.100711263-015-0816-y

Sasibhooshan, R., Kumaraswamy, S., & Sasidharan, S. (2023). Image caption generation using Visual Attention Prediction and Contextual Spatial Relation Extraction. *Journal of Big Data*, *10*(1), 18. doi:10.118640537-023-00693-9

Simonyan K. & Zisserman, A. (2014). Very deep convolutional networks for large-scale image recognition. *CoRR*, abs/1409.1556.

Sufian, A. Ghosh, A. Naskar, A., & Sultana, F. (2019). Bdnet: Bengali handwritten nu- meral digit recognition based on densely connected convolutional neural networks. *CoRR*, abs/1906.03786.

Sultana, F., Sufian, A., & Dutta, P. (2018). Advancements in image classification using convolu- tional neural network. In *2018 Fourth International Conference on Research in Computa- tional Intelligence and Communication Networks (ICRCICN)*, (pp. 122–129). IEEE.

Szegedy, C., Liu, W., Jia, Y., Sermanet, P., Reed, S., Anguelov, D., Erhan, D., Vanhoucke, V., & Rabinovich, A. (2015). Going deeper with convolutions. In *The IEEE Conference on Computer Vision and Pattern Recognition (CVPR)*. IEEE.

Teuwen, J. (2020). *Convolutional neural networks, Elsevier and MICCAI Society Book Series, Handbook of Medical Image Computing and Computer Assisted Intervention*. Academic Press.

Thalagala, S., & Walgampaya, C. (2021). Application of AlexNet convolutional neural network architecture-based transfer learning for automated recognition of casting surface defects. *2021 International Research Conference on Smart Computing and Systems Engineering (SCSE)*, Colombo, Sri Lanka. 10.1109/ SCSE53661.2021.9568315

Wang, J., Zhu, H., Wang, S. H., & Zhang, Y.-D. (2021). A Review of Deep Learning on Medical Image Analysis. *Mobile Networks and Applications*, *26*(1), 351–380. doi:10.100711036-020-01672-7

Wu, J.-N. (2016). Compression of fully-connected layer in neural network by Kronecker product. *2016 Eighth International Conference on Advanced Computational Intelligence (ICACI)*, Chiang Mai, Thailand. 10.1109/ICACI.2016.7449822

Yadan, O., Adams, K., & Taigman, Y. (2013). *Multi-GPU Training of ConvNets*. Eprint Arxiv.

Yim, J., Ju, J., Jung, H., & Kim, J. (2015). Image Classification Using Convolutional Neural Networks With Multi-stage Feature. In J. H. Kim, W. Yang, J. Jo, P. Sincak, & H. Myung (Eds.), *Robot Intelligence Technology and Applications 3. Advances in Intelligent Systems and Computing* (Vol. 345). Springer. doi:10.1007/978-3-319-16841-8_52

Zeiler, M. D., & Fergus, R. (2014). Visualizing and understanding convolutional networks. In D. Fleet, T. Pajdla, B. Schiele, and T. Tuytelaars (Eds.), Computer Vision – ECCV 2014 (pp. 818–833). Springer International Publishing. doi:10.1007/978-3-319-10590-1_53

Zhang, R., Isola, P., & Efros, A. A. (2016). Colorful image colorization. *CoRR*, abs/1603.08511.

Zhao, Y., Man, K. L., Smith, J., Siddique, K., & Guan, S.-U. (2020). Improved two-stream model for human action recognition. *J Image Video Proc.*, *2020*(1), 24. doi:10.118613640-020-00501-x

Zhu, Y., Yao, C., & Bai, X. (2016). Scene text detection and recognition: Recent advances and future trends. *Frontiers of Computer Science*, *10*(1), 19–36. doi:10.100711704-015-4488-0

Chapter 9
Die Casting Process Using Automated Machine Learning

Abhinav Koushik
Vellore Institute of Technology, Chennai, India

Denisha Miraclin
Vellore Institute of Technology, Chennai, India

Swapnil Patil
Wipro Technologies Ltd, Pune, India

Milind Dangate
Vellore Institute of Technology, Chennai, India

ABSTRACT

Castings that are near to net forms are made using the extremely complex manufacturing technique known as die casting. Despite the method's lengthy history—more than a century—a system engineering method for characterizing it as well as the information that each cycle of die casting can create has not yet been completed. Instead, a tiny subset of knowledge deemed to be essential for die castings has attracted the attention of industry and academia. The majority of the research that has been published on artificial intelligence in die casting has a specific focus, which restricts its usefulness and efficacy in an industrial casting. This study will examine the die casting process through the perspective of systems design and show practical uses of machine learning. In terms of technical definition and how people interact with the system, the die casting process satisfies the criteria for complex systems. The die casting system is an adaptive, self-organizing network structure, according to the technical definition.

INTRODUCTION

Die casting, often known as die-casting, is a very difficult industrial process. Die casting is made up of several systems that control mechanical, thermal and hydraulic

DOI: 10.4018/978-1-6684-9804-0.ch009

processes to produce castings that are almost net-like (Andresen, 2005). The design, configuration and administration of these systems have a bearing on casting quality and machine performance. For process management and optimisation, the die casting industry formerly only used a tiny percentage of the system data (Blondheim, 2020).

According to the North American Die Casting Association (NADCA), sales of aluminium die casting will reach $8 billion in 2019. This is more than 80% of the $9.67 billion estimate provided by the American Foundry Society (AFS) (Folk, 2019, pp-16-19) for all aluminium castings. The average internal scrap rate for components manufactured by the industry's existing control and optimisation processes is 8%, and equipment utilisation is 68% (NADCA, 2014).

Die casting has a variety of expostulations as it transitions from traditional data collecting to slice- bite analytics on vast information sets. One of the first expostulations is the introductory understanding of how blights are produced and the bracket of expiring enterprises. Collecting, analysing, storing, and utilizing voluminous quantities of data is grueling . also, a lot of trouble must go into expiring serialisation and traceability across the force chain. also, artistic hurdles must be beat for the use and relinquishment of daedal logical approaches. (Wuest et al., 2016, pp.23-45)(Baier et al., 2019. p.16) (Sun et al., 2020) (Landry et al .,2018) (Blondheim, Jr, 2018,2020)

From a system engineering perspective, die casting will generate orders of magnitude more data than it does at the moment. Each cycle in the company would now store thousands of data points instead of the hundreds that used to exist (Blondheim, 2020). For anyone tasked with optimising the die casting process, this abundance of data becomes daunting. In order to understand the data needed to address practical challenges for the die casting system, a framework for data creation is required. Machine learning is needed to analyse, optimise, and manage the pace and volume of data created by the die casting system.

Die Casting Basics

Metal castings with almost flawless shapes are produced using the HPDC manufacturing method, often in large numbers. Liquid metal is poured into a mould that can be used repeatedly at high pressures and speeds. A structure that typically weighs under 20 pounds and has traditionally been made by die casting is required to generate data. Castings weighting 40 pounds or more are used more frequently in the industry as a result of recent technological advancements, growing demand for massive block engines (Alvarez, 2020), and architectural die cast components (North American Die Casting Association, 2009). High-level die casting process phases are shown in Table 1.

Each of the procedures uses other machinery in order to complete some functions, such as holding, delivery, colding and removal of metal, which is also included in the Die Casting Machine. These systems will take the steps necessary to generate a casting, via interfaces and communication with the die cast machine. For small castings, but two or three minutes for large castings the diecast cycle takes a couple of seconds.

The size, speed, and degree of automation of the equipment, as well as the amount of time needed for the casting to harden, all affect cycle time. In an example arrangement in Figure 1 extracted from Table 1, a large tonnage die casting machine with operational stages installed and marked is shown.

Aluminium, Mg, Zn, and aluminium are often used as alloys in die casting, however other alloys including Sn, Cu, can be utilized in specific applications (Andresen, 2005; Doehler, 1951; NADCA, 2018). Die castings are used to produce goods from a variety of industrial sectors, such as those in the automobile, agricultural machinery, recreation, office furniture, toys, aircraft, home hardware, home appliances, and electrical equipment industries . These sectors make use of die casting's benefits to produce castings that are extremely intricate and nearly net-shaped. Figure 2 displays an illustration of a sizable aluminum die-cast block made by Hg.

For designers, HPDC offers a number of benefits. Die casting makes it possible to fill thin components over a long distance by operating at high speeds and pressures.

Table 1. Lists the steps in the high degree die casting process

	Step	**Content**
1	Lubrication of the die with a spray.	In order to lubricate the surfaces of the die, a spray method shall use it in an open position. This lubrication will aid the release of aluminium from steel dies and offer a certain thermal cooling.
2	Closing of the Die	Under tonnage, the die halves close and lock through a mechanical or hydraulic mechanism.
3	Metal Delivery	Typically, a machine or a metal pump delivers metal through the chamber connected to a die.
4	Metal injecting	To create the casting, The liquid metal is propelled by means of hydraulics out of the chamber and into the die.
5	Intensification Pressure	The injection system switches to a HPP when the mould is filled, it is used to shift into mould.
6	Time for Cooling/Dwell	The cooling systems are cycled to remove the heat from the die and to promote the melting of the fluid material once it has hardened.
7	Die Open	The casting is still on the die as the two die halves are opened by a mechanical or hydraulic mechanism.
8	Extraction and casting Ejection	The casting is pushed off the die surfaces by an internal ejection system and extracted from the cell, usually by a robot.
9	The preparation of Extraction Mobile Casting	The casting is frequently further validated and processed after it comes out of the die before being given to an operator for packing and final inspection.

Figure 1. Illustrates a die cast cell architecture

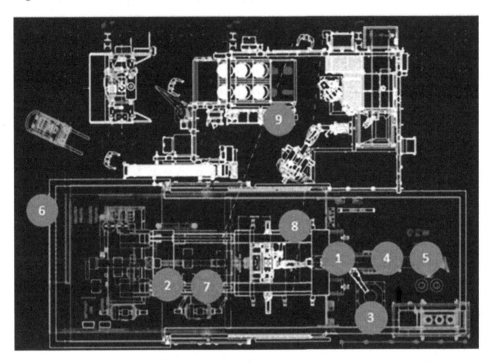

Figure 2. An illustration of a die-cast V8 engine block

Designers may now reduce the size of a component without compromising its strength or usefulness. Some of the most complex casting patterns are produced with this casting, and the dimensional outcomes are quite reliable. In order for the delicate steel die that forms the casting to perform its work, this is necessary. Die casting provides a large range of material and alloy options, as was previously mentioned. These alloys only partly meet certain industrial requirements.

Another benefit is cycling time, which may produce castings much more rapidly than any other kind of manufacturing process, such as casting with sand, lost foam, or fixed mould. The typical range is between 1,000 and 1,000,000. Low component costs, little machining needs, surface smoothness, and pressure tightness are further advantages.

Like any production process, using die casting has trade-offs. In order to achieve quick and low cycle times component prices, businesses must spend a significant amount of capital in tools and equipment. Making decisions while designing for die casting is thus difficult (Doehler, 1951). Design adjustments made to a casting after the work is in use result in costly element alterations & short tool life. In addition, the equipment is harmed by the temperature cycling necessary in die casting. At the end, the costly dies need constant upkeep and ultimately replacement (Herman & Kirkman, 2011). Finally, utilising created patterns, the casting must be taken out of the die steel. More surface draught is required as a result, and an undercut feature cannot be included (Doehler, 1951; Herman & Kirkman, 2011). Because its benefits continue to outweigh its disadvantages, die casting is a process that is extensively utilised in foundries for the design and manufacturing of components. Once the concept of die casting has been define.

Metal Delivery, Holding, and Metallurgy

Extraordinary changes take place at elemental level during the transition from a material phase. A series of different components are formed into diescasting alloys. The impact of various elements on the process of solidification varies. For example, silicon is a primary alloying component of aluminium die cast alloys. Si is responsible for the fluidity and castibility of liquid metals but also has an influence when solid metal temperature increases, as shown in Figure 16. As a result, compared to manufacture with a lower Si level, different forms of filler may be created at high Silicon levels. Silicon is used one of elements in commercial purpose (Herman & Kirkman, 2011). Others may have an impact on the automated properties of metal, though others may have an impact on the process (Apparao & Birru, 2017, pp.1852-1859).

The alloy is produced, then kept in an oven till it is put into the it. A separate system, the oven , which is linked to the ladle system, is designed to keep a certain volume of metals at the right heat. A control system maintains the required metal temperatures in the furnace. In order to prevent oxides and other contaminants from entering the casting, the ceramic filter system is often utilised. The ladling mechanism transports metal from the combustion chamber to the machine during each cycle. For the distribution of metal, there are numerous alternatives. Figure 3 depicts three possible outcomes: a dosage pump, a 2-axis metal delivery device, and a 7-axis robotic structure. The metal in the storage furnace is also replenished by a mechanism for feeding metal from a smelting region within the foundry. To lessen metallurgical oxides and flaws, degassing devices may be added to the burner or the metal replenishing system. If clean metal is to be injected onto the die casting machine, an oxide film that develops at the point where the liquid metal comes into contact with the atmosphere in the holding furnace has to be manually removed by workers.

Important components of the die casting process are the metal holding and ladling mechanisms. When these 2 systems affect the cell's overall cycle time, subpar castings can be made. A discrete event is the delivery of metal. The amount of metal removed causes the level in the furnace to decrease after each cycle. The ladle bucket may take longer to fill as metal is taken out of the furnace, depending on the controls and timer settings. The longer it took to fill, the more was removed. The extended cycle period of the ladle system could act as a pacemaker for the duration of the total cell cycle.

Figure 3. Shows three different ladles used to transport metal: a 2-axis ladle in the centre, a 7-axis robot ladle on the right

System of Chamber, Hamber, and Injection

When utilising a die, a sizable hydraulic system is needed to deliver the molten metals from the cavity into the die casting mould. In order to guarantee a consistent infusion of the molten metals onto the die throughout the tool phase, the filled process is typically modelled using simulation. The chamber holds the liquid metal after it has been supplied from the ladle and is ready to be shot into the die. The tool design procedure involves determining the room diameter and length for the injection system while taking into account the part capacity and target metal pressure. Figure 4 depicts how the chamber, die, and shot rod mechanism interact. Two steps comprise the injection process (Aluminum Alloys, 2020)

The 1st stage is sometimes known as the low beat. By pushing the tip and firing rod forward, the slow shot seals the partially filled chamber of liquid metal into a huge hard cylinder. This main purpose is to prevent the liquid or air injected into the casting from becoming trapped in turbulence or waves. Usually, acceptable shock frequency is increased to reduce the probability of waves (Aluminum Alloys, 2020). Figures 5, 6, and 7 are graphs of waveforms at slow firing rates which are too slow, too quick, and right, respectively. A quick shot is the general name for the second stage. Often referred to as the fast fire, the second stage. The metal is forced very quickly into the die in the second stage from the chamber. Less than 100 milliseconds of filling time are possible for castings that weigh more than 40 kilogrammes. Early on in the picture, the first and second phases are different.

If the slow projectile's speed is too great, turbulent waves form (Figure 6).

When the injection procedure is finished and the metal starts to freeze, the tool, if assembled properly, eliminates oxygen from the mould. Following then, the injection

Figure 4. Die-chamber diagram

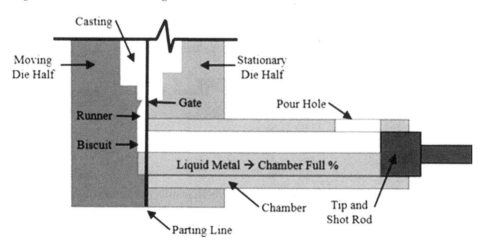

Figure 5. Air is trapped in waves when the slow shot velocity is too sluggish

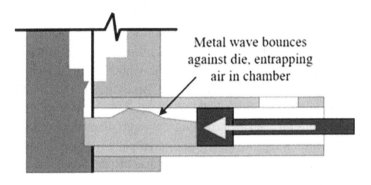

Figure 6.

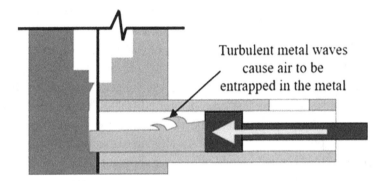

Figure 7. Proper wave formation permits the entire volume of air inside the chamber to escape

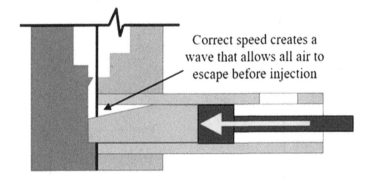

mechanism starts an intensification process, which results in a final volume of liquid metal being produced in the chamber. The hydraulics of the casting device force liquid metal into the die as it is being set up. This method fills in any holes left by the phase change's shrinkage. When the injection process is finished and the metal starts to freeze, the tool, if assembled properly, eliminates the air from the mould. Following then, the injection mechanism starts an intensification process, which results in the final amount of liquid metal being produced in the chamber. Setting up the casting while the machine's hydraulics push liquid metal into the die. This technique helps fill in any gaps due to shrinking of the phase change.

Slide Pulls, an Ejection System, and Die Clamping

In order to prevent separation during the injection process, die halves are kept locked together with hydraulics and mechanics. In addition, the casting shall be removed by means of hydraulics from the die. The quality of the cast could be affected by decisions taken at the design stage of the process.

One choice, for instance, is how much clamping force is used to keep the die halves together. The clamping tonnage is limited by machine capacity and die design. The moving and stationary plates of the die cast machine are connected by four tie bars.

One tie bar may be under higher stress than the other due to the anticipated area of the casting not being distributed evenly across the tie bars, which might make it challenging for the die to remain closed. The heat from several cycles is absorbed, increasing the temperature of the die. Some components of the die may be clamped more firmly than others as a result of this shift in the tool steel.

The casting is given a dwell length for settling in the tool. The casting could fuse or get bound to the die steel after an extended resting period. After the dwell period, the device unlocks the die and initiates the ejection procedure. The first thing to do is to remove unwanted die slides that might have impacted the castings'

Figure 8. Shows a graph of a sample shot injection's pressure and velocity

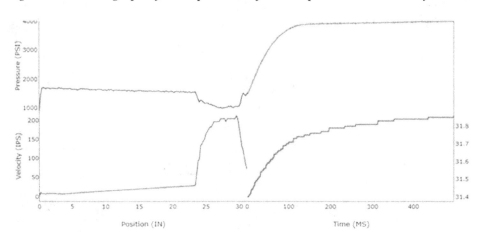

geometry. For complicated component designs, several slides might be necessary. A very extended resting time increases the possibility of the casting sticking or welding to the die steel.

After then, the die's ejection mechanism is under hydraulic pressure. A series of pins built into the die's ejection mechanism forces the casting out of the mould. A machine normally the retrieved casting is taken out of the cell. Setting the system's hydraulic pressure is necessary. A die with the ejector pins extended is shown in Figure 10. It is possible to identify potential tool failures or changes to the overall process by monitoring the pressure profile in the cylinders for slide pulls and ejections.

Heat Management Equipment

Heat regulation of the die steel has a significant impact on casting quality and production rates. warmth is generated as the fluid metal solidifies and is transferred to the die. High-pressure jet cooling, hot water, hot oil, and channels cut into the die are used to regulate the temperature of the die. The equipment used is made up of individual components of the overall thermal management apparatus. If certain process steps need control of temperature, the device is connected to a die casting machine and can receive on or off signals. For each of these systems, it is important to make a choice about temperature settings, start and stop times. A number of

Figure 9. Die with slides in (left) and out (right) positions, and hydraulic cylinders

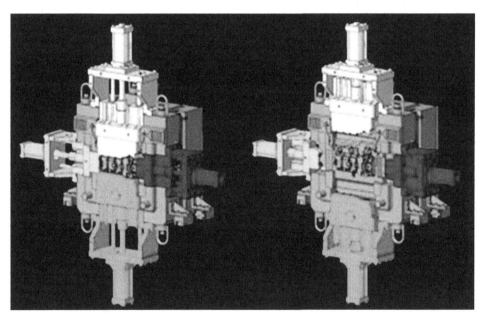

Figure 10. Shows a die example with the ejection pins extended

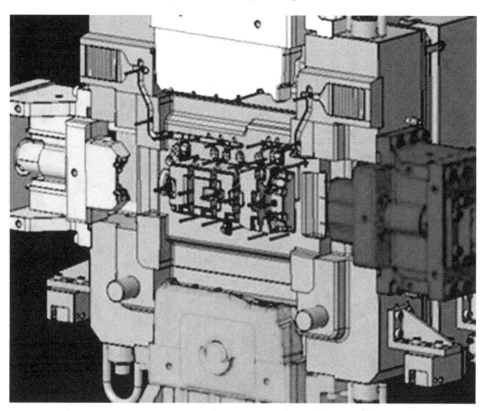

temperature units, each with different control zones, may be set up in a complicated casting system that can provide heating medium to 100s of individually cooled way inside the die. Figure 11 shows an example of a warm water and cool unit.

When specific production steps need the regulation of heat, the device communicates with the casting die process and receives on/off signals. With each of these systems, decisions must be made regarding thermostat applications start and stop times, and other factors of each with multiple control zones that supply cooling fluid to the die's hundreds of individual coolant passageways. Figure 11 may provide an illustration of a hot water unit and a jet cool unit.

The steaming water device (on the left) and the water jet cooling device (on the right) are both in use in Figure 11.

Die spray is another method for controlling the die's temperature. Unlike cooling lines, die spray controls the temperature on the die's outside surface. The basic objective is to lubricate the die surface in order to facilitate the casting's release during ejection. Goal rates and the mixing and distribution infrastructure at the plant

Figure 11.

influence the die lube to water ratio. In the die casting cell, a multi-axis robot or a spray manifold on specialised spray equipment applies the die lubricant.

Die spray manifolds typically use one of two methods. The first is a universal spray manifold, which has a small number of nozzles but can be used with many different instruments and often produces large amounts of spray. In the second technique, a spray manifold with a large number of nozzles is used to accurately guide the spray where it is required. Each technique has a varied effect on both long-term maintenance and performance as well as optimum lubricant use. An example of a spray system with two axes and six axes robot can be seen in Figure 12. The amount of spray sprayed to the die is influenced by the duration of each nozzle, nozzle direction, nozzle obstruction, and movement of the spray manifold. The amount of cooling also varies with flow rates and lubricant temperature. Monitoring these factors can make it easier to spot spray system problems and process modifications.

Die temperatures can be recorded using thermal image cameras on the die surface or thermal couplings embedded in the die near the cavity surface.

Figure 12 shows spray systems using a 6-axis robot and a 2-axis manifold.

Tool Design, Assembly, and Setup

The elaborate die casting tooling design is responsible for a significant portion of the process' complexity. The v-block engine may need 5,000 separate pieces to put together a big block of die. These missionaries need to be correctly designed, put together, and produced on every run using this die cast mission. Components may range from tiny fittings to massive steel holding blocks weighing tonnes.

The injection settings, gate system, component design, and venting system all have an impact on how much metal flows through the die. The direction of the component within the mould, enclosed portions, and the final cast's fill area are some of the flow parameters that affect part design and shape. The designer must then consider how the metal will go into the mould as well as how the air will exit the empty space. The metal is put into overflows intended to catch the first steel face when it passes through the die after it has filled the mould. Since the metal in the vent system lowers before it hardens, the liquid metal should virtually be prevented from escaping, allowing all the air to escape. Refer to Figure 14.

Figure 12.

Figure 13. The key nomenclature of die characteristics

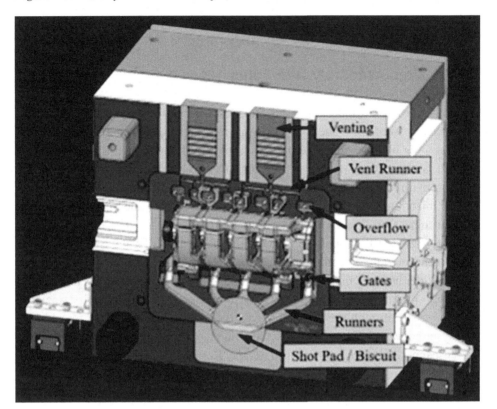

Figure 14 shows the casting's bicuity, runner, gating, and venting system.

It is difficult to manage the air and metal flow through a casting. The die casting industry makes use of methods like flow modelling in order to aid in tool design and gain a better comprehension of how various gated and ventilation systems affect the filling process. In order to improve the design, simulations are run at a number of various variables. Figure 15 illustrates a flow simulation. Through the cookie and runner mechanism, metal is injected into the casting from the chamber. It typically takes this process about 50 and 100 milliseconds during the injection phase.

One of the most important design issues is the heat control of the die Temp. The die casting business used a range of cooling techniques to aid with this. The thermal thing of the cycle is controlled by these systems by injecting cooling medium via dozens to hundreds of distinct, specially created channels. Figure 16 illustrates the intricate nature of these cooling lines.

Figure 16 shows intricate thermal cooling lines used in die design.

one line is connected backwards, cooling cannot flow through the channel, which will influence thermal management and porosity creation. Systems are

Figure 14.

Figure 15. Injection of simulated metal fluid

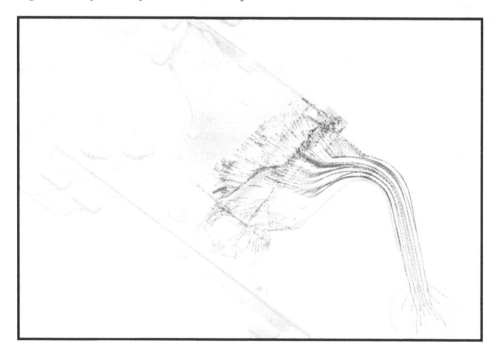

Figure 16.

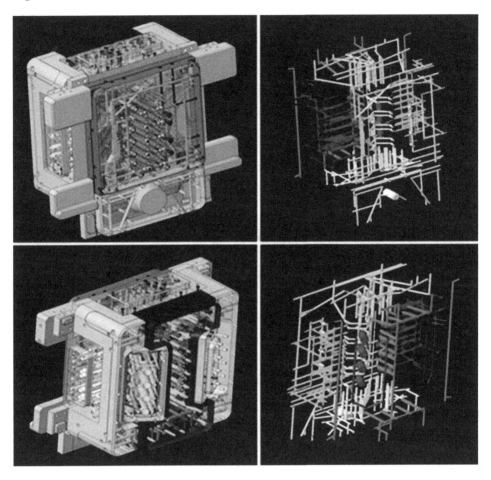

required to verify that the tool is assembled and configured correctly. Readings of pressure, flow rates, and temperature reductions confirm that the die's thermal management is reliable. In Figure 17, is an example of a section of thermal lines on a manufacturing tool. Each time the die is established or maintained, these lines must be placed properly.

Figure 17 shows a moving portion of a huge die with warm water and cold lines.

Environment and Equipment Performance

A lot of die cast equipment's speed, pressures and timing is determined by how efficient the system's motors and pumps are. Two to six distinct hydraulic pumps are used in die casting machines and pressure of the hydraulic systems used for

Figure 17.

gripping, inserting, ejecting or pulling is usually exerted. Monitoring this equipment can produce data streams for temperatures, revolutions per minute (RPM).

Natural factors might also affect the die casting process. The die temperature and associated cooling rates may change depending on the temperature, airflow, and humidity of the surrounding environment. Input water temperatures and recovery times within the cooling units attached to dies may change, as a result of indirect effects on plant wide water systems due to air temperature.

Result of System Complexity

A complicated system underlies die casting. In order to see and specify all the processes and related missions, it merits a rigorous, system engineering approach. We'll talk more about complexity and the systems approach in the context of die casting. An in-depth knowledge of the available data can be achieved by breaking down the complex process using a systems approach. It tackles some of the flaws in the literature currently available on machine learning and die casting optimization.

Process Optimization Literature Review

Die casting process optimisation research is not brand-new. Several authors have developed optimised process parameters to lower errors using the Taguchi technique(Hsu & Do, 2013, pp.1-9) (Balasubramaniam et al., 1999). To optimise parameter selections, several writers have employed statistical techniques such analysis (Q. Han et al., 2017, pp.38-43) (Tsoukalas , 2008,pp.2027-2033) and learning methods like algorithmic evolution (Q. Han et al., 2017, pp.38-43) or neural networks (Tsoukalas , 2008,pp.2027-2033). Although these methods are useful and might benefit the industry, they also have drawbacks that should be recognised and addressed from an industrial standpoint.

Numerous publications conduct their research using poorly selected experimental design inputs. For instance, the second stage plunger speed used in the Tsoukalas article (J. Zheng et al., 2009,pp. 667-674) is 1.2, 2.5, or 3.8 m/s. The above rates represent hole fill periods of forty milliseconds to 127 milliseconds according to the casting capacity and pusher area specified in the study. Industry standards dictate that fill duration must be reduced in order to account for surface abrasion and porosity problems. Less permeability but better surface polish result with longer fill times. Better surface polish is achieved with shorter fill times, but porosity performance is compromised (Aluminum Alloys,2020). It is not unexpected that the optimization carried out for this article reached the same exact result given the diversity of parameters studied. Without the need for analytics, testing, or optimization, one might get the same set points as the author by using the NADCA's published industrial calculations (Aluminum Alloys,2020). The bulk of the literature that we looked at had input ranges that were significantly larger than anything that industry would ever consider. In the end, the majority of the publications using the optimization approach suggested just adhered to normative business practises.

The die casting process generates a lot more input parameters than what's usually measured. The most popular approach in the industry is to measure the intensification pressure and the injection velocity systems using the most commonly used approach (Herman,2012). Usually, 20-30 inputs are calculated from the time series data Blondheim, D, Jr. (2020). Most of the published research makes assumptions about the most important inputs and then relies on a small subset of those inputs to collect data. Usually, 3-5 inputs were used (Hsu & Do, 2013, pp.1-9) (Balasubramaniam et al., 1999) (J. Zheng et al., 2009,pp. 667-674) (Herman,2012). Since most of this research is just exploratory and relies on small study populations, it makes sense that this approach doesn't take into account the inputs that could be important for optimization. Han et al., for example, used over 20 input variables in their analysis of optimizations (Tsoukalas , 2008,pp.2027-2033), but again, this is just a small subset of the data that die casting could potentially provide.

It has described in the literature on die casting process optimisation are useful for the industry. Aoptimised results typically match the fundamental estimates that are advised by the sector. For die casting, a better data collection and optimisation procedure is needed.

CONCLUSION

To get the concluded and way of optimization in die casting, there is a discrepancy between mathematical techniques and practical implementations. The intricate die casting system has to be treated with a systems engineering perspective in order to narrow this gap. To choose the most appropriate applications, it is also necessary to have a solid grasp of faults and classification. automated education.

The die casting production system's application of complexity theory, the need for a systems engineering-based strategy, and the creation of the die casting process are all described in length in this chapter. It will be shown that in order to analyze and locate critical techniques are necessary owing to the enormous quantity and speed of data created in die casting. In-depth research on the erratic nature of permeability making in die castings revealed that the factors that the industry typically controls to raise the better of its components had little effect on the permeability formation's erratic behaviour. This gives us the opportunity to stress the intricate structure of a die casting mechanism in two different ways. The importance of the Critical notion is discussed in relation to the impact that defect categorization has on individuals.

Applications for machine learning that are used in the manufacture of die casting. Four case examples of artificial intelligence are provided before a basic overview of automated training and some of the difficulties in manufacturing are given. The dissertation is ended with an analysis of the takeaways and a list of prospective areas for further investigation.

REFERENCES

Aluminum Alloys 101. (2020). https://www.mercalloy.com/aluminum-alloys-101/

Alvarez, S. (2020). *Tesla Model Y single-piece rear casts spotted in Fremont factory.* https://www.teslarati.com/tesla-model-y-unibody-casts-sighting-video/

Andresen, B. (2005). *Die Casting Engineering: A Hydraulic, Thermal, and Mechanical Process.* Marcel Dekker.

Apparao, K. C., & Birru, A. K. (2017). Optimization of Die casting process based on Taguchi approach. *Materials Today: Proceedings*, *4*(2), 1852–1859. doi:10.1016/j.matpr.2017.02.029

Baier, L., Johren, F., & Seebacher, S. (2019). Challenges in the deployment and operation of machine learning in practice. *Proceedings of the 27th European Conference on Information Systems (ECIS).*

Balasubramaniam, S., Kannan, S., & Shivpuri, R. (1999). *Improving the Quality in Die Casting Production Using Statistical Analysis Procedures.* Presented at the 1999 NADCA World of Die Casting, Cleveland, OH. Available: http://www.diecasting. org/archive/transactions/T99-071.pdf

Blondheim, D., Jr. (2018). *Unsupervised Machine Learning and Statistical Anomaly Detection Applied to Thermal Images.* Available: http://www.diecasting.org/archive/ transactions/T18-071.pdf

Blondheim, D., Jr. (2020). *Artificial Intelligence, Machine Learning, and Data Analytics: Understanding the Concepts to Find Value in Die Casting Data.* Presented at the NADCA Executive Conference, Clearwater, FL.

Doehler, H. H. (1951). *Die Casting.* McGraw-Hill Book Company.

Folk, J. (2019). U.S. Aluminum Casting Industry – 2019. *Die Casting Engineer,* 16–19. Available: https://www.diecasting.org/archive/dce/71916.pdf

Han, Q., McClure, D., Wood, D., & Yang, D. (2017). Statistical Analysis of the Effect of Operational Parameters on the Scrap Rates of Crossmember Casting. *Die Casting Engineer,* 38–43. Available: http://www.diecasting.org/archive/dce/111738.pdf

Herman, E. A. (2012). *Die Casting Process Control E-410.* North American Die Casting Association.

Herman, E. A., & Kirkman, J. S. (2011). *Designing Die Casting Dies Series - E-506.* North American Die Casting Association.

Hsu, Q.-C., & Do, A. T. (2013). Minimum Porosity Formation in Pressure Die Casting by Taguchi Method. *Mathematical Problems in Engineering, 2013,* 1–9. doi:10.1155/2013/920865

Landry, J., Maltais, J., Deschênes, J.-M., Petro, M., Godmaire, X., & Fraser, A. (2018). *Inline Integration of Shotblast Resistant Laser Marking in a Die Cast Cell.* Available: https://www.diecasting.org/archive/transactions/T18-123.pdf

Midson, S. (2014). Report on the 2014 Die Casting Benchmarking Survey Part 2 of 3: Operations. In *Report on the 2014 Die Casting Benchmarking Survey.* North American Die Casting Association.

NADCA Product Specification Standards for Die Casting. (2018). 10th ed.). North American Die Casting Association.

Product Design for Die Casting E-606. (2009). (6th ed., Vol. E-606). North American Die Casting Association.

Sun, Kopper, Karkare, Paffenroth, & Apelian. (2020). Machine Learning Pathway for Harnessing Knowledge and Data in Material Processing. *Inter Metalcast.* doi:10.1007/s40962-020-00506-2

Tsoukalas, V. D. (2008, December). Optimization of porosity formation in AlSi9Cu3 pressure die castings using genetic algorithm analysis. *Materials & Design, 29*(10), 2027–2033. doi:10.1016/j.matdes.2008.04.016

Wuest, T., Weimer, D., Irgens, C., & Thoben, K.-D. (2016, January). Machine learning in manufacturing: Advantages, challenges, and applications. *Production & Manufacturing Research, 4*(1), 23–45. doi:10.1080/21693277.2016.1192517

Zheng, J., Wang, Q., Zhao, P., & Wu, C. (2009, October). Optimization of high-pressure die-casting process parameters using artificial neural network. *International Journal of Advanced Manufacturing Technology, 44*(7–8), 667–674. doi:10.100700170-008-1886-6

Chapter 10

A Chatbot–Based Strategy for Regional Language–Based Train Ticket Ordering Using a novel ANN Model

Kiruthika V
ⓘD https://orcid.org/0000-0003-1915-6315
Vellore Institute of Technology, Chennai, India

Sheena Christabel Pravin
Vellore Institute of Technology, Chennai, India

Rohith G
Vellore Institute of Technology, Chennai, India

Aswin B.
Vellore Institute of Technology, Chennai, India

Ompirakash S
Vellore Institute of Technology, Chennai, India

Danush Ram R
Vellore Institute of Technology, Chennai, India

ABSTRACT

Chatbots are becoming increasingly crucial in modern society. Typically, a large group of individuals will purchase train tickets together. This requires considerable effort and time. Multiple inquiries from a user are part of the booking procedure. In this research, the authors create an intelligent, user-friendly chatbot for booking train tickets in the native language. In this study, a Tamil-speaking chatbot is developed to assist with train ticket purchases. The authors employed NLP techniques to create

DOI: 10.4018/978-1-6684-9804-0.ch010

an effective and user-friendly conversational interface. The above poll indicates that chatbots have been used in a variety of contexts with positive results. This method will make purchasing tickets much less of a burden for residents of remote areas, who will appreciate it. The ANN model is used to train the chatbot to discern the consumer's desires and respond accordingly. The proposed method has a success rate of 85% and will benefit consumers by expediting and simplifying ticket transactions.

1. INTRODUCTION

Excellent software that can simulate and handle user inquiries is a chatbot. Its use in a wide variety of consumer-focused contexts has been on the rise in recent years. Communicating with others is simplified and improved by chatbots. Many industries have found widespread use for chatbots, and their popularity continues to grow. Emails and phone calls to inquire about something are laborious and cause unneeded delays. Chatbots save time and energy by providing instantaneous responses to inquiries. They are easy to use and accomplish their goal without sacrificing quality. When questions are answered quickly, customers are relieved and satisfied. Conversational interfaces, or chatbots, are increasingly being used in business to improve operational efficiency, resulting in significant cost savings for both the business and the country. By automating responses to common customer questions, chatbots help businesses save time and money by responding to fewer customer service requests. A company can scale, personalize, and be proactive with the help of chatbots. Having access to customers' private information has the potential to vastly improve results, as suggested by the available evidence in the literature Liu et al., 2017. Marketing campaigns that employ chatbots to encourage the purchase and use of consumer goods have seen widespread implementation to date. The literatures that used Chatbots in various fields are Aishwarya and Chawla, 2020 in Education, Chinedu and Abejide, 2021, in student services Petrovic et al., 2020, in website management, Siddharth et al., 2015 in healthcare, Jovanovic et al., 2021, in individualised communication and Darius and Sophie, 2018, in transactions and Rossmann et al., 2020 in customer service.

Railways, electricity, bus services, gas booking, and many more applications could all benefit by incorporating chatbots to improve communication and resolve customer issues more quickly and effectively. This research suggests creating a chatbot to help with booking train tickets. There is currently a lot of progress being made in the field of Natural language processing for creating pipelines and grammar checks in different regional languages. So using a chatbot that is based on a specific language can increase the efficiency with which train tickets are booked. It would be much more convenient for customers to book tickets if they could do so in their native language. Those who are less comfortable with English would greatly benefit from the introduction of a chatbot programmed in a regional language such as Tamil or Hindi. This motivated to design a regional based chatbot.

In this research, a Tamil-speaking chatbot is built to assist with purchasing train tickets. The goal is to supply a minimal set of questions and dialogues for a train ticket booking system. The created chatbot will patiently respond to any inquiries or concerns that the clients may have and will also remember certain information in order to buy the ticket. People in outlying locations will appreciate this innovative method since it will make purchasing tickets much less of a hassle.

The salient features of this chatbot are

- This chatbot, built upon natural language processing and ANN, allows users to formulate queries using their own vocabulary. The chatbot is equipped with a conversation flow that assists users in navigating through the multiple steps required to complete a certain action.
- Efficient ticket reservation facilitated by a user-friendly user interface.
- It is more convenient for customers since they are not in need to log in to the system.
- The system enables the user to generate a transcript of the discussion, offer a set of pre-determined response options for efficient selection, direct the user through the conversation process, automatically extract relevant information from user input, facilitate information retrieval using search and filtering mechanisms, and deliver concise and comprehensible answers.
- The system also possesses the capability to automatically generate responses in instances where clients inquire about certain queries.

2. RELATED WORKS

A comprehensive analysis of chatbots in a range of contexts were conducted. The process followed by the developers was also extensively investigated to rate the question-answer sets. For the purpose of assisting the elderly, a chatbot was created by Su et al., 2017. The sentences become patterns after being extracted from a database. To facilitate conversation with the elderly, information was extracted using a multi-layered LSTM-based model. As predicted by the model, accuracy was 79.96%. Using machine learning techniques, a chatbot was created to answer banking clients' questions. During the conversation, the chatbot provided acceptable responses to the questions asked by the clients in English. Better accuracy was achieved with Random Forest and Support Vector Machines which was reported in the literature Kulkarni et al., 2017. Frequently asked queries in a university setting inspired the creation of a chatbot by Ranoliya et al., 2017. The questions posed online were taken straight from the FAQ. In this research, Machine Learning [**ML**] and Latent Semantic Analysis [**LSA**] were employed. In this study, ML was used to answer broad inquiries, whereas LSA was used to answer questions about specific services. ML is easy to use because it only consists of a few different sorts of tag; nonetheless, the ML code needs to be updated anytime the number of utterances to be matched rises.

The authors Lee et al., 2018 created a system to automatically generate questions based on content in childrens' literature. About a hundred student narratives were used to develop the questions. The user's query accuracy was evaluated using logistic regression. A group of researchers have created a ticketing chatbot service that uses Facebook's Wit.AI. The service places an emphasis on the serverless feature by making use of a webhook was highlighted by Handoyo et al., 2018. The webhook was activated when the incoming message arrived, and the response was transmitted to the client side via GET and POST requests. Named Entity Recognition [**NER**] is a process that takes place whenever an incoming message is examined to see whether or not it contains any matched named entities. These named entities can include things like the time, location, date, and so on. Wit.AI is completely free to use and does not place any restrictions on the number of requests that can be made. It also has the ability to speed up the processing time due to the fact that the chat history is quickly captured and trained. The negative is that it is unable to deal with situations that are off-topic, and the input often involves typing errors. Researchers Kazi et al., 2018 created a bus E-ticketing system. Login and selection of a seat are enabled. The seat is paid for and an E-ticket is generated. E-tickets stored in electronic devices prevent users from losing their paper tickets. The device also shows consumers how many seats are available. The study conducted by Cha and Lee, 2018 employed a Convolutional Neural Network [CNN] model for the purpose of text classification. The study has demonstrated that Convolutional Neural Networks are not only effective in the task of image classification, but also in text classification. The convolutional layer has the capability to generate feature maps that contain the embedded information of the keyword. The feature maps containing the weights of the keywords are subjected to a fully connected layer in order to generate the relevant features that will be used by the softmax classifier for making predictions. The fully connected layer discards inactive characteristics prior to reaching the softmax classifier in order to prevent extraneous information from interfering with the accuracy of predictions. Based on a study conducted by Prabowo et al., 2018, comparing the performance of LSTM and simple RNN in generating Bahasa Indonesia Conversation, it was found that LSTM outperformed simple RNN. The Long Short-Term Memory [LSTM] model exhibited superior performance compared to the Recurrent Neural Network [RNN] in terms of both response time and the ability to deliver the anticipated answer. The reason for this distinction is in the design of the Long Short-Term Memory [LSTM] model, which is specifically engineered to retain information about the sequential sequence of words. In contrast, Recurrent Neural Networks [RNNs] operate under the assumption that each word is independent of its neighbouring words.

The effect of conversational recommendation systems was analysed. In order to improve the feedback elicitation procedure, dialogue-based conversational recommender systems [DCRSs] were used by Cai et al., 2022. The research found that when the recommender system made recommendations for various purposes, the communication and engagement between the chatbots and consumers improved. Aishwarya et al., 2021 created a chatbot for medical purposes that is powered by AI. In response to a list of symptoms, the suggested method identified the most likely condition. The device also recorded the patient's medical history available in a database, even before the creation of the chatbot. The chatbot provided helpful responses to frequently asked questions and aided the patient in making informed decisions. Medical chatbots have been created by Madhu et al., 2017. The chatbots were taught their skills using a structured database. Chatbots have the potential to aid in illness prediction by providing a list of remedies based on the patient's reported symptoms. It may also provide information about the medicine's composition and its possible applications. Human-robot interactions were the subject of a study by Marita et al., 2021. Users from a variety of countries were randomly selected to participate in Skype interviews. Neither piece of feedback was identical. Numerous people claimed to have both happy and bad feelings. In this article, we explore the difficulties caused by a lack of shared context for interpreting chatbot responses. The research group Pophale et al., 2021, created a chatbot to detect the feelings of an adult. The software assisted in deciphering people's mental states and intuiting their feelings based on their textual exchanges.

From the existing research, the use of natural language processing [NLP] allows for the possibility of advancement in the field of bot-human communication. In multiple contexts, chatbot solutions fuelled by NLP have produced promising results. The interface demonstrates both user-friendliness and effectiveness. They reduce the need for human labour while facilitating productive conversations between businesses and their clients. The development of these chatbots involved the use of machine learning and deep learning techniques. The outcomes of chatbots created using machine learning and deep learning methodologies are impressive. Utilising Natural Language Processing [NLP] facilitates the development of bot-human communication. The integration of artificial neural networks [ANNs] and natural language processing [NLP] in the form of a hybrid model shows great promise and represents a significant step forward in the field of avatars based on regional information.

From the above related works, the research gap bridged are

- A Tamil-speaking ticket-buying chatbot developed in regional language is a pioneer effort. The intention is to provide the bare bones of a ticket-buying process for a train. The resulting chatbot will patiently address any questions or concerns raised by the customers and keep track of relevant data until the purchase is complete. This novel approach will greatly simplify the process of buying tickets for customers living in remote areas.
- During the course of our investigation, we made use of various NLP techniques in order to design a conversational interface that is not only efficient but also simple to use. Chatbots have already been implemented in a variety of settings, and the results have been promising. They reduce the need for human labour while simultaneously enabling businesses to have fruitful dialogues with their customers.
- The methods of machine learning and deep learning were utilised during the construction of these chatbots. The use of natural language processing [NLP] makes it possible to make advancements in bot-human communication. The proposed study utilises an algorithm that is built on artificial neural networks [ANNs] in order to create chatbots, which represents a novel approach to this area of research.

3. PROPOSED ARCHITECTURE

The study proposes to develop a system called as the train ticket booking system (TTBS) to get user's data about passenger name, source and other travel details to enable automatic ticket booking. The flowchart of TTBS system is given in Figure 1.

The detailed illustration of Figure 1 is depicted as follows-

- The user provides vocal input in Tamil. In order to provide input, the user only needs to utilise the microphone and cease recording by pressing the stop recording button.

The voice input is processed beforehand and then provided as input to the model. Subsequently, the chatbot's response will be displayed on the console.

- There are two functionalities available to users inside this chatbot. The first functionality pertains to the common form of conversation, which typically involves asking the name, date of birth, and other related details. It involves

Figure 1. Block diagram of the chatbot system

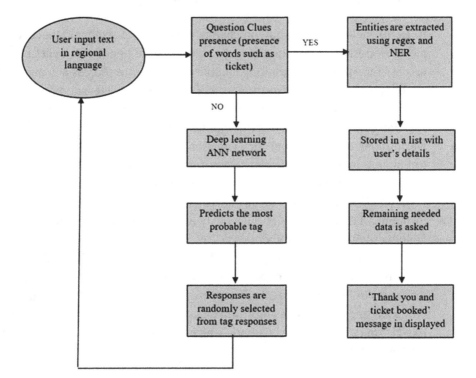

engaging in small-t conversations with the user, during which their input is analysed and categorised based on the trained intents.

- The second functionality is to consider the acquisition of train ticket data for the purpose of booking. It involves the gathering of ticket data, wherein we gather information pertaining to the following four questions: "How many tickets are being purchased?", "On which date is the boarding scheduled?", "What is the initial point of departure?", "What is the final destination?", and "What is the name of the passenger?".

- The selection between the first and second approaches is made by the bot. The bot conducts a search for the terms "train" and "ticket" in the user's input. In the event of finding the terms, the second functionality is selected; otherwise, the first is chosen.

- The Natural Language Toolkit [NLTK] library comprising the NER [Named Entity Recognition] model is utilised in our study for information extraction. In the event that the user provides input such as "I would like to purchase two tickets." The extraction process will prompt for the omitted information subsequent to identifying the text elements that have been emphasised.

Once all the necessary values have been obtained, the system will generate a confirmation indicating that the ticket has been successfully booked, accompanied by a message expressing gratitude.

3.1 Data Pre-Processing and Implementation Details

The dataset used to train the neural network was created using the basic conversations of a train ticket booking session. The TTBS dataset has six sets of responses and patterns. Each response and pattern have 1–4 examples. The total word count of the dataset is 145 words. To begin with, our model has been trained using English text. The user provides input in Tamil speech, and we use Google's speech recognition model, implemented using the Python module, to turn it into Tamil text. The Tamil text is subsequently translated into English using Google's translation package. We developed a foundational English model that was trained with 30 sentences, encompassing five intents. The architecture of the translation pipeline is to translate Tamil voice into English text, with each sentence consisting of approximately 1–4 words. In order to train the model, a separate pipeline was developed to transform a collection of patterns associated with each intent into vector representations. Subsequently, the vectors are used as input for the model in order to facilitate the training or testing process.

As previously indicated, selecting the second option will result in the extraction of data. Specifically, we aim to extract four entities, which are the "number of tickets," "passenger names," "source," and "destination."

This dataset is stored in a JSON file. In this data, each class contains a pattern of speech and its response. The dataset cannot be directly fed to ANN because networks only understand numbers, so data should be vectorized. In order to train the ANN model, this dataset also undergoes the same preprocessing as mentioned above. The resultant vectorized words are fed to the TensorFlow sequential ANN model for training the network.

The TTBS system recognises the speech using a SciPy wave reader until a certain stop time with the help of a JavaScript and HTML user interface. This wav file is converted to Tamil text through b64 decoding. This text was converted from the native language to English through the Google Translate package. The resultant English text is pre-processed. The input from the user is received and translated into English. This resultant English text undergoes the following steps, as described in Figure 2. At this step, the presence of QC (question clues) is checked. QC is a list of words related to train ticket booking. If QC is present, user details are extracted from user input or requested if some details are missing, and the conversation is ended. If QC is absent, user input is fed to the ANN network to predict the most probable response. This response will be displayed in Tamil. Currently, this system is implemented in

Google Colab with the help of GPUs and CPUs. Followed by this, the list of words undergoes a process called lemmatization. Lemmatization is a text normalisation technique used to reduce words to their simple or root form (lemma). Lemmatization refers to word related works carried out using proper vocabulary and morphological analysis of words, with an intention to remove inflectional word-endings. After lemmatization, a process called vectorization is performed where the list of words is converted into numbers by substituting previously assigned unique numbers for each unique word. These preprocessing techniques are exclusively done with the help of the Natural Language Toolkit (NLTK) library. NLTK is a collection of programmes and libraries for statistical and symbolic natural language processing in English. NLTK is available in the Python programming language. Preprocessed data sample code for understanding the TTBS dataset preprocessing is shown in figure 3.

3.2. Question Clue Check (QC)

Question Clues are a set of words whose presence indicates the user's need for ticket booking. Examples of QC words are ticket, train, etc. If QC words are present in the English text of user input, the system applies named entity extraction (NER) to extract booking information from the text. After extracting all the needed details, the system prints a Tamil response, ending the conversation. If QC words are absent, then the vectorized input is sent to the pretrained ANN model to predict the response.

Figure 2. Flow diagram for preprocessing

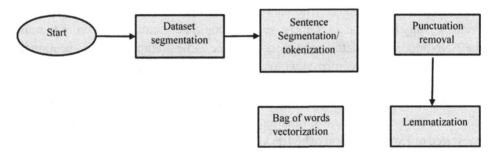

Figure 3. Preprocessed data sample code for understanding the TTBS dataset processing

```
data = {"intents": [
            {"tag": "greeting",
             "patterns": ["Hello", "How are you?", "Hi there", "Hi", "Whats up"],
             "responses": ["Hello"]
            },
```

3.3. Named Entity Recognition

NER [Named entity Recognition] is a method that is used for information extraction. The term Named Entity helps to recognize names of organizations, people and geographic locations in the text, currency and time. This NER library uses part of speech [POS] tagging method to aid the tagging process for tags such as Location, Name etc. Figure 4 shows a sample of Named Entity Recognition.

The information extracted using NER should provide all the needed train ticket booking details. If the required information is not extracted, then the system specifically asks certain questions to inquire about the details. If QC words are present, a predefined response will be printed in Tamil, ending the session. But if QC words are absent, then vectorized input is fed to an artificial neural network (ANN) model, and the output response is displayed as Tamil text.

3.4. Design of TTBS System Model

The preprocessed data is used to train the chatbot system. The dense layer receives information from all the neurons of the preceding layers and helps in classifying the given entity based on the information from the convolutional layers. Multiple numbers of such neurons are available in each layer. The dropout layer helps nullify the outcome of certain neurons while leaving the others unmodified when proceeding to the subsequent layers. The details of the Model is given in Table.1.

The details on the testing and training of the layers are

- Training data- 30 sentences or patterns (6 intents) and Testing data-20 Sentences
    - Input layer -- dense, 256 neurons per layer, 1d input shape, activation RELU,
    - Hidden layer -- dense 256 neurons per layer, activation RELU

Figure 4. An illustration on named entity recognition [NER]

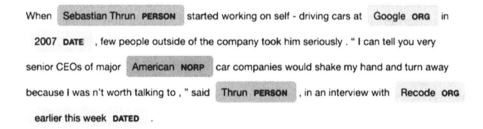

Table 1. Details of the ANN model

Layer Type		Number of Layers
Input	Dense layer	256
	Dropout layer	256
Hidden	Dense layer	256
	Dropout layer	256
Output	Dense layer	6

- ◦ Output layer -- dense, output layer, activation softmax,
- ◦ 4 optimizers -- Adam, learning rate -- 0.01, decay -- 1e-6
- ◦ Loss -- categorical cross-entropy
- ◦ Epoch and neurons per layer are variable

In this study, the dense layer shapes were fixed based on the highest accuracy that was obtained. The sequential API helped in creating a model that had a better understanding of the queries that were presented to the system. The dropout layers helped prevent certain information from proceeding to the subsequent layers. A careful study was made in fixing the number of dense and dropout layers. The activation function computes the weighted sum with bias and helps in deciding the activation of the neuron. The activation decides whether a neuron should be activated or not by calculating a weighted sum and further adding bias to it. It helps introduce non-linearity into the neuron's output. RELU is the most popular activation function, which is used in the hidden layer of NN. This study uses the RELU activation function, as it helped improve the performance of the outcome by providing an in-depth analysis of the features fed to the network. SoftMax is used at the last layer of the neural network and has the capability to handle several classes. It helps to calculate the likelihoods distribution of the event over 'n' different events. This system uses the SoftMax (output layer) activation function. SoftMax is used because this TTBS system incorporates a multiclass classification system. An optimizer is a function that adjusts the various attributes of the network model. Deep learning models based on stochastic gradient descent can be trained using the Adam optimizer. The Adam optimizer can be used to handle noisy problems as it is a combination of the best properties of the AdaGrad and RMSProp algorithms. This system uses an Adam optimizer with a learning rate of 0.01 as it helped in answering most of the queries posted by the user. It helped improve the accuracy and overall loss of the TTBS, yielding a better performance.

4. RESULTS AND DISCUSSION

A voice input is received from the user by the TTBS system. With Google speech recognition and the Google translate package, the system converts the Tamil speech to Tamil text and Tamil text to English text, respectively. For recording the audio on screen, Tamil Chatbot uses JavaScript code, and to encode it to a wav file, we use 64_encode and other necessary packages such as JSON, IO, ffmpeg, HTML, and Audio.

Figure 5 shows a sample recording for the translation process. Once the recording is subjected to TTBS system, a sequential model containing a specified combination of dense and dropout layers is developed in this study. The model was developed by trying different combinations of dense and dropout layers. Increasing the number of layers contributed to better accuracy. TTBS's accuracy had increased with the experiments on the neurons per layer, the number of epochs, and adding of dropout layers. The results of the accuracy analysis are presented in Table 2.

From Table.2 first case, without the dropout layer (64 neurons per layer), an accuracy of only 57% was obtained. Only very few data along with their response was recognized by the system. There was a lack of better understanding of the query-response combination as the number of layers was smaller. Trials were made with a dropout layer (128 neurons per layer), and it yielded an accuracy of 71%. A moderate increase in accuracy was predicted with an increase in the number of layers, and this

Figure 5. A sample voice recording for translation

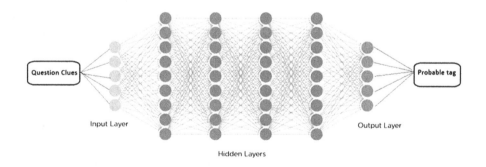

Table 2. Accuracy variations while designing the TTBS model

S.No	Traits	Accuracy
1	Without Dropout layer	57%
2	With Dropout layer (128 neurons per layer)	71%
3	With Dropout layer (256 neurons per layer)	85%

Table 3. Performance analysis for different number of layers in TTBS model

Class	Without Dropout Layers			With Dropout Layers (128 neurons per layer)			With DropoutLayers (256 neurons per layer)		
	Precision	Recall	F-Score	Precision	Recall	F-Score	Precision	Recall	F-Score
0	100	33	50	100	40	57	100	67	80
1	100	50	67	100	50	67	100	50	67
2	100	50	67	100	50	67	100	50	67
3	67	100	80	100	100	100	100	100	100
4	100	33	50	100	40	57	100	67	80

gave the inference that an increase in the number of layers contributed towards an increase in accuracy. Further trials were made with a dropout layer (256 neurons per layer), and the accuracy considerably improved to 85%. This indicated that there was a better understanding of the query-response combination. When the dropout layers were further increased, the accuracy did not increase further and became saturated. A detailed analysis of the performance metrics such as precision, recall, and F-score was also predicted from the resultant confusion matrix. The results are presented in Table 3. From Table 3, it can be inferred that better performance metrics could be obtained for all the classes for dropout layers (256 neurons per layer). In certain classes, significant changes were found in performance indices as the number of neurons increased. The trained model helps in giving the required response for the user's input query. The response is displayed by the chatbot on the screen for the user's inference. The respective translated Tamil reply is printed on the console.

The screenshot of the reply from the chatbot is shown in Figure 6. Also, if the user gives a sentence containing a question clue, such as "ticket," then data is extracted and stored in the list for further ticket booking.

The NER recognises the user input during the booking of a train ticket and stores the information. The stored information can be used by the TTBS system for subsequent ticket bookings. The user may refrain from entering the data once again when he uses the TTBS for future bookings of train tickets. Figure 7 shows the results of NER, where the user data is stored in a list for future retrieval. The TTBS presented in this study uses the Tamil language as input. But this system can be used to implement the booking of tickets in any regional language with the

Figure 6. Sample outcome from the TTBS chatbox model

நன்றி விரைவில் சந்திப்போம்

| Recording... press to stop |

Figure 7. User data stored data in a list in the TTBS chatbox model

help of the simple Google speech recognition and Google translator packages. The proposed TTBS model and the NER functions will be the same irrespective of the language as it is trained for English text only.

The strength of the proposed system are

- With the help of the simple Google speech recognition and Google translation packages, a system can be set up to let people book tickets in any local language. Since it has only been trained on English text, the suggested TTBS model and the NER functions will be the same no matter what language is used. It is easy to use and will help the common man book a ticket in his own language.
- The interface is straightforward and user-friendly. The process of reserving tickets is straightforward and concise. The questions and their corresponding solutions have been organised into categories. By default, the responses to the inquiries are concealed. The questions have been categorised based on their respective topics. The response or resolution supplied is concise and unambiguous.

- The system incorporates the functionality of forwarding customers to a live agent in cases where the chatbot is unable to provide a satisfactory response to their request. This is due to the inherent importance of the aforementioned feature, as it serves a crucial role in situations where the system fails to resolve customer issues, which cannot be left unresolved. Consequently, it becomes necessary for the system to generate notifications andalert live agents to engage in direct communication with the users.

The limitations of the proposed system are

- Large quantum of training datasets are required and ineffective communication with the chatbot leads to miscommunication.
- In order to obtain the solution, it is necessary for users to thoroughly read and comprehend all of the questions provided. The approach presented lacks the use of visual aids, which are known to enhance users' comprehension.
- In order to select topics from the menu, users are required to scroll upwards within the chat for the purpose of making their selection. It is not possible to change the language with a single click.

However, these limitations are posed to the researchers as a gap that we have identified from the proposed work. In future, it is feasible to develop comparable systems and employ them in diverse customer-centric environments.

5. CONCLUSION

In this research, an innovative TTBS to answer customers' questions about purchasing train tickets online is designed and tested. User-posted inquiries are incorporated into the research and processed by the system using the query context. In the event that the question hints do not include the query, an ANN model created with appropriate hyperparameters is trained to predict the response. The improved performance is seen in the 85% accuracy provided by the constructed ANN model. The created system may be accessed in a convenient manner and is user-friendly. People living in more remote places would greatly benefit from this innovative method, which would make it simpler and more accessible for them to buy tickets. A noise cancellation technique integrated through the get audio function might improve the work's accuracy in converting audio to text. It is possible to create equivalent systems in a number of regional languages and to use them in a number of customer-focused contexts.

REFERENCES

Aishwarya, B., Pathak, A., & Hattiambire, S. (2021). AI Medical Chatbot. *Journal of Emerging Technologies and Innovative Research, 8*(3), 61–64.

Aishwarya, R., & Chawla, V. (2020). Chatbots in Marketing - A morphology of literature. *Proceedings of the European Marketing Academy, 64187*, 1–11.

Cai, W., Jin, Y., & Chen, L. (2022). Task-Oriented User Evaluation on Critiquing-Based Recommendation Chatbots. *IEEE Transactions on Human-Machine Systems, 52*(3), 354–366. doi:10.1109/THMS.2021.3131674

Cha, J., & Lee, J.-H. (2018). Extracting Topic Related Keywords by Backtracking CNN based Text Classifier. *2018 Joint 10th International Conference on Soft Computing and Intelligent Systems (SCIS) and 19th International Symposium on Advanced Intelligent Systems* (ISIS), (pp. 93-96). IEEE.

Chinedu W.O., & Abejide, A.I.(2021). Chatbots applications in education: A systematic review. *Computers and Education: Artificial Intelligence, 2,* 1-10.

Darius, Z., & Sophie, H. (2018). Chatbots – An Interactive Technology for Personalized Communication, Transactions and Services. *IADIS International Journal, 15*(1), 96–109.

Jovanovic, M., Baez, M., & Casati, F. (2021). Chatbots as Conversational Healthcare Services. *IEEE Internet Computing, 25*(3), 44–51. doi:10.1109/MIC.2020.3037151

Kazi, S., Bagasrawala, M., Shaikh, F., & Sayyed, A. (2018). Smart E-Ticketing System for Public Transport Bus. *2018 International Conference on Smart City and Emerging Technology (ICSCET).* (pp. 1-7). IEEE. 10.1109/ICSCET.2018.8537302

Kulkarni, C. S. (2017). Bank Chat Bot–An intelligent assistant system using NLP and machine learning. *International Research Journal of Engineering and Technology, 4*(5), 2374–2377.

Lee, C. (2018). Automatic Question Generation from Children's Stories for Companion Chatbot. *IEEE International Conference on Information Reuse and Integration,* (pp. 491-494). IEEE. 10.1109/IRI.2018.00078

Liu, Xu, Z., Sun, C., Wang, B., Wang, X., Wong, D. F., & Zhang, M. (2017). Content-oriented user modeling for personalized response ranking in chatbots. *IEEE/ACM Transactions on Audio, Speech, and Language Processing, 26*(1), 122–133. doi:10.1109/TASLP.2017.2763243

Madhu, D. (2017). A novel approach for medical assistance using trained chatbot. *International Conference on Inventive Communication and Computational Technologies*, (pp. 243-246). IEEE. 10.1109/ICICCT.2017.7975195

Marita, S. (2021). My Chatbot Companion- a Study of Human-Chatbot Relationships. *International Journal of Human-Computer Studies*, *149*, 102601. doi:10.1016/j. ijhcs.2021.102601

Petrovic, A., Zivkovic, M., & Bačanin, D. N. (2020): Singibot - A Student Services Chatbot. *Proceedings of International Scientific Conference on Information Technology and Data Related Research*, (pp. 318-323). IEEE.

Pophale, S., Gandhi, H., & Gupta, A. K. (2021). Emotion Recognition Using Chatbot System, In: V.K. Gunjan, & J.M. Zurada (eds) *Proceedings of International Conference on Recent Trends in Machine Learning, IoT, Smart Cities and Applications. Advances in Intelligent Systems and Computing*, (pp. 1-9). IEEE.

Prabowo, Y. D. (2018). LSTM And Simple RNN Comparison In The Problem Of Sequence To Sequence On Conversation Data Using Bahasa Indonesia. *The 1st 2018 INAPR International Conference*, (pp. 51-56). IEEE.

Ranoliya, N., Raghuwanshi, Singh. S.(2017). Chatbot for university related FAQs. *International Conference on Advances in Computing, Communications, and Informatics*, (pp. 1525-1530). ACM.

Rossmann. (2020). The Impact of Chatbots on Customer Service Performance. In: Spohrer, J., Leitner, C. (eds) Advances in the Human Side of Service Engineering. AHFE 2020. Advances in Intelligent Systems and Computing, 1-7. Springer. doi:10.1007/978-3-030-51057-2_33

Siddharth. (2015). An E-Commerce Website based Chatbot. *International Journal of Computer Science and Information Technologies*, *6*(2), 1483–1485.

Su, M., Wu, C., Huang, K., Hong, Q., & Wang, H. (2017). A chatbot using LSTM-based multi-layer embedding for elderly care. *2017 International Conference on Orange Technologies*, (pp. 70-74). IEEE. 10.1109/ICOT.2017.8336091

Chapter 11

Authentication by Palmprint Using Difference of Block Means Code

G. Ananthi
Mepco Schlenk Engineering College, India

G. Shenbagalakshmi
Mepco Schlenk Engineering College, India

A.T. Anisha Shruti
Mepco Schlenk Engineering College, India

G. Sandhiya
Mepco Schlenk Engineering College, India

ABSTRACT

Biometrics is an automatic identification of people with their physiological and behavioural characteristics. There are various modes used in biometrics, such as face, iris, retina, fingerprint, palmprint, palm vein, ear, handwriting, speech, gait, and so on. All these types of biometrics have some shortcomings. Palmprint identification is the biometric methodology used in this chapter, has several advantages over other biometric features which includes user friendliness, environment flexibility, and discriminating capacity. For several years, palmprint identification has been employed in a variety of applications. In the proposed system, the difference of block means approach is used to recognize palmprint which only requires fundamental operations (addition and subtractions), resulting in a significantly lower computing cost compared to existing systems. Even with low-resolution images, the palmprint authentication method yields substantially better results. CASIA Multispectral Palmprint database is used in the experiments. The proposed approach achieves better accuracy.

DOI: 10.4018/978-1-6684-9804-0.ch011

INTRODUCTION

In olden days, the authentication was done with passwords, code words (something to remember), and cards (something to hold or carry). The problems with these classic methods are the person has to memorize the secret words and remember to carry the cards. In the password scheme, often he / she has to change the passwords against brute force. For various applications, different credentials have to be used and remembered to avoid cracking the passwords. To overcome these issues in the authentication, in the digital era, biometrics was introduced. Biometrics is an automatic identification of people with their physiological and behavioural characteristics. There are various modes used in the biometrics such as face, iris, retina, fingerprint, palmprint, palm vein, ear, hand writing, speech, gait and so on. All these varieties of biometric modes have some shortcomings such as due to skin issues and the nature of the jobs, about 2% of the population is unable to provide clear fingerprint images in fingerprint authentication; similarly, because of temporary or chronic injuries hand geometry may provide minimal information, resulting in inaccurate human detection or identification; for iris and retina recognition, the user acceptability is less; the face images and fingerprint are easily hacked by the intruders; voice and gait (way of walk) of one person can be mimicked by others. Palmprint refers to the image of the palm region of the hand. In olden days, palmprint was acquired by using ink. In the digital era, it is acquired with the digital cameras. Palmprint is the pattern in the skin surface of palm of the hand. The palm region includes the patterns: points, principal lines, wrinkles, epidermal ridges, and texture. Palmprint identification is the biometric methodology used in this article, which has several advantages over other biometric features such as user friendliness, environment flexibility, and discriminating capacity even to discriminate the twins. For several years, palmprint identification has been employed in a variety of applications. In the proposed system, first the pre-processing is done to remove the noise in the input image. In the pre-processed image, the most interested region ie., the region which includes the most discriminating features is segmented as region of interest (ROI). Then in the ROI, blocks of size 8x8 is considered and the mean of the block is computed and the difference of block means is computed to create a feature vector. The authentication task includes two phases namely training and testing phase. The entire palmprint database is divided into 2:1. 2/3 of the total images are used for training purpose ie., to construct the model. The remaining 1/3 of the total images are used for testing ie., to test the correctness of the constructed model. During the training phase, for all the training images the features are extracted by following the steps mentioned above and stored as templates. During the testing phase, for the test images also the features are extracted as earlier and then these currently extracted features are compared with the template of features using Euclidean distance and

Hamming distance measure. The advantage of difference of Block Means approach is that it only requires fundamental operations (mostly addition and subtractions), resulting in a significantly lower computing cost as compared to existing systems. Even with low-resolution images, the palmprint authentication method yields substantially better results. The CASIA Multispectral Palmprint database is used in the experiments. The proposed approach achieves an accuracy of 99.75% which is comparably better than the state-of-the-art methods.

BACKGROUND AND LITERATURE REVIEW

Currently the recognition systems that involve biometric have gained popularity in digital security and forensics due to their quick and easy method to authenticate individuals which has proven to be much more efficient than other methods. These biometric based methods require some physical and behavioural traits of individuals such as iris, face, voice, gait, palmprint, fingerprint and palm veins to uniquely identify individuals, even twins.

Among all these different ways to authenticate by biometric, palmprint has some advantages over others as they occupy the most area from the hand which has a significant number of patterns that can be used for the purpose of recognition. Palm features such as ridges, flexion creases, wrinkles, and minutiae are located on a hand and are permanent and unique to an individual. All these palmprint features have been studied for over twenty years, methods have been proposed with high accuracy on publicly available palmprint databases. The flow of the recognition system using palmprint consists of a sequence of modules that are responsible for pre-processing, extraction of the palm region of interest (ROI), and matching. The modules are designed to extract desired features at each stage and forward that information gained to the next subsequent stages. Multispectral images are used to collect more information to improve the accuracy.

In general processing, the noise is removed from the palmprint image using a Low pass filter such as Gaussian filter. Then the image is converted to binary by applying the OTSU algorithm. By using a tracking algorithm to track the Boundary, the ROI of the palm image is extracted. In the extracted ROI, a filter like Gabor is applied in order to extract the texture features.

Existing coding methods such as PalmCode method, CompCode scheme, Radon transform (FRAT), Modified Radon transform (MFRAT), Difference of Vertex normal vectors (DoN) and Robust line orientation code (RLOC) mostly focused on the texture, contour, and edge features. They provided high identification accuracy and computational complexity, making our proposed system applicable in real-time applications. In this proposed work, the Difference of Block Means (DBM) method is employed. This method does not require any additional filtering operations, and requires only basic operations. Additionally, it yields high performance on well aligned/segmented low-resolution palmprint images.

Zhang, D., Kong, W.K., You, J., Wong, M. (2003) developed a system for online person authentication using palmprint biometric. They developed a rule called fusion rule which was used to select the elliptical Gabor filters for coding the phase information. Kong, A., Zhang, D., Kamel, M (2006) performed feature level fusion for human authentication with different modules in their work such as palmprint acquisition, palmprint feature representation, stack filter and tuning process, generation of mask, and palmprint matching. Owing to feature level fusion, the result they obtained was better comparable. They faced a main challenge in extracting the lines from palmprint images as they are unclear.

Xiang-Qian, W., Kuan-Quan, W., Zhang, D (2002) performed palmprint recognition based on the wavelet method. The authors reported that the main features of a palmprint image are not uniform and cannot be discriminated against by multi-resolution methods. Principal lines and wrinkles are non-oscillating patterns whereas ridges are oscillating patterns. Histogram of oriented gradient (HOG) is not an appropriate tool to find line orientations and line responses of pixels. Because of wavelet based feature extraction, the authors achieved good recognition results.

W. Jia R. -X. Hu, Y. -K. Lei, Y. Zhao and J. Gui (2014) proposed a new method called Histogram of oriented lines (HOL), which made use of the line-shape filter such as real part of Gabor filter and modified finite radon transform (MFRAT) to extract line responses and orientation of pixels. After preprocessing, HOL was computed as the features and was matched.

Karhunen-Loeve transform was proposed by Lu, G., Zhang, D., Wang, K (2003), which is a technique that combines the original palmprint images with a small set of eigenvectors. These eigenvectors are the representations of the training. The subspace projection technique was used to reduce the dimensionality of the features and Euclidean distance measures or classifiers were used to perform matching. The authors achieved a 98.691% recognition rate.

Zhang, L., Li, L., Yang, A., Shen, Y., Yang, M. (2017) explained a novel approach called CR_CompCode which achieved high recognition accuracy while having a less computational complexity. The authors constructed a very large palmprint image dataset with 12000 high quality contactless palmprint images. A recognition rate of 98.78% was obtained with an identification time of 12.48 ms.

Latent and apparent direction information for human recognition was performed by Fei, L., Zhang, B., Zhang, W., Teng, S (2019) and Ananthi, G., Raja Sekar, J., VigneshKumaran, N (2020). The apparent direction was extracted from the surface layer of the palmprint whereas the latent direction features were extracted from the energy map layer of the apparent direction. The authors worked with four different palmprint databases such as PolyU, IITD, GPDS and CASIA palmprint databases and achieved promising results.

Genovese, A., Piuri, V., Scotti, F., Plataniotis (2019) used local texture descriptors and Convolutional Neural Network (CNN) to extract features. The authors designed PalmNet which applied Gabor filter in CNN and extracted the discriminating palmprint features. They did not use the class labels during training. PalmNet supported different palmprint databases and proved its efficiency.

Liu, Y. Kumar, A (2020) developed a deep learning-based system for identifying the persons using palmprint through R-CNN architecture. The constructed model supported a generalization property. With IITD palmprint database, 99.2% accuracy was obtained. Matkowski, W.M., Chai, T., Kong, A.W.K. (2020) used an end-to-end deep learning algorithm, which included two networks namely alignment network and a feature extraction network, and both were end-to-end trainable. This work was compared with other online palmprint recognition methods and it has been evaluated with three databases (IITD, CASIA and PolyU) and two new palmprint databases such as NTU-PI-v1 and NTU contactless palmprint database. For the palmprint images collected in an uncontrolled and uncooperative environment also, the authors received better recognition results.

Shalini Agarwal,Pawan Kumar Verma, Mohd Amir Khan (2017) proposed a method which generated Region of interest (ROI) of captured image then applied a median filter and Histogram equalization on ROI. The exact ROI extraction was done to minimize the problem (larger false rejection rate) of displacement of palm over the scanner. Gabor filter was used for extracting the detailed information from the ROI image as Gabor filter is an efficient tool for texture representation. The final classification was done with the support vector machine (SVM) classifier.

Ananthi, G., Raja Sekar, J., Lakshmipraba, N (2018) performed human authentication with palm dorsal vein biometric. The pre-processing step improved the quality of the image by assigning high values to the vein pixels and low values to other pixels. After applying the thinning algorithm, the bifurcation points were extracted as features and matching was done with the Euclidean distance metric.

Ananthi, G., Raja Sekar, J., Apsara, D., Gajalakshmi, A. K., Tapthi, S (2021) computed the score for prediction using score-level fusion of the individual scores found with salient and discriminative descriptor learning method (SDDLM) and gray-level co-occurrence matrix (GLCM) method. This fused score improved the recognition rate and reduced the computational burden.

Ananthi, G., Raja Sekar, J., Arivazhagan, S (2022a) performed palm vein based human authentication by using curvelet multiresolution transform. From the curvelet subbands, standard deviation and mean features were extracted and two different scores were computed. Those two scores were fused using a weighted sum rule. The authors achieved a comparable recognition rate and equal error rate (EER).

Ananthi, G., Raja Sekar, J., Arivazhagan, S (2022b) did palm vein authentication using scale invariant feature transform (SIFT) and Gabor filter. Palm vein was extracted using a 3-valley point maximal palm extraction strategy and then the SIFT and Gabor features were extracted. The scores obtained from these features were ensembled using a weighted sum rule to find the final score. The results which were superior to the state-of-the-art methods were obtained.

Unlike Deep learning-based approaches, the palmprint recognition system adds extra complexity to enhance the performance by performing calculations in parallel as there are a number of calculations. This work introduces a new, more efficient, and low computational cost technique namely Difference of Block Means (DBM) which involves basic operations like addition and subtraction only.

The flow of the paper is structured as: Section 3.1 discusses pre-processing, Section 3.2 discusses ROI extraction, Section 3.3 explains about how feature extraction is done and finally Section 3.4 discusses how the palmprint matching is done.

MAIN FOCUS OF THE CHAPTER

The idea of this work is to do human authentication using his / her palmprint biometric. For biometric based authentication, the user need not carry or remember anything. Simply he / she is recognized with what he / she has or possesses. From the input palm vein image, the region of interest is segmented and the features are extracted with difference of block means code. Then feature matching is done with the Hamming distance metric.

PROPOSED METHOLOGY

Figure 1 shows the architecture diagram of the proposed system. The input palmprint image is first preprocessed to remove the noise and then it is binarized so that by locating the peak and valley points, the region of interest is extracted properly. After ROI extraction, feature extraction is done with difference of block means (DBM) method. The extracted DBM code features are matched with Hamming distance method. Based on the distance value, the query palmprint image is either validated or rejected.

Pre-Processing

The input to the system is a raw palmprint image. This image may suffer from noise and blurring effect that occurs because of the image acquisition setup. The

Figure 1. System architecture to authenticate individual by palmprint

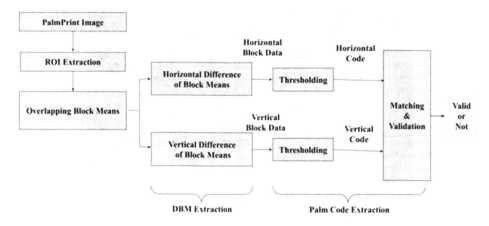

unwanted noise in the palmprint image is removed by applying the Gaussian low-pass filter. Low-pass filters are generally called as blurring filters as they remove the high frequency components from the image. As Gaussian filter is strong in eliminating spike or salt- and-pepper noise, it is applied to eliminate the noise in the input palmprint image. The noise removed image is binarized by using OTSU algorithm. Otsu algorithm finds the global threshold value to do binarization. From the binarized image, the needed region of interest is extracted as mentioned in the algorithm ExtractROI_Palmprint.

ROI Extraction

Region of interest (ROI) extraction plays an important role in biometrics as this process segments the interested region from the input image which is further used for the feature extraction. In the binarized image, all the boundary points are located. Among the resulting boundaries, the largest boundary represents the palm boundary. In the located largest boundary, the peak and valley points are located, and the ROI is segmented as stated in the algorithm ExtractROI_Palmprint. The processes involved in ROI extraction is shown in figure 2.

Feature Extraction

The segmented ROI, *R*, is divided into overlapping blocks of size 8 x 8, with overlapping factor of 4 pixels in both horizontal and vertical direction. From each of these overlapping blocks, the mean value is computed and stored in a matrix. This block means information is used for the description of the palmprint information in

Figure 2. Procedure to extract ROI

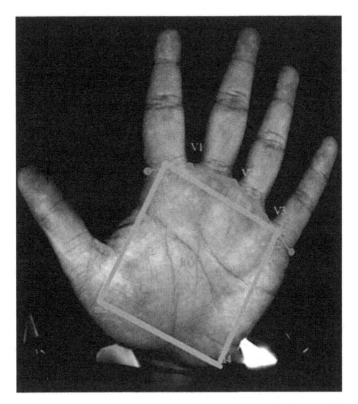

each direction. For obtaining the final palmprint code in each respective direction, thresholding is done.

Let A be the matrix representing block means of the ROI of size $M \times N$. From A, containing the statistical mean features, two more matrices, namely $A1$ and $A2$ are computed to hold the horizontal and vertical differences of block means respectively. While computing the horizontal difference, the mean values in the same row and adjacent columns are subtracted, and for vertical difference, the mean values in the adjacent rows of the same column are subtracted as in Eqns. (1) and (2).

$$A1(x, y) = \{ A(x, y + 1) - A(x, y), \ y < N \tag{1}$$

$$A(x, 0) - A(x, y), \ y = N$$

$$A2(x, y) = \{ \ A(x + 1, y) - A(x, y), \ y < M \tag{2}$$

$$A(0, y) - A(x, y), \ y = M$$

Algorithm ExtractROI_Palmprint(P$_{Img}$, R)

Input: A pre-processed palmprint image, P_{Img}.

Output: ROI image, R, segmented from P_{Img}.

With salient-point detection algorithm, locate three-key-points, V_1, V_2, V_3 at finger web locations.

Connect the key-point V_2 with V_1 and V_3. Extend those two lines to intersect with the palm boundary. Mark the midpoints of the extended lines as A and B.

Four edges of length $||AB||$ is computed by the principle of geometric square and the ROI is segmented.

The segmented ROI is normalized to the size of 256 x 256, yields R.

From the computed horizontal and vertical difference of block means, the horizontal and vertical codes, *Chor* and *Cver* are derived with thresholding method with threshold being set as 0. If the difference of mean is greater than the threshold, then the code for the corresponding pixel position is taken as 1 otherwise 0. The horizontal and vertical codes, *Chor* and *Cver* are computed as in equations (3) and (4).

$$Chor(x, y) = \{1, A1(x, y) \geq 0 \tag{3}$$

0, *otherwise*

$$Cver(x, y) = \{1, A2(x, y) \geq 0 \tag{4}$$

0, *otherwise*

These obtained horizontal and vertical code features are further matched in the subsequent process.

Matching

After completing the feature extraction process, they are matched using different distance matching metrics such as Euclidean distance and Hamming distance measures. Let the horizontal code for the training and test image be *Chortr* and *Chortst*. The Euclidean distance, distE, between these two matrices is computed as in equation (5).

$$dist E = \sqrt{\sum i \ \sum j (Chortr(i, j) \ \sum Chortst(i, j))2} \qquad (5)$$

Hamming distance, distH, between the matrices *Chortr* and *Chortst* is computed as the sum of the exclusive-OR of the individual corresponding pixel values as in equation (6).

$$dist H = \sum i \ \sum j \ Chortr(i, j) \oplus Chortst(i, j) \qquad (6)$$

The accuracy of the system with different distance measures is computed and compared. To take all the minimal geometric changes into consideration, the binary palmprint codes are shifted by fifteen pixels in all possible directions. Suppose, C1 and C2 be the pairs of palmprint code computed as in equation (7).

C1 = (Cver, 1,Chor, 1)

C2 = (Cver, 2,Chor, 2) \qquad (7)

The horizontal distance, dhor(C1,C2) and the vertical distance, *dver(C1,C2) are* computed as in equations (8) and (9).

$$d\,(C, C\,) = min\,\{dist$$

hor 1 2

$$d\,(C, C\,) = min\,\{dist$$

ver 1 2

From the horizontal and vertical distances, the palmprint matching distance, matchdist, is calculated as the average of these two distances as in equation (10).

$$matchdist(C, C\,) = dhor(C1,C2) + dver(C1,C2)$$

Query image is assigned with the class label of the training palmprint image with which the query image has a minimal matching distance, matchdist. The steps involved in the matching process is shown in figure 3.

RESULTS AND DISCUSSION

The entire work was carried out with CASIA multispectral palmprint database. The database is described below.

CASIA Multispectral Palmprint Database

This dataset consists of totally, 7200 palm images which were collected from 100 individuals using a multiple spectral imaging device that was designed especially for this purpose. The illuminator has several wavelengths that provide values to the six different spectrums which include 460 nm, 630 nm, 700 nm, 850nm, 940nm and white light respectively. In this database, the images acquired under wavelengths 460, 630, and 700 nm denote the palmprint images and the others are palm vein images. All the images have certain degree of differences in hand postures to increase the intra-class diversity. In the proposed work, totally 1800 left palmprint images were used.

Discussion

The input palmprint image was preprocessed with Gaussian lowpass filter. Then by applying the Otsu algorithm, the global threshold was found and the image was binarized. After that, the ROI was segmented with the novel algorithm ExtractROI_ Palmprint. The segmented ROI was divided into 8x8 blocks and the mean of the block was computed as the features. The extracted features were matched with the Euclidean distance metric and the Hamming distance metric.

System Performance

From the input palmprint image, the ROI is segmented first. Then, it is split into small blocks of size 8 x 8 and the overlapping block mean value is computed. Then the directional block means horizontal and vertical codes are extracted as features. Two-third of the images are trained while one-third are tested. To work with a greater number of samples, the training and testing are performed in several combinations. The performance of the proposed system with the Hamming distance and Euclidean distance measure are shown in Table 1 and 2 respectively. From these tables, it is clear that the Hamming distance measure outperforms.

Figure 3. Steps involved in matching process

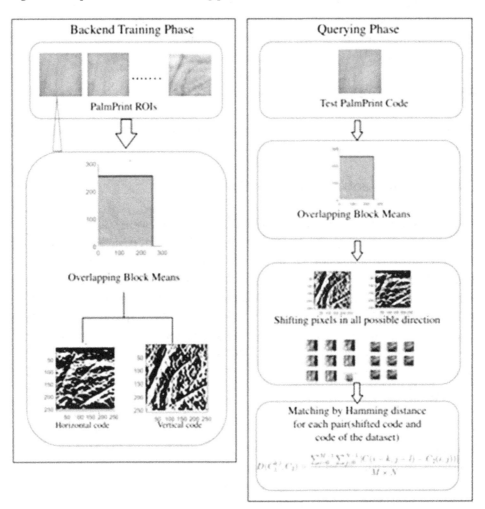

Table 1. The performance of the proposed DBM code by using Hamming distance

Training Image	Testing Image	Correctly Predicted	Incorrectly Predicted	Accuracy (%)
400	200	195	5	97.5
800	400	398	2	99.75
1200	600	596	4	99.33

From the above two results, it is evident that the Hamming distance is a suitable measure to perform palmprint matching. The proposed work also outperforms the state-of-the-art methods with less computing complexity. This is proved from table 3.

Table 2. The performance of the proposed DBM code by using Euclidean distance

Training Image	Testing Image	Correctly predicted	Incorrectly predicted	Accuracy (%)
400	200	190	10	95
800	400	396	4	99
1200	600	595	5	99.16

Table 3. Performance comparison with the state-of-the-art methods

S.No.	Method used	Authors	Year	Accuracy (in %)
1.	CR_CompCode, a Collaborative Representation scheme	Zhang, L., Li, L., Yang, A., Shen, Y., Yang, M	2017	98.78
2.	PalmNet-GaborPCA	Genovese, A., Piuri, V., Scotti, F., Plataniotis	2019	99.77
3.	End-to-End Palmprint Recognition Network (EE-PRnet)	Matkowski, W.M., Chai, T., Kong, A.W.K	2020	99.54
4.	**Proposed method, Difference of block means code**		2023	**99.75**

FUTURE RESEARCH DIRECTIONS

This system has used the publicly available database for palmprint images. To include more diversity in the intraclass, the self-built or database can be created and tested.

CONCLUSION

The proposed work uses the difference of block means (DBM) which uses minimal mathematical operations. Thereby they can be applied to several online and real-time applications. And in this work, based on the comparative study we get to know that hamming distance is the best suitable distance metric in matching stages. The system achieves the best accuracy of 99.75%.

REFERENCES

Agarwal, S., Verma, P. K., & Khan, M. A. (2017). An Optimized Palm Print Recognition Approach using Gabor filter", International Conference on Computing, Communication and Networking Technologies (ICCCNT), Delhi, India. *10.1109/ICCCNT.2017.8203919*

Ananthi, G., Raja Sekar, J., Apsara, D., Gajalakshmi, A. K., & Tapthi, S. (2021). Enhanced Palmprint Identification Using Score Level Fusion [IJARSCT]. International Journal of Advanced Research in Science, Communication and Technology, 4(3), 76–81. doi:*10.48175/IJARSCT-V4-I3-011*

Ananthi, G., Raja Sekar, J., & Arivazhagan, S. (2022). Human palm vein authentication using curvelet multiresolution features and score level fusion. The Visual Computer, 38(6), 1901–1914. doi:10.100700371-021-02253-9

Ananthi, G., Raja Sekar, J., *& Arivazhagan, S.* (2022). Ensembling Scale Invariant and Multiresolution Gabor Scores for Palm Vein Identification. Information Technology and Control, 51(4), 704–722. doi:10.5755/j01.itc.51.4.30858

Ananthi, *G., Raja Sekar, J., & Lakshmipraba, N.* (2018). PALM DORSAL SURFACE AND VEIN PATTERN BASED AUTHENTICATION SYSTEM. International Journal of Pure and Applied Mathematics, 118(11), 767–773.

Fei, L., Zhang, *B., Zhang, W., & Teng, S. (2019). Local apparent and* latent direction extraction for palmprint recognition. Elsevier on Information science, 473, 59-72. doi:10.1016/j.ins.2018.09.032

Genovese, A., Piuri, A., Scotti, V., & Plataniotis, F. (). PalmNet: gabor-PCA convolutional networks for touchless palmprint recognition. IEEE transaction on Information Forensic and Security, 14, 3160 - 3174.

Jia, W., **H**u, *R.-X., Lei, Y.-K., Zhao, Y., & Gui, J. (2014). Histogram* of oriented lines for palmprint recognition. IEEE Transactions on Systems, Man, and Cybernetics, 44(3), 385–395. doi:10.1109/TSM*C.2013.2258010*

Kong, A., Zhang, D., & Kamel, M. (2006). Palmprint identification using feature-level fusion. Science Direct, 39(3), 478–487.

Liu, Y., & Kumar, A. (2020). Contactless palm*print identifi*ca*tion* using deeply learned residual features. IEEE Transaction on Biometric, Behavior and Identity Science, 2(2), 172–181. *doi:10.1109/TBIOM.2020.2967073*

Lu, G., Zhang, D., & Wang, K. (2003). Palmprint recognition using eigen palms features. Pattern Recognition Letters, 24(9-10), 1463–1467. doi:10.1016/S0167-8655(02*)00386-0*

*Matkowski, W.M., C*hai, T., Kong, A.W.K. (2020). Palmprint recognition in uncontrolled and uncooperative environment. IEEE transaction on Information Forensic and Security, 15, 1601 – 1615.

*Xiang-Qian, W., Kuan-Quan, W., & Zhang, D. (2002). Wa*velet based palm print recognition. Intern. Conf. Mach. Learn. Cybern, 3, 1253–1257.

Zhang, D., Kong, *W. K., You, J., & Wong, M. (2003).* Online palmprint identification. IEEE Transaction on Pattern Analysis and Machine, 25(9), 1041–105*0. doi:10.1109/ TPAMI.2003.1227981*

Zhang, L., Li, L., Yang, A., Shen, Y., & Yang, M. (2017). Towards contactless palmprint recognition: A novel device, a new benchmark, and a collaborative representation based identification approach. Pattern Recognition, 69, 199–212. doi:10.1016/j.patcog.2017.04.*016*

Chapter 12
Credit Risk Analysis and Prediction

Akhil Raman Sarepalli
Vellore Institue of Technology, India

Maheshwari S
Vellore Institue of Technology, India

ABSTRACT

Credit scoring is used to divide applicants into two groups: those with good credit and those with bad credit. When a bank gets a loan request, borrowers with strong credit have a high likelihood of repaying debt. The likelihood of default is higher for applicants with bad credit. The profitability of financial organisations depends on the accuracy of credit scoring. Financial institutions will experience less of a loss if their credit scoring of applicants with poor credit is even 1 percent more accurate. This study seeks to solve this categorization issue by examining the risk of granting a loan to the applicant using the applicant's socioeconomic and demographic attributes from German credit data. In terms of overall accuracy, the authors evaluated the efficiency of several ML techniques like decision tree, logistic regression model, neural network, SVM, as well as random forest. The authors compared and evaluated several models for the model optimization process, integrating the impacts of balancing the AUC (area under the ROC curve)and accuracy values.

INTRODUCTION

Motivation

Credit granting to consumers is an important operation of the banking sector. Credit risk management assesses the information that is available and determines a customer's reliability to protect the financial institution from fraud.

DOI: 10.4018/978-1-6684-9804-0.ch012

Datasets

A collection of datasets helpful for assessing machine learning algorithms may be found at the UC Irvine Machine Learning Repository.The German credit data and another dataset from UCI - ML 1 repository were both used for this study. The Australian dataset comprises 14 characteristics and 690 instances, compared to 20 features and 1,000 examples in the German sample. A customer's level of credibility is the response variable, which is a binary decision. The loan's purpose, the credit score, and client information are some of the shared attributes between the two datasets -age, occupation, account duration, and salary.

Credit Risk

A critical phase of knowledge discovery is data mining, which looks for patterns in data using theories, processes, and tools. In order to ensure that tools and procedures are correctly corresponded to the data and the purpose of pattern recognition, it is essential to understand the fundamental principles of the methodology. There may be a number of tool choices for a certain data collection. When a bank receives a loan application, the bank must decide based on the applicant's profile whether to authorize the loan or not. The bank's decision includes two different categories of risks:

- If the borrower has good credit risk or is likely to pay back the loan, then the bank loses business by rejecting the loan application.
- The bank can experience a loss by making the loan if the customer has a poor credit risk, which means they are unable to pay back the debt.

OBJECTIVE AND SCOPE OF PROJECT

Objective

- The bank needs a decision rule that specifies who gets to approve loans and who doesn't to reduce loss from the bank's standpoint. Before deciding on a borrower's loan application, loan managers take into account the applicant's socioeconomic and demographic data.

Scope

- We will be looking into a Credit dataset.
- We will derive relations between a person's socioeconomic lifestyle with his credit ratings.
- Based on these trends and patterns we will analyze the data.
- Using Models, we will be able to predict whether a client is creditworthy or not.

TOOLS AND TECHNIQUES

To analyse the data, we used the following analytical approaches and methodology:

1. Statistic summary for each variable
2. Finding the frequency of each factor's contributing standard violation
3. Using box plots and graphs to depict data graphically.
4. Using correlation and regression analysis, key metrological variables are identified
5. The development of models using multiple linear regression and neural networks
6. Tools utilized: R, & Excel
7. Techniques: Histogram, Box Plot, Line Chart, Bar Chart, Visual Clues, Infographics, Artificial Neural Network, Multiple Linear Regression, Correlation Matrix.
8. For our investigation, we employed Microsoft Excel and R Programming environment.

METHODOLOGY

The following activities—which are not always in that order—will be part of the analytical technique:

a. Data collection.
b. Data description and data preparation
c. Model Development
d. Final Model

Data Collection

Dr Hans Hofmann of the University of Hamburg contributed the dataset including the German Credit data. It is accessible to the general public through the UCI ML repository

When we look at the German dataset, we see that it is a data frames with 21 variables and 1,000 observations in total. The dataset's response variable is the Class label, a binary variable that indicates credit risk or creditworthiness with values of bad and good. We'll outline the 20 features and their attributes in this section:

- Credit rating
- Account balance
- Credit Duration
- Previous Credit
- Credit Purpose
- Credit Amount
- Saving
- Employment duration
- Installments
- Guarantor
- Marital status
- Current assets
- Residence duration
- Age
- Bank credits
- Apartment type
- Dependent
- Occupation
- Foreign worker
- Telephone
- Glimpse of our dataset

Data Description and Preparation

Figure 1 shows a glimpse of our dataset.

Dealing With Missing Values

The German credit dataset has no null values, so we can continue with data preparation (see Figure 2).

Data Preparation

Changes to the values, format, or structure of data are called data transformation. Data may be modified at two points in the data pipeline for projects including data

Figure 1. Dataset sample

Figure 2. Checking null values

analytics. For our dataset, we have to convert all the categorial variables to factors and the numerical values are kept the same

Categorial variables include credit rating, savings, previous credit payment status, instalment rate, employee duration, guarantor, marital status, current assets, residence duration, other credits, bank credit, apartment type, occupations, dependency, telephones, and foreign workers. Numerical variables include credit amount, credit duration months, and age.

Exploratory Data Analysis

To get a better understanding of our dataset and the interdependences of the different variables in our dataset we will perform exploratory data analysis, by the end of this section we will remove the unnecessary attributes from the dataset and reduce the factors in certain attributes to improve our prediction models.

Job Data

Figure 3. Job data analysis

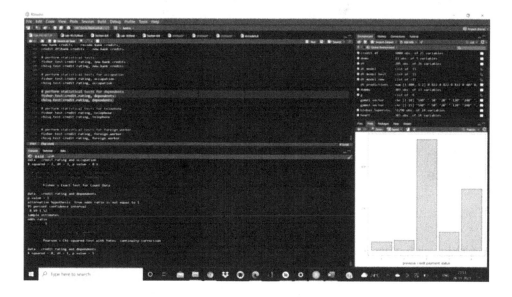

Inference

In occupations:

1- Unskilled with permanent residence
2- Unemployed with no permanent residence
3- Self-employed/executive/higher civil servants
4- Skilled workers/civil servants

From the plot, we can observe that people under category 3 are taking a higher number of loans and higher loan amounts.

Other Credit Data

Figure 4. Other credit data analyses

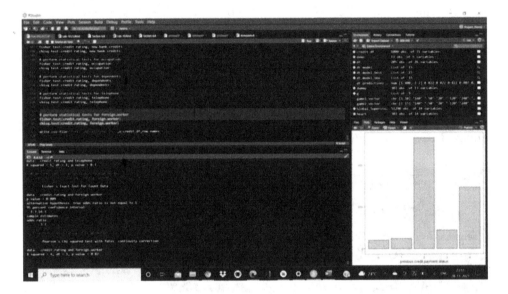

Inference

In other credits:

1- Credits with other banks
2- 2-In stores
3- 3-No further credits

We can observe in our dataset most of the clients have no further credits

Credit Purpose

German credit dataset consists of 10 different credit purposes, we will conduct data transformation and merge these credit purposes to improve our prediction models (see Figure 5):

Figure 5. Credit purpose analyses

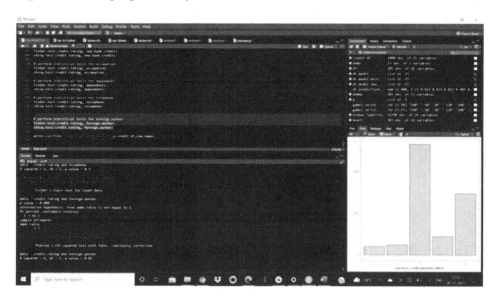

0-Others
1-new car
2-used cars
3-furniture items
5-Household applications
6-repair
7- No significance
8-vacation
9-training
10-business

After performing the transformation, the related contingency table is:

1-New car
2-old car
3-Home applications
4-Others

Credit Worthiness

Figure 6. Credit worthiness Analysis

Contingency table plot

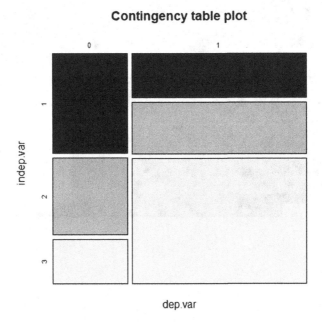

Inferfence

We can observe if the credit purpose is for a new car most of the clients have good credit ratings. For the category others which consists of vacation, business, and repair we can see that more Clients with a bad credit rating have loans having a higher credit amount.

Credit Duration

See Figure 7.

Inferfence

We can observe that the median credit duration is higher for people with a bad credit rating.

Figure 7. Credit duration Analysis

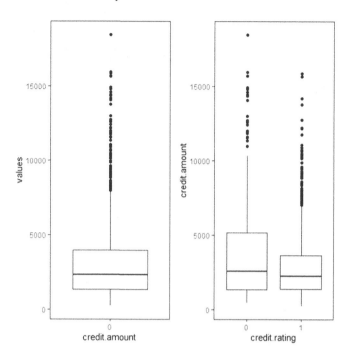

Previous Credit Payment Status

Figure 8. Credit payments Analysis

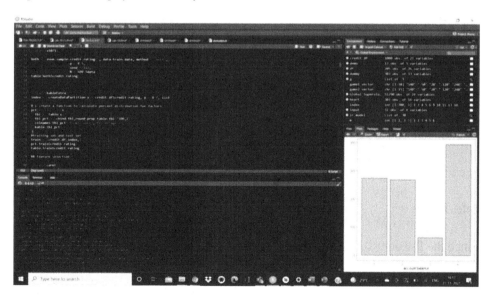

Inferfence

Category 0,1 and 3 are in low frequencies, to make the analysis part easier we conduct data transformation and merge 0 and 1 into 2 and 3 with 4.

Statistical Tests For Residence Duration

Figure 9. Statistical tests for residence duration

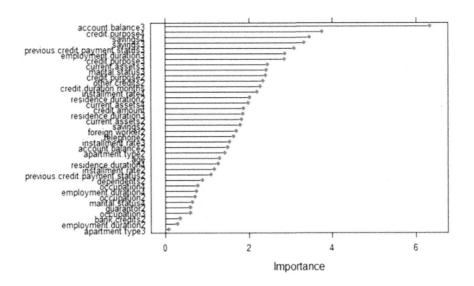

Inferfence

Since the P-value≤0.05, there is no link between residence duration and credit rating.

Statistical Tests for Occupation

See Figure 10.

Inferfence

Since the P-value≤0.05, there is no link between occupation and credit rating.

Figure 10. Statistical tests for occupation

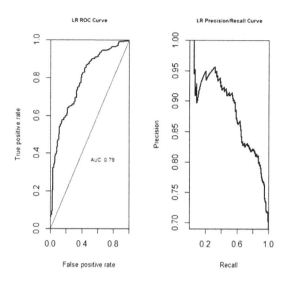

Statistical Tests for Dependents

Figure 11. Statistical tests for dependents

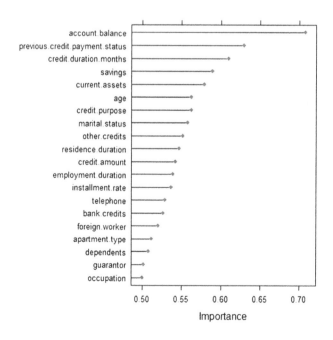

Inferfence

Since the P-value≤0.05, there is no link between dependents and credit rating.

Statistical Tests for Foreign Worker

Figure 12. Statistical tests for telephone

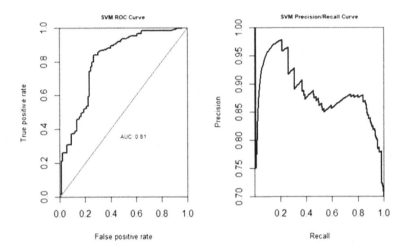

Inferfence

Since P-value≤0.05, there is no link between telephone and credit rating

Statistical Tests for Foreign Worker

See Figure 13.

Inferfence

Since the P-value≤0.05, there is no link between a foreign worker and credit rating.

Account Balance

See Figure 14.

Figure 13. Statistical tests for telephone

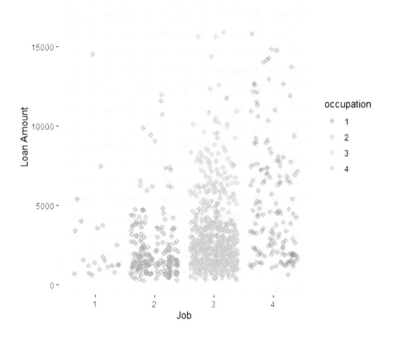

Figure 14. Account balance

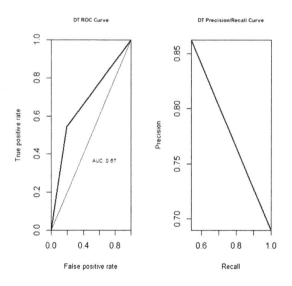

Inferfence

We can infer that since the P-value is less than 0.05, there is a strong correlation between Account Balance and credit rating.

Credit Amount

Figure 15. Statistical tests for telephone

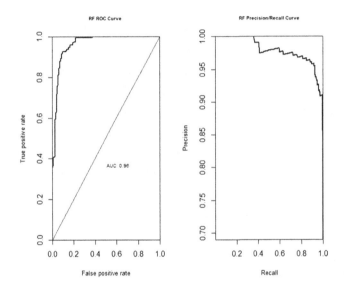

Inferfence

From the boxplot, we can observe that the outlier values are higher for bad credit clients when compared to clients with a good credit rating. We can infer that the median value from the credited amount is higher for people with a bad credit rating. Distribution of credit amount Right skewed.

Data Partition

A population is categorized into smaller groups called as strata as part of a sampling technique called stratified random sampling. This is helpful for datasets that are unbalanced and may be utilized to offer a minority class greater weight. In stratified random sampling, groups are created on the basis of common characteristics or attributes among the participants.

In this instance, we'll utilize the strata Good/Bad and divide the data into train and test sets of 70% and 30%, respectively. To divide the data into balanced portions, use the caret method **createDataPartition**.

Figure 16. Statistical tests for telephone

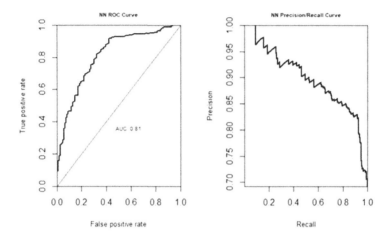

Predictive Model Development

Logistic Regression

A categorical dependent variable may be predicted using the method of logistic regression using one or more observed characteristics. A logistic function is used to represent the probability defining the potential outcomes as a function of the observable factors. Logistic regression seeks to do this by directly estimating the P{Y|X} distribution from the training set.

We applied this model to the training set in our research using the stats package's **glm** method. The **predict** function of the same package was then used in the testing stage to assess our fitted model on the testing data.

- Deviance Residuals:

Min	1Q	Median	3Q	Max
-2.5044	-0.6905	0.3700	0.7033	2.1270

- Confusion Matrix and Statistics

	1	0
1	184	46
0	26	44

Accuracy: 0.76
95% CI: 0.7076, 0.8072
No Information Rate: 0.7
P-Value [Acc > NIR]: 0.01249
Kappa: 0.3898
Mcnemar's Test P-Value: 0.02514
Sensitivity: 0.8762
Specificity: 0.4889
Pos Pred Value: 0.8000
Neg Pred Value: 0.6286
Prevalence: 0.7000
Detection Rate: 0.6133
Detection Prevalence: 0.7667
Balanced Accuracy: 0.6825
'Positive' Class: 1

Feature Selection

The automated selection of your data's characteristics that have the greatest influence on the output or prediction variable that you are interested in is the basis of the feature selection approach.

If your data includes irrelevant properties, many models, especially those that employ linear techniques like logistic and linear regression, may become less accurate.

Performing feature selection before data modelling has three advantages:

- **Reduces Overfitting**: Less redundant data minimizes the likelihood that decisions will be on the basis of noise.
- **Improves Accuracy**: Modeling accuracy increases when misleading data is reduced.
- **Reduces Training Time**: Algorithms train more quickly with fewer data.

In the credit dataset, the top 5 most important variables are account balance, credit duration, previous credit amount, bank credits, and savings.

Building Model Using Feature Selection

Figure 17. Feature selection

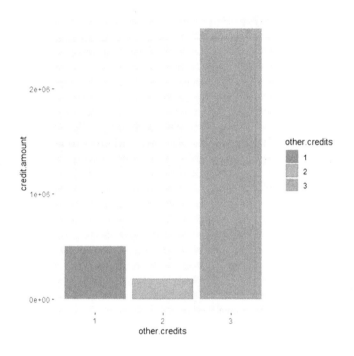

Confusion Matrix and Statistics

	1	0
1	183	51
0	27	3

Accuracy: 0.74
95% CI: 0.6865, 0.7887
No Information Rate: 0.7
P-Value [Acc > NIR]: 0.072279
Kappa: 0.3299

Mcnemar's Test P-Value: 0.009208
Sensitivity: 0.8714
Specificity: 0.4333
Pos Pred Value: 0.7821
Neg Pred Value: 0.5909
Prevalence: 0.7000
Detection Rate: 0.6100
Detection Prevalence: 0.7800
Balanced Accuracy: 0.6524
'Positive' Class: 1

Inference

By observing the results of both the logistic regression models, we can infer that logistic regression with feature selection is better when compared to a model with feature selection. Using the logistic regression model, we will plot the ROC curve along with the AUC value.

Figure 18. Logistic regressions

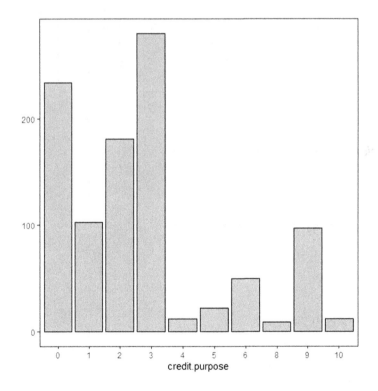

AUC values ranged between 0 and 1. The AUC of a model with 100% inaccurate predictions is 0.0, whereas with 100% right predictions is 1.0.

The two factors listed here make AUC desirable:

- AUC is **scale-invariant**. It assesses how well the predictions are scored rather than their exact values.
- AUC is **classification-threshold-invariant**. It assesses how effectively the model predicts the future, regardless of the classification threshold utilized.

For our case, the AUC value is 0.79 which is decent

Support Vector Machines

SVM techniques divide the classes from one another using linear conditions. To maintain the two classes as distinct from one another as feasible, it is intended to use a linear condition. For binary classification, SVMs were designed by Cortes & Vapnik 1995. Overlapping classes, class separation, problem solution, and nonlinearity—which is a quadratic optimization problem—can all be broadly outlined as tasks in their methodology.

The primary task, Class separation, entails locating the best-separating hyperplane between the two classes by optimizing the distance between these points that define the boundaries of the classes [refer given Figure]; the points that define the boundaries are known as support vectors, and the optimal separating hyperplane is placed in the centre of the margin. Follow Karatzoglou et al. [2005] or Wien and Meyer [2015] for further information.

The award-winning C++ implementation by Lin & Chang [2001], libsvm, is accessible using the package e1071.

The **svm** function which was developed to be as user-friendly as possible, was employed in our research (we compared the outcomes of the **ksvm** function of the kernlab package). The test set is applied to predict how well the models will perform, while the training set is employed to fit the models.

Call

Svm[formula = formula.init, data = train, kernel = "radial", gamma=1, cost=100]

Confusion Matrix and Statistics

	1	0
1	210	90
0	0	0

Accuracy: 0.7
95% CI: 0.6447, 0.7513
No Information Rate: 0.7
P-Value [Acc > NIR]: 0.5284
Kappa: 0
Mcnemar's Test P-Value: <2e-16
Sensitivity: 1.0
Specificity: 0.0
Pos Pred Value: 0.7
Neg Pred Value: NaN
Prevalence: 0.7
Detection Rate: 0.7
Detection Prevalence: 1.0
Balanced Accuracy: 0.5
'Positive' Class: 1

Feature Selection

Figure 19. Feature selection

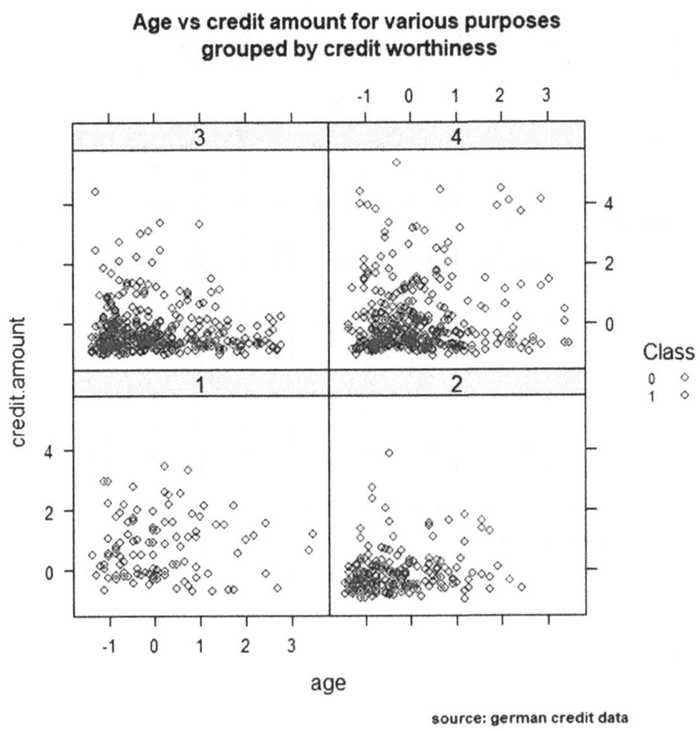

Figure 20. Support vector machines

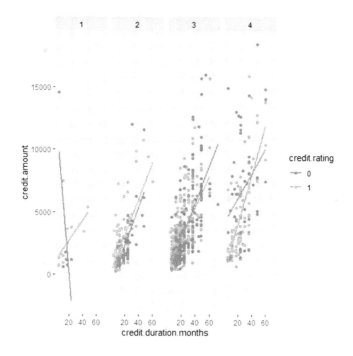

Figure 21. Support vector machines

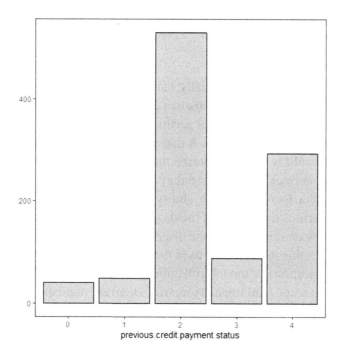

Confusion Matrix and Statistics

	1	0
1	188	52
0	22	38

Accuracy: 0.7533
95% CI: 0.7005, 0.8011
No Information Rate: 0.7
P-Value [Acc > NIR]: 0.0238850
Kappa: 0.3509
Mcnemar's Test P-Value: 0.0007485
Sensitivity: 0.8952
Specificity: 0.4222
Pos Pred Value: 0.7833
Neg Pred Value: 0.6333
Prevalence: 0.7000
Detection Rate: 0.6267
Detection Prevalence: 0.8000
Balanced Accuracy: 0.6587
'Positive' Class: 1

Decision Trees

The data is segmented hierarchically using decision trees, linking the distinct segmentations at leaf level to the distinct classes. At every stage, a split criterion is used to generate the hierarchical partitioning. A predicateon a single property can be used in the split criteria, or it may include conditions on many attributes. A multivariate split is used to describe the latter, while a univariate split is used to describe the former. The main strategy involves trying to recursively partition the training data to optimize the ability to distinguish between the different classes over various nodes. When the degree of skew among the various classes in a particular node is maximum, the discrimination between the different classes is optimized. In this research, we used the rpart function of the rpart package to develop classification tree model with training data. The **rpart** function divides the node by default using Gini impurity metric. There are more different occurrences within a node the higher the Gini coefficient. We projected the fitted tree on the testing data using predict technique.

Figure 22. Decision tree

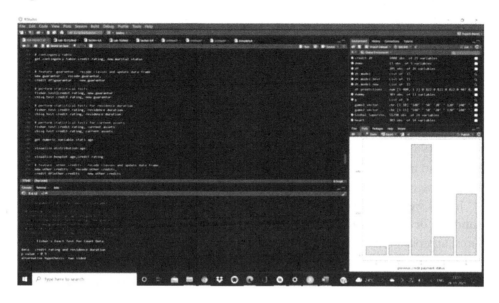

Confusion Matrix and Statistics

	1	0
1	172	50
0	38	40

Accuracy: 0.7067
95% CI: 0.6516, 0.7576
No Information Rate: 0.7
P-Value [Acc > NIR]: 0.4283
Kappa: 0.2739
Mcnemar's Test P-Value: 0.2410
Sensitivity: 0.8190
Specificity: 0.4444
Pos Pred Value: 0.7748
Neg Pred Value: 0.5128
Prevalence: 0.7000
Detection Rate: 0.5733
Detection Prevalence: 0.7400

Balanced Accuracy: 0.6317
'Positive' Class: 1
AUC value is 0.67

Random Forest

It may be seen as a variant Bagging method. It employs the decision tree technique to construct the fundamental classifiers and follows the main Bagging steps. In addition to majority voting and Bootstrap sampling, which are utilized in Bagging, Random Forest also includes random feature space selection while developing training sets to encourage the variety of base classifiers.

In this work, we made our random forest models using training data using the **randomForest** function of randomForest version, which executes Breiman's random forest approach (on the basis of original Fortran code of Breiman and Cutler). The latter model was then predicted using the **predict** function on the test set.

Call

RandomForest[formula = formula.init, data = train, importance = T, proximity = T]

Type of random forest: classification
Number of trees: 500
No. of variables tried at each split: 4
OOB estimate of error rate: 23%
Confusion Matrix and Statistics

	1	0
1	270	21
0	7	102

Accuracy: 0.93
95% CI: 0.9004, 0.953
No Information Rate: 0.6925
P-Value [Acc > NIR]: < 2e-16
Kappa: 0.8303
Mcnemar's Test P-Value: 0.01402
Sensitivity: 0.9747

Specificity: 0.8293
Pos Pred Value: 0.9278
Neg Pred Value: 0.9358
Prevalence: 0.6925
Detection Rate: 0.6750
Detection Prevalence: 0.7275
Balanced Accuracy: 0.9020
'Positive' Class: 1

Neural Network

A graph of linked units that represents a mathematical tool of biological neurons is known as an ANN or neural net. These units are also known as nodes, processing units, or just neurons. The strength of the links between the units is represented by weights on unidirectional or bidirectional arcs that connect them. This was inspired by the biological paradigm, in which the strength of the synapses between neurons either inhibit or facilitate the transmission of signals, is represented by the connection weights.

Figure 23. Neural network

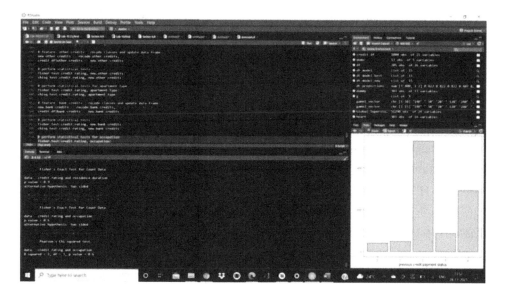

We mostly utilised the nnet package developed by Ripley in 2016 in this work. The NeuralNetTools Analysis and Visualization Tools for Neural Net as well as neuralnet packages were also taken into consideration.

Confusion Matrix and Statistics

	X1	X0
X1	248	52
X0	29	71

Accuracy: 0.7975
95% CI: 0.7547, 0.8358
No Information Rate: 0.6925
P-Value [Acc > NIR]: 1.542e-06
Kappa: 0.4985
Mcnemar's Test P-Value: 0.01451
Sensitivity: 0.8953
Specificity: 0.5772
Pos Pred Value: 0.8267
Neg Pred Value: 0.7100
Prevalence: 0.6925
Detection Rate: 0.6200
Detection Prevalence: 0.7500
Balanced Accuracy: 0.7363
'Positive' Class: X1

Model Selection

For selecting the best model we will be comparing accuracy, specificity, sensitivity and AUC value of the models.

From table 1 we can say for selecting the best model, we will be comparing the accuracy, specificity, sensitivity and AUC value of the models. By comparison, we

Table 1. Results

MODEL	ACCURACY	SPECIFICITY	SENSITIVITY	AUC VALUE
logistic regression	0.76	0.8	0.45	0.8
support vector machine	0.75	0.9	0.5	0.79
decision tree	0.7	0.8	0.44	0.67
random forest	0.94	0.97	0.84	0.96
neural network	0.8	0.9	0.57	0.81

can conclude that Random Forest is best suited for our analysis, it has the highest accuracy, a very good AUC value and decent specificity and sensitivity values.

The decision tree is the worst model with accuracy being equal to no information rate.

CONCLUSION

Finally, we have seen wide range of applications of ML in the domain of credit risk. We create a taxonomy that connects financial and computational algorithms. We also provide a quick overview of the fundamentals of statistics and machine learning methods. We categorize public datasets based on their accuracy. The rather limited and historical data utilized in this case is one restriction of the study. A good model would use tens of thousands, if not millions, of customer records and would be regularly updated to reflect the latest information. Due to access to relevant data and computing limitations, this was not possible in the scenario. Additionally, to make more accurate predictions, more complex models may certainly be created. This example demonstrates how reasonably accurate models may be created with only a few lines of code using popular statistical modelling techniques.

Chapter 13
Eye Gaze Capture for Preference Tracking in a Scalable Environment

G. Ananthi
Mepco Schlenk Engineering College, India

G. Shenbagalakshmi
Mepco Schlenk Engineering College, India

M. Pujaa
Mepco Schlenk Engineering College, India

V.M. Amretha
Mepco Schlenk Engineering College, India

ABSTRACT

Nowadays, eye gaze tracking of real-world people to acknowledge what they are seeing in a particular page is trending; but its complexity is also growing fast, and the accuracy is not enough. In the proposed system, the image patch of the eye region is extracted from the input image using the Viola Jones algorithm for facial feature detection. Then SqueezeNet and U-Net are combined to train the model for pixel classification of iris and pupil from the eye image patch with a training dataset that contains manually labelled iris and pupil region. After extracting the iris and pupil features, the eye gaze tracking is formulated by using 2D pupil center extracted by applying Mean-Shift algorithm and 3D eyeball center. The system achieved an accuracy of 99.93% which is best comparable to the state-of-the-art methods.

DOI: 10.4018/978-1-6684-9804-0.ch013

INTRODUCTION

Nowadays, eye gaze tracking of real-world people to acknowledge what they are seeing in a particular page is trending as it is emerging fast; but its complexity is also growing fast and the accuracy is not enough. Earlier, the researchers used IR illumination glasses to track the contents in a page that the user was seeing. But IR illumination glasses were expensive. Recently, Wang, C., Shi, F., Xia, S., Chai, J (2016) introduced a method for tracking the eye movement through normal monocular RGB camera (webcams, mobile phone camera, etc) by extracting iris and pupil features through random forests classification. As random forests consume so much memory, Wang again introduced the method of extracting iris and pupil features by using DCNN. Thus, using DCNN reduced the memory size and semantic segmentation of iris and pupil was achieved through fewer parameters. This made eye gaze tracking possible in devices with less memory like mobile phones.

Our aim is to identify which products attract user's attention the most. This paper introduces eye gaze tracking for preference tracking. Our idea is to extract iris and pupil features from the input image by using Deep convolutional neural network and producing heatmap in a page and to calculate which product that a user has seen the most.

To achieve this goal, the image patch of the eye region is extracted from the input image using the Viola Jones Algorithm for facial feature detection. Then SqueezeNet and U-Net are combined to train the model for pixel classification of iris and pupil from the eye image patch with a training dataset that contains manually labelled iris and pupil region.

After extracting the iris and pupil features, the eye gaze tracking is formulated by using 2D pupil center extracted by applying Mean-Shift algorithm and 3D eyeball center.

Lastly, after the eye gaze capture, the camera image plane and the screen image plane are mapped through linear transformation by instructing the user to focus on pre-defined points on the screen and then the eye gaze points are visualized on the screen by producing heatmaps using Gaussian kernel. A timer is set to cool down the previous focus points on the screen. Time is calculated to find the duration, the product seen. The product that was seen for more amount of time is declared the most viewed product.

BACKGROUND AND LITERATURE REVIEW

In Wang, C., Shi, F., Xia, S., Chai, J (2016), important facial features to reconstruct the 3D head poses were detected and random forest classifier was used for extracting iris and pupil pixel in each frame to formulate the 3D eye gaze tracker in the maximum a posterior (MAP) framework, which inferred the most probable state of 3D eye gaze. Forrest N. Iandola, Song Han, Matthew W. Moskewicz, Khalid Ashraf, William J. Dally, Kurt Keutzer (2017), Badrinarayanan, V., Kendall, A., Cipolla, R (2017), Lemley, J., Kar, A., Drimbarean, A., Corcoran, P (2019) introduced a calibration-free method for appearance-based gaze estimation that is suitable for consumer applications and low-cost hardware with real time requirements, using a Convolutional Neural Network. Yihua Cheng, Feng Luand Xucong Zhang (2018) used AsymmetricRegression-Evaluation Network (ARE-Net) to improve the gaze estimation performance to its full extent and overcome two eye asymmetries. In Daniel Melesse, Mahmoud Khalil, Elias Kagabo, Taikang Ning, Kevin Huang (2020), image acquisition was achieved using a low-cost USB web camera. To determine the point of gaze, the Viola Jones algorithm was used to extract facial features from the image frame. The gaze is then calculated using image processing techniques to extract gaze features. Fydanaki, A., Geradts, Z (2018) introduced OpenFace, the first open-source tool capable of facial landmark detection, head pose estimation, facial action unit recognition, and eye-gaze estimation. Yan, B., Pei, T., Wang, X (2019), Lu, F., Gao, Y., Chen, X (2016), Helhamer, E., Long, J., Darrell, T (2017) converted contemporary classification networks (AlexNet, VGG net, and GoogLeNet) into fully convolutional networks and transfer their learned representations by fine-tuning to the segmentation task. Based on Wood, E., Baltrušaitis, T., Morency, L., Robinson, P (2018), for the system to redirect the eye gaze, it tracked the eye region by fitting a multi-part eye region model onto video frames using analysis-by-synthesis, thus recovering eye shape, texture pose, and gaze simultaneously. Then eye gaze redirection was done by warping the eyelids in the original image and synthesizing a 3d model of the eyeball. In Nazanin Beheshti, Lennart Johnsson (2020), Fydanaki, A., Geradts, Z (2018), Chi, J., Wang, D., Lu, N., Wang, Z (2020), the iris radius was calibrated based on the binocular strategy and estimates the iris center using the calibrated iris radius, and then calibrate the cornea radius by a set of non-linear equations under the constraint of equivalent distances from the cornea center to the iris edge points. The final layer of Deep Convolutional Neural Networks (DCNNs) was not sufficiently localized for accurate object segmentation. This was due to the invariance properties. To overcome this, in Chen, L., Papandreou, G., Kokkinos, I., Murphy, K., Yuille, A (2018) a combination of the responses at the final DCNN layer and a fully connected Conditional Random Field (CRF) was done.

In Bulat, A., Tzimiropoulos, G (2020), Hassanpour, M., Malek, H (2020), ImageNet pretrained SqueezeNet achieved an accuracy of approximately 75 percent over 10 classes on the Tobacco-3482 dataset. Network can learn meaningful features that are useful for document classification. In an Adversarial Approach there is an inherent difference of distributions between images coming from graphics engine and real world. Such domain difference deteriorates test time performances of models trained on synthetic examples. In Wang, Z., Chai, J., & Xia, S (2021), Guosheng Lin, Anton Milan, Chunhua Shen, Ian Reid (2016), Avisek Lahiri, Abhinav Agarwalla, Prabir Kumar Biswas (2018) this issue was addressed with unsupervised adversarial feature adaptation across synthetic and real domain for the special use case of eye gaze estimation which is an essential component for various downstream HCI tasks. Cheung, Y., Peng, Q (2015) implemented eye gaze tracking using web camera. Eye gaze movement is accomplished by integration of eye vector and head movements. Akshay S, Aswathy Rames, Ashika P (2019) related the stimulus and eye gaze of a person with the help of heatmap. It can be used as a tool to understand the differences in viewing behavior of the participants. The color variations in heatmaps show the time spent by the viewer. Guillermo Jimenez-Perez (2019) used U-Net architecture, a fully convolutional network. The detection performance showed a precision of 89.27%, 98.18% and 93.60% for the detection of the P, QRS and T waves, respectively, and a recall of 89.07%, 99.47% and 95.21%. Naqvi, R., Arsalan, M., Batchuluun, G., Yoon, H., Park, K (2018) used a CNN-based model using a near-infrared (NIR) camera, six NIR light-emitting diodes (LEDs) and one zoom lens for driver gaze classification purpose. They used stochastic gradient descent (SGD) optimizer with 16 epochs. Vora, S., Rangesh, A., Trivedi, M. M (2018) used AlexNet, VGG-16, ResNet50 and SqueezeNet for gaze classification. They achieved a classification accuracy of 95.18%.

Shin, C., Lee, G., Kim, Y., Hong, J., Hong, S.-H., Kang, H., Lee, Y (2018) performed gaze depth calculation for VR and AR systems. They used neural network model for gaze depth prediction. They obtained an accuracy of 90.1% for the individual models and 89.7% for the generalized model. Choi, I.-H., Kim, Y. G., Tran, T. B. H. (2016) performed driver gaze zone identification using CNN approach. They worked with their own dataset and classified gaze as one of the nine different gaze zones.

MAIN FOCUS OF THE CHAPTER

For this digital modernized world, and for marketing purposes, what the people see is more important. In this work, the tracking of eye gaze is done with DCNN and heatmap. For segmenting the iris and pupil region, the frame of the video is given as input to the DCNN. With the tracked eye gaze, heatmap is generated by mapping eye gaze to the screen coordinates using Gaussian kernel.

PROPOSED METHODOLOGY

Fig.1 shows the schematic diagram of proposed system design. The input given is a live video, which is split frame by frame and fed to the DCNN for semantic

Figure 1. Schematic diagram of the proposed system

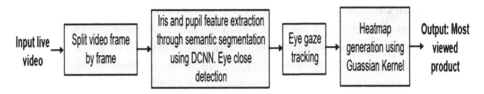

segmentation of iris and pupil region and eye close detection. With extracted iris and pupil region, eye gaze tracking is implemented. Then the tracked eye gaze is mapped to the screen and the most viewed product is found through heatmaps generated using Gaussian Kernel. The three major modules of the proposed system are:

Iris and pupil extraction
Eye gaze tracking
Eye gaze capture and heatmap generation

The following sections discuss all the three modules.

Iris and Pupil Extraction

To track the eye gaze, initially the iris and pupil features are needed to be extracted. The iris and pupil features are extracted from the image patch of the eye region. The image patch is obtained using the Viola Jones algorithm. The algorithm constructs a strong classifier with the combination of several weak classifiers. The final classifier is computed as in Eq. 1 and Eq. 2:

$$h(x) = sgn(\sum^{M} \alpha_j h_j(x)) \tag{1}$$

where,

$$sgn(x) = \{$$

$$1, x > 0$$

$$0, x = 0$$

$$-1 \ x < 0 \tag{2}$$

$h(x)$ is the strong classifier. $h_j(x)$ is a simple weak classifier and its weight is α_j. The image patch is resized to a size of 24 x 48 for the semantic segmentation.

After extracting the eye image patch using Viola Jones Algorithm, the image patch is given as input to the Deep Convolutional Neural Network (DCNN) for iris and pupil extraction. The DCNN comprises the properties of both SqueezeNet and U-Net.

Here, the U-Net's encoder-decoder framework is used for segmentation. The encoder/expanding path in a U-Net usually consists of 3x3 convolutional layers for segmentation. These 3 x 3 convolutional layers are replaced with the fire module of a SqueezeNet to reduce the memory size. The expanding path of the U- Net does downsampling through a 2 x 2 strided convolutional layer. In the same way, the decoder/contracting path does upsampling through a 2 x 2 transposed convolutional layer which is replaced with the fire module that comprises the transposed layer.

The fire module in the expanding path contains a squeeze layer -convolutional layer with kernel size of 1 x 1 and an expand layer – 2 convolutional layers with kernel sizes of 1 x 1 and 3 x 3. And the fire module in the contracting path contains a squeeze layer – transposed convolutional layer of kernel size 1 x 1 and an expand layer – 2 transposed convolutional layers of kernel sizes 1 x 1 and 2 x 2. The number of channels is multiplied into 2 in each module in the expanding path and divided by 2 in each module in the contracting path. The neural network uses the Softmax layer to find the probability that the pixels are present in the iris and pupil region or not. The pixel classification further does the semantic segmentation. Fig.2 shows the DCNN architecture for the proposed work. Fig.3 shows the fire modules.

Figure 2. DCNN architecture. The architecture is a combination of U-Net and SqueezeNet. The 3 x 3 convolutional layer in the U-Net architecture is substituted with the SqueezeNet's fire module.

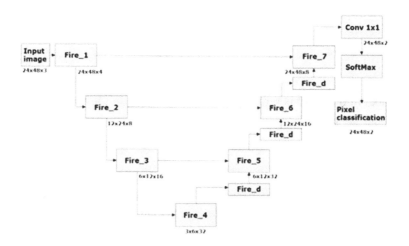

Figure 3. The fire modules substituted in the place convolutional layer in the contracting and expanding paths (Fire) and transposed convolutional layer in the expanding path (Fire_d)

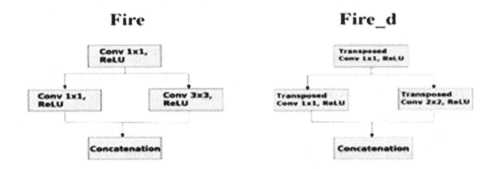

The network is trained with a manually labelled iris and pupil region dataset. The loss function used to measure the difference between the ground truth and segmentation result is Cross-Entropy and for optimizing the model Stochastic gradient descent is used. The equation for Cross-Entropy is given in Eq. 3:

$$E = - \sum_i [t_i \log(P_i) + (1 - t_i)\log(1 - P_i) \tag{3}$$

where, P_i is the output of the neural network. t_i is the ground truth, the label assigned to the pixel (x_i,y_i) manually in the Image Labeller of MATLAB as in Eq. 4:

$1, (x, y) \in R$

$t = \{$

$0, otherwise$ $\tag{4}$

The label of the pixel is set as $t_i = 1$ for the pixel belonging to the iris and pupil region R and set as $t_i = 0$ for other regions.

Eye Gaze Tracking

After extracting iris and pupil features, the 2D pupil center is extracted through Mean-Shift algorithm. Mean-Shift algorithm is explained as below:

Create random points and window W.
Determine the average inside W.
Position the search window to the middle.
Repeat Steps 2 and 3 until convergence is achieved.

The Kernel function for the Mean-Shift Algorithm is mentioned in Eq. 5:

$k(x, x) = (P$

$(x$

$\times p$

$i \, map \, i$ (5)

The pixels obtained from the segmentation process are considered as random points and the Mean-Shift algorithm is applied on these points. The mean/center point found is considered as the 2D pupil center. Once the pupil center is extracted, the parameters for eye gaze tracking are calibrated as in Eq. 6:

$V = \{\theta, \phi\}$ (6)

Here, θ and ϕ are the spherical coordinates of the iris center on the eyeball. θ and ϕ respectively denote angle of elevation and azimuth angle. θ and ϕ are updated frame by frame.

Then, the eyeball center is kept at origin presuming that the pupil center is 12 pixels away from the eyeball center. Now, from the center of the eyeball to the pupil center, a 3D line is plotted. This line is projected on a plane in front of the eye and the point of intersection between the line and the plane is found. Fig.4 shows the design of eye gaze tracking.

Figure 4. Design of eye gaze tracking

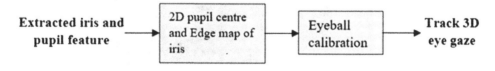

Eye Gaze Capture and Heatmap Generation

Eye gaze tracking is further used for eye gaze capture. In this proposed work, the captured eye gaze is used for finding the most viewed product in a webpage. To do so, initially the viewer is asked to focus their eyes on some predefined fixed points on the screen (center of the screen, top, bottom, left, right, top left, top right, bottom left, and bottom right). After getting the intersections between the eye gazes and the camera image plane that was produced by seeing the predefined fixed points, the image plane and the screen plane are mapped using linear transformation.

Once the screen plane and the image plane are mapped, heatmaps are generated using Gaussian Kernel, wherever the viewer sees the screen. A timer is set to cool down the heatmap on the previous focus points. Also, how much time the viewer has seen a product is calculated and the product that was viewed for the most amount of time is declared as the most viewed product.

Experimental Results

Web camera was used to capture the live video streams for experimentation purposes. The computer system, Intel(R) Core (TM) i5-10500 CPU @ 3.10GHz with 8 GB RAM was used to carry out the work. The sample frames extracted from the input videos are shown in Fig.5. The initial learning rate was 1e-4. The batch size was 32. To optimize the training loss, Stochastic Gradient Descent is used. The momentum used is 0.99. For normalization, the weight decay is 1e-7. The learning rate drop factor is 0.1 for a period of 200 epochs.

Figure 5. Sample video frames

Fig.6 shows the result of iris and pupil region segmentation process. On applying the Viola Jones algorithm over the input image frame (a), the eye patch (b) of size 24 x 48 is extracted. Then 2D pupil center is obtained using mean-shift algorithm (c). From the marked pupil center, iris and pupil region are segmented (d).

Figure 6. Segmenting iris and pupil region (a) input frame (b) segmented eye (c) marked pupil center (d) marked pupil and iris

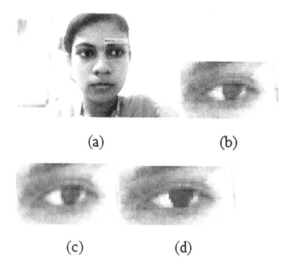

The neural network was trained for 20000 iterations with 3040 images, annotated manually. From training, the obtained training accuracy is 97.8190% and the training loss is 0.1055. The Jaccard distance between the obtained segmentation and actual segmentation is approximately 0.8. Fig.7 shows the distance between the obtained and the actual image.

Figure 7. The Jaccard distance between the obtained image and actual image

Table 1 shows the Jaccard similarity coefficient obtained for the sample eye image patches.

Table 1. Jaccard Similarity Coefficient for the sample input eye image patches

Input Image	ObtainedSegmentation vs.Actual Segmentation	Jaccard Similarity Coefficient
		0.7600
		0.7170
		0.7347
		0.8936
		0.8723

With 2D pupil center and considering the eyeball center as origin (assuming that the eyeball center is located 12 pixels away from pupil center), 3D eye tracking is done by plotting a 3D line from eyeball center (origin) to 2D pupil center. It is shown in fig.8.

Figure 8. 3D line from eyeball center to pupil center

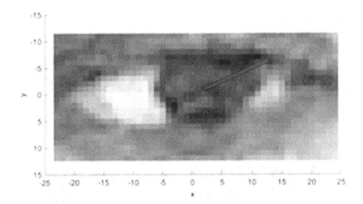

The angle of elevation and Azimuth angle (θ and ϕ) are updated frame by frame. A sample of updating (θ and ϕ) is shown in Figure 9. For i^{th} sample frame in fig.9 (a), θ and ϕ are updated respectively 2.6779, - 1.2141, and for $(i + 1)^{th}$ frame in figure 9 (b), it is 2.3562 and -1.3393 respectively.

Figure 9. Updating θ and ϕ in (a) ith frame (b) (i + 1)th frame

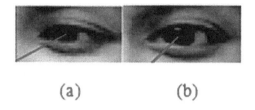

(a)   (b)

The point of intersection between the projected line and the image plane is found. Then the obtained intersection point is linearly transformed to plot that point on the screen plane. The Considered image plane is of dimension, 80 x 64 and screen plane is of dimension, 1000 x 800, to find where the viewer sees on the screen.

Fig.10 shows the tracking of user preference on the page.

For comparison purposes, the work was carried out with and without calibration. The results obtained are shown in table 2. From table 2, it is clear that calibration with θ and ϕ parameters results in better accuracy compared to calibration-free method.

Figure 10. Tracking the user preference

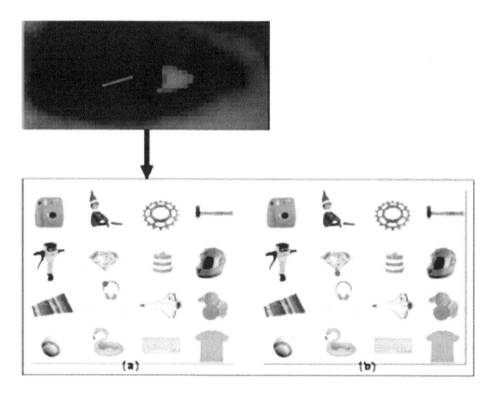

Table 2. Accuracy in calibration and calibration-free method

	Accuracy (in %)	Head movement
Calibration-based (with θ and φ parameters)	99.93%	No
Calibration-free	95.59%	Yes

The proposed work is compared with the-state-of-the-art techniques in Table 3. From table 3, it is evident that the proposed work is comparably better for preference tracking.

Table 3. Comparison with the state-of-the-art methods

S.No.	Authors	Year	Architecture	Accuracy
1.	Choi et al.	2016	Own architecture	95%
2.	Shin et al.	2018	Own architecture	90.1%
3.	Vora et al.	2018	AlexNet, VGG-16, ResNet and SqueezeNe	95.18%
4.	Naqui et al.	2018	VGGFace16	99.6%
5.	Our proposed work	2023	SqueezeNet and U-Net	**99.93%**

FUTURE RESEARCH DIRECTIONS

This system has used the live videos acquired from the web camera. To make the system scalable, video acquired from different means can be used in the future.

CONCLUSION

The live video sequence is acquired with web camera and split into frames. From the input image frame, eye region is extracted by using the Viola Jones algorithm. In the eye region, pupil and iris pixel classification was carried out with SqueezeNet and U-Net. After extracting the iris and pupil features, the eye gaze tracking was formulated by using 2D pupil center extracted by applying Mean-Shift algorithm and 3D eyeball center. The proposed system tracks the user preference on a particular page with an accuracy of 99.93% which is best comparable to the state-of-the-art methods.

REFERENCES

Akshay, S. (2019). Aswathy Rames, Ashika P, "Visual Search Capability using Heatmaps. *International Journal of Engineering and Advanced Technology*, *8*(5), 1811–1814.

Badrinarayanan, V., Kendall, A., & Cipolla, R. (2017). SegNet: A Deep Convolutional Encoder-Decoder Architecture for Image Segmentation. IEEE Transactions on Pattern Analysis and Machine Intelligence, (pp. 2481-2495). IEEE. doi: . 2644615 doi:10.1109/tpami.2016

Beheshti, N., & Johnsson, L. (2020). Squeeze U-Net: A Memory and Energy Efficient Image Segmentation Network. *IEEE/CVF Conference on Computer Vision and Pattern Recognition Workshops*, (pp. 1495-1504). IEEE. .10.1109/CVPRW50498.2020.00190

Bulat, A., & Tzimiropoulos, G. (2020). Hierarchical Binary CNNs for Landmark Localization with Limited Resources. *IEEE Transactions on Pattern Analysis And Machine Intelligence*, (pp. 343-356). IEEE. doi: . 2018.2866051. doi:10.1109/tpami

Chen, L., Papandreou, G., Kokkinos, I., Murphy, K., & Yuille, A. (2018). DeepLab: Semantic Image Segmentation with Deep Convolutional Nets, Atrous Convolution, and Fully Connected CRFs. *IEEE Transactions on Pattern Analysis and Machine Intelligence*, *40*(4), 834–848. doi:10.1109/TPAMI.2017.2699184 PMID:28463186

Cheng, Y., & Feng, L. X. Z. (2018). Appearance-Based Gaze Estimation via Evaluation-Guided Asymmetric Regression. European Conference on Computer Vision, (pp. 105-121). Springer. 10.1007/978-3-030-01264-9_7

Cheung, Y., & Peng, Q. (2015). Eye Gaze Tracking with a Web Camera in a Desktop Environment. *IEEE Transactions on Human-Machine Systems*, *45*(4), 419–430. doi:10.1109/THMS.2015.2400442

Chi, J., Wang, D., Lu, N., & Wang, Z. (2020). Cornea Radius Calibration for Remote 3D Gaze Tracking Systems. *IEEE Access : Practical Innovations, Open Solutions*, *8*, 187634–187647. doi:10.1109/ACCESS.2020.3029300

Choi, I.-H., Kim, Y. G., & Tran, T. B. H. (2016). *Real-time categorization of driver's gaze zone and head pose - using the convolutional neural network*. Proc. HCI Korea, Korea.

Forrest, N. (2017). *Iandola, Song Han, Matthew W. Moskewicz, Khalid Ashraf, William J. Dally, Kurt Keutzer, "Squeezenet: Alexnet-Level Accuracy with 50x fewer parameters and <0.5mb Model Size. ICLR.*

Fydanaki, A., & Geradts, Z. (2018). Evaluating OpenFace: An open-source automatic facial comparison algorithm for forensics. *Forensic Sciences Research, 3*(3), 202–209. doi:10.1080/20961790.2018.1523703 PMID:30483670

Jimenez-Perez, G. (2019). *Alejandro Alcaine, Oscar Camara, "U-Net Architecture for the Automatic Detection and Delineation of the Electrocardiogram* (Vol. 46). Computing in Cardiology.

Hassanpour, M., & Malek, H. (2020). Learning Document Image Features with SqueezeNet Convolutional Neural Network. *International Journal of Engineering, 33*(7). doi:10.5829/ije.2020.33.07a.05

Helhamer, E., Long, J., & Darrell, T. (2017). Fully Convolutional Networks for Semantic Segmentation. *IEEE Transactions on Pattern Analysis And Machine Intelligence,* (pp. 640-651). IEEE. doi: . doi:10.1109/tpami.2016

Lahiri, A., Agarwalla, A., & Biswas, P. K. (2018). Unsupervised Domain Adaptation for Learning Eye Gaze from a Million Synthetic Images. *11th Indian Conference on Computer Vision, Graphics and Image Processing.* ACM. . 3293423, 2018.10.1145/3293353.3293423

Lemley, J., Kar, A., Drimbarean, A., & Corcoran, P. (2019). Convolutional Neural Network Implementation for Eye- Gaze Estimation on Low-Quality Consumer Imaging Systems. *IEEE Transactions on Consumer Electronics,* (pp. 179-187). IEEE. doi: . 2019.2899869. doi:10.1109/tce

Lin, G. (2016). RefineNet: Multi-Path Refinement Networks for High-Resolution Semantic Segmentation. arXiv:1611.06612.

Lu, F., Gao, Y., & Chen, X. (2016). Estimating 3D Gaze Directions Using Unlabeled Eye Images via Synthetic Iris Appearance Fitting. *IEEE Transactions on Multimedia, 18*(9), 1772–1782. doi:10.1109/TMM.2016.2576284

Melesse, D., Khalil, M., Kagabo, E., Ning, T., & Huang, K. (2020). Appearance-Based Gaze Tracking Through Supervised Machine Learning. 15th IEEE International Conference on Signal Processing, (pp. 467-471). IEEE. . 9321075, 2020.10.1109/ICSP48669.2020.9321075

Naqvi, R., Arsalan, M., Batchuluun, G., Yoon, H., & Park, K. (2018). Deep learning-based gaze detection system for automobile drivers using a NIR camera sensor. *Sensors (Basel), 18*(2), 456. doi:10.339018020456 PMID:29401681

Shin, C., Lee, G., Kim, Y., Hong, J., Hong, S.-H., Kang, H., & Lee, Y. (2018). Evaluation of gaze depth estimation using a wearable binocular eye tracker and machine learning. *Journal of the Korea Computer Graphics Society, 24*(1), 19–26.

Vora, S., Rangesh, A., & Trivedi, M. M. (2018). *Driver gaze zone estimation using convolutional neural networks: A general framework and ablative analysis.* Arxiv. https://arxiv.org/abs/1802.02690, 2018.

Wang, C., Shi, F., Xia, S., & Chai, J. (2016). Realtime 3D eye gaze animation using a single RGB camera. *ACM Transactions on Graphics, 35*(4), 1–14. doi:10.1145/2897824.2925947

Wang, Z., Chai, J., & Xia, S. (2021). Realtime and Accurate 3D Eye Gaze Capture with DCNN-Based Iris and Pupil Segmentation. *IEEE Transactions on Visualization and Computer Graphics, 27*(1), 190–203. doi:10.1109/TVCG.2019.2938165 PMID:31478861

Wood, E., Baltrušaitis, T., Morency, L., Robinson, P., & Bulling, A. (2018). GazeDirector: Fully Articulated Eye Gaze Redirection in Video. *Computer Graphics Forum, 37*(2), 217–225. doi:10.1111/cgf.13355

Yan, B., Pei, T., & Wang, X. (2019). Wavelet Method for Automatic Detection of Eye-Movement Behaviors. *IEEE Sensors Journal, 19*(8), 3085–3091. doi:10.1109/JSEN.2018.2876940

Chapter 14
Groundwater Contamination Forecasting Using Automated Machine Learning

Sathya Narayanan
Vellore Institute of Technology, Chennai, India

Denisha Miraclin
Vellore Institute of Technology, Chennai, India

Milind Dangate
Chemistry Division, School of Advanced Sciences, Vellore Institute of Technology, Chennai, India

Deepak Chaudhari
Allied Informatics Inc., USA

ABSTRACT

Because of the subsurface's inherent geologic unpredictability, it is difficult to forecast the fate and transit of groundwater contaminants. To solve the equation for advection, dispersion, and reactivity, forecasting the flow of pollutants has been done using simplified geology and accepted assumptions. It may soon be possible to use extensive groundwater quality data from long-term polluted sites to feed machine learning algorithms that predict the spread of pollution plumes and enhance site management. The objective of this study was to first utilise extensive historical data from groundwater monitoring well samples to better understand the complex relationships between groundwater quality parameters, and then to construct a useful model for predicting the time until site closure.

DOI: 10.4018/978-1-6684-9804-0.ch014

INTRODUCTION

Goal of the United Nations' Sustainable Development Agenda is "By 2030, enhance the purity of water through decreasing pollution, eradicating dumping, and limiting release of dangerous substances and chemicals, halving the amount of wastewater that is untreated, and significantly boosting recycling and safe reuse globally." In order for this interdisciplinary objective, it is also important to clean up contaminated water. According to (Gleick, 1993), groundwater accounts for 99 percent of the world's fresh, liquid water supply (Groundwater, 1979). Shallow groundwater, which is used extensively for rural and municipal drinking water, has been contaminated due to industrialisation and the slow control of chemicals. Understanding how precious resource is harmed and how it will be used for good use, whether by human intervention or natural processes, requires the collecting and analysis of modern data. Goal of (EPA) is "to protect human health and the environment," however this goal can't be achieved without first conducting a thorough and open evaluation of groundwater data.

The battle to identify and trace the spread of contaminated plumes in soil and groundwater has advanced greatly since the emergence of contamination hydrology as a distinct field of study. Nonetheless, it is challenging to have a precise understanding due to the subsurface's inherent unpredictability. While the (ADR) equation has been around since the 1970s and offers a theoretical basis for contaminant transport, the underlying mechanisms are often obscured by complexity (Groundwater, 1979). This complicates both the study of subterranean pollution and the identification of groundwater plumes. With varying degrees of success, tracer experiments have compared model results with ground-truth samples. These problems originate from the irrational assumptions included in the governing equation.

The mechanisms that regulate the decomposition of contaminants have made strides in the lab and in the field, but it remains difficult to generalize results to specific sites because of the many site-specific elements that impact these processes (Elder, 2002). However, models built on empirical data may provide ground-breaking opportunities for improving our understanding of pollutant fate and transit at specific places as the quantity of data collected from contaminated areas grows. Emerging contaminants might possibly influence the regulatory goals at multi-contaminant sites or have an impact on previously unregulated regions. To identify the underlying structure and forecast the movement and fate of pollutants, new techniques must be developed.

At a large site in New Jersey, for instance, PMF was utilized to pinpoint attenuated plume components (Capozzi, 2018). Attenuation of 1,4-dioxane was shown using linear discriminant analyses on data from the California public database Geotracker

(Adamson, 2015). Using matrix factorization has been shown to be a very helpful method in forensics for tracking out the sources of plumes.

Various statistical machine-learning techniques, such decision trees and neural networks, have been used in the analysis of the revised data. Cleansing costs were calculated using a combination of decision trees and text mining of petrol station data (Farrel, 2007). As a way to predict variables like breathability as well as distribution parameters, which are inputs to reactive transportation models, neural networks have also been used to this kind of data. Skewed hydrological data may be used using machine learning techniques, as these investigations have demonstrated. To properly appreciate how machine learning may enhance our comprehension of complicated systems in the environment, more ground has to be covered. Fluorescent soil samples and images may be analyzed using pattern recognition, and curative choices can be backed by the creation of suggestion systems.

Econometrics-based time series forecasting techniques that use machine learning have lately become more prominent, especially when applied to the earth sciences. For the research and monitoring of polluted areas, time series data on pollutant concentration in monitoring wells is required. However, despite its widespread use in understanding this data, non-parametric trend analysis, such as the Mann-Kendall technique, is unsuitable for projecting future concentrations. Future groundwater levels, air pollution, and surface water pollution may all be predicted using earth science (Aguilera, 2019). when used to analyze things like weather, temperature, air pollution, and groundwater levels.

The research is on time series models, which may be trained using historical data to make predictions about the future. Given the complexity of depicting the various variables that influence fate and progress over such extended time frames, this might be useful. A major drawback of this method is that unlike a numerical flow model, which employs mathematics to precisely identify the procedures in the model, any mechanistic interpretations relies on the data and a detailed grasp of the chemical and physical steps involved.

Historical Datasets From Legacy Sites

A lot of commercial waste was simply dumped into nearby bodies of water before the EPA, RCRA, and CERCLA were established in the 1970s and '80s, respectively. After large-scale plants were found to have discharged in the past, state and federal regulating programmes were implemented. Groundwater monitoring wells and boreholes were drilled to collect groundwater samples for analysis, site evaluation, and potential remediation. Based on this data, the management of the site noticed patterns in pollutant concentration and problem regions. Several of these sites are still under observation, have sample data archives dating back decades, since environmental pollution tends to linger for quite some time. Twelve important cultural sites in North America provided historical sample data that was gathered for this study. Over a thousand monitoring wells have provided samples for the cleaning effort at the largest of these sites since the late 1980s. We have made every effort to close any data gaps introduced by advances in technology and improvements in sampling methods. Samples are still gathered from monitoring wells and transported to a laboratory for chemical analysis, therefore the procedures used to get this data have essentially stayed the same. Probes and field testing kits (like Hach sets) were used to check several parameters outside. Monitoring well mixing, sample mistakes, and poor quality control might all skew the findings of these investigations.

Data Analysis

When analytical substances are seldom found, this value is stated as the threshold for detection limits of the method of analysis. The lowest concentration at which a deviation from the method blank can be recognized with typically 99% confidence is referred to as the detection limit. Whether you know it as the quantitation limit or the reporting limit. The letter "J" indicates that the concentration of the analyte is between the reporting limit and the detection limit of the method used. QA and QC of scientific analytical data often reveals additional red flags like these, which might make the understanding of output difficult. These are provided with the outcomes of the analytical tests in order to alert the public to potential issues with the quality standards of the labs. Labs that have earned (NELAP) certification are subject to stringent rules regarding quality assurance and quality control. When submitting analytical samples to regulatory organizations, you must provide this certification to show that your results meet the requirements of the law.

Field Data

Probes, quick tests, and field research are common methods of gathering information in the field. Numerous probes have been employed to measure groundwater temperatures, oxygen content, oxidation-reduction potential, and depth. Because carbon dioxide would off-gas into the atmosphere at a partial pressure that is lower when brought to the surface, the pH of the subsurface samples would increase (Groundwater, 1979). Several variables, such as soil organic matter, infiltration, water table depth, may affect the chemical make-up of underground water. Field quick tests are often used to analyse nitrate and nitrite, iron, and other compounds that might provide light on the geochemical properties of groundwater. There is a trade-off between the accuracy of findings from materials analysed in a laboratory and those obtained using these kits, which are useful for characterising materials in the field. Some people, while it varies from person to person, employ colorimetric judgement. Instead of recording and using these data in quantitative research, they may be more useful as qualitative indications in certain circumstances.

These observations, even when made by qualified geologists, are frequently incorrect due to subtle differences in makeup that could result in differing (USCS) classifications. This is a typical issue that may make it harder to build and understand a mental image of a site.

Modern Site Management Techniques

In the short history of remediating contaminated sites, there have been a number of notable modifications to the characterization and cleaning procedures. Because it was largely spawned by the environmental movement and the subsequent passage of laws, contaminated hydrology has a more recent history than many other scientific subjects. In many respects, the core investigative approaches of classifying soils, examining samples in a lab, and applying the ideas of subsurface movement to polluted plumes are identical. Technology has expanded the methods and equipment for collecting such samples, and understanding the limitations of early methodology has led to the development of more sophisticated methods for collecting samples and assessing toxins.

The monitoring of well drilling has a number of purposes, and this is true despite the fact that the drilling of wells for both irrigation and drinking water has been the subject of substantial research. Many iterations of refinement have resulted in the present state of the art for building methods. Recognising that dangerous pollutants frequently exist in very low quantities makes precise identification without dilution an essential consideration. A better knowledge of the fine resolutions at which contaminant dispersion may be considerably altered in a complicated heterogeneous subsurface was achieved by the use of multi-level samplers (Groundwater, 1979). Due to substantial groundwater inputs from locations outside of the target stratum, a very long well screen may dilute the sample. The complex characteristics of the groundwater plume are not well represented by the composite site sample, which was created over a long period of time. For instance, due to the design's emphasis on places with the greatest toxin concentrations, it may be challenging to decide. Because it may contaminate a previously uncontaminated groundwater zone, knowing its interval is critical. In fact, problems with pollution are often brought on by improper well installation.

A comparable transformation has occurred in our understanding of how pollutants themselves deteriorate, going beyond the design and installation of efficient monitoring wells. Naturally occurring attenuation by microorganisms has garnered more attention since the beginning of restoration at legacy sites than the formerly prevalent practise treating water. Many modern cleanup techniques include changing the subsurface geochemical environment and/or adding organisms and micronutrients in order to promote the microbially-mediated degradation of prevalent pollutants. The concept of reverse diffusion from low-permeability zones has helped to clarify problems with pump-and-treat techniques (Chapman, 2005).

There are several other approaches that have been developed to increase operational efficiency, such as genetic algorithms, reactive transport modelling software, and optimisation problems. In order to filter out pollutants or pathways, detailed conceptual site models are often created employing consideration of pollution transmission. The 14-compartment model is an example of a model that uses this kind of separation to help choose which sections to study.

The use of genetic programs to identify well sites that may not be required in analyzing plume behavior and should be eliminated is one optimization technique that has been proposed for ongoing surveillance. People who are well-versed in crucial regulatory or adjudicative facts may be given more agency via the use of these algorithms, which may also be used in combination with experts to enhance decision-making (Babber-Sebens, 2008). Decision assistance systems like MAROS and ASSIST (Aziz, 2003) are founded on genetic algorithms for optimizing problems. Considering the fact that this field of study has spawned a large number of tools. In order to help with site management, computer models with parameters that roughly match subsurface conditions have been created in a number of forms. Computer models of geologic topography have substantially advanced our understanding of subterranean fluid movement due to the formulation of the advection-dispersion equation and the intricacy of groundwater flow. The most utilized methodology is the USGS-developed open-source MODFLOW numerical finite-difference model. REMchlor and PREMchlor are two well-known instances of reactive problem integration in fundamental models. Due to the large quantity of data required to run the models, they are not practical for application at less contaminated sites. For larger sites, however, these methods may be used to construct a comprehensive conceptual site model that produces an approximation of the plume's eventual position.

Overview of Machine Learning

The area of machine learning tools to predict the future. Whether machine learning algorithms are supervised—trained using the user's input to create the "right" responses—or unsupervised, in which they just employ input data to uncover connections. Classification, regression, and logistical regression are just a few examples of the functions that algorithms may accomplish. Clustering, reduction of dimensionality, and prediction may all be accomplished using the same method. With a brief summary of numerous essential methodologies, the foundation of the task following may be more readily understood. The intention of this piece is not to give exhaustive coverage of every technique.

Dimensionality Reduction

It is feasible to comprehend the connections between various characteristics when highly dimensional data is simplified using a family of machine learning methods known as "dimensionality reduction." In enormous data sets with numerous variables that vary, this method is vital for identifying the interrelationships between them. The dimensionality reducing technique utilized to analyze the data in this research was the principal component analysis (PCA). PCA generates values that are linear function of the initial value using either an eigenvector or a single-valued solution in order to identify the variables that contribute the most variation to the data set. The most important parts are the novel variables that explain the most variation. The PC scores reflect the relative importance of the various factors in the development of the new factors. Computers now make it feasible to apply principal component analysis (PCA) to enormous multi-dimensional data sets, despite the fact that this technique, which is based on straightforward linear algebra, has been around since 1900s.

Forecasting Time Series

Time series data is essential for keeping an eye on polluted areas. The Mann-Kendall approach, which is ineffective in predicting future concentrations of substances, is often used to analyse this data. The need for precision in corporate analytics and marketing has led to the creation of sophisticated forecasting models. In 2018, Facebook released Prophet, a remarkable model that expands upon a decomposable time series model and includes components that may be interpreted by humans. The authors of this approach argued that "forecasting at scale," It is essential in many businesses for many analysts that possess expertise in their particular areas but may lack training in mathematical frameworks for predicting to be able to provide accurate predictions using an interpretable and tunable model. The model is designed for "analyst in the loop" uses, in which a human analyst swiftly anticipates data from many datasets, checks for abnormalities, and makes adjustments to the model to address them. This model is now being used more often by a number of earth scientific subdisciplines, including hydrology, atmospheric science, and others.

The Prophet model is based on both secular and religious holidays. It may be written as $g(t) + s(t) + h(t) + Et = y(t)$.

The seasonal component $s(t)$ is included in this equation with the holidays represented by $h(t)$. The error, represented by Et, is assumed to follow a normal distribution. The trend term, which is based on an equation for the carrying capacity of an ecosystem, will be utilized to signal decline rather than expansion in this instance. Changepoints, which are automatically identified in prior data, may be manually adjusted to vary their expansion rate. The historical data of the to-be-predicted variable are known as endogenous variables. Numbers from other sources, with an external relationship to the dependent variable, are called exogenous variables.

The smooth standard Fourier series provides the basis upon which the seasonal component of the model is constructed. The analyst has the ability to predetermine the occurrence of seasonal patterns, which may occur on a daily, weekly, monthly, quarterly, or annual basis. The purpose of vacation component is to take into consideration out-of-the-ordinary situations that may startle the prediction but also need the user's close attention. An individual may create a list of previous and future dates that will be recognized as holidays, in addition to the conventional holidays observed in some nations. The vacation component of the study serves as a proxy for real-world scenarios like receiving remedial treatment.

By examining each component separately, the effect of each on the overall forecast may become clear. The predictions' accuracy may be evaluated using the mean absolute percentage error (MAPE) and the approach of simulating prior forecasts, which generates forecasts inside the current data time line that can be compared with the actual data. One of the most valuable aspects of the prophet model is its flexibility in identifying and addressing prediction issues via the adjustment of model parameters. Automatic detection of anomalies is strongly suggested to identify any erroneous forecasts.

The prophet package for the R programming language has allowed these forecasting techniques to be included in the fable package. Using this program, the analysis for this study was completed. The inclusion of several time series models enables the creation of an efficient programming environment by removing the necessity for the testing of these models to be conducted in a variety of different packages and languages. Simple models such as naive and mean were employed and evaluated for utility in addition to the models chosen for in-depth study, but ultimately they fared much worse.

Numerical models need a transport model and mechanically applicable reactions to precisely represent subsurface phenomena. Future values in a time series may be predicted using a model trained with historical data using Prophet. Neither the past data nor the forecast can be explained mechanically. This is helpful since it becomes difficult to adequately demonstrate the multiplicity of elements that impact destiny and migration for big regions over lengthy time periods. One drawback of this approach is that interpretation is less dependent on mathematics that represent the chemical and physical reactions occurring in the model and more dependent on the data and a wide knowledge of the procedures involved.

The oversight of contaminated areas is one of the many fields that might benefit from machine learning's revolutionary effects.

The two primary obstacles to machine learning are poor data quality and a lack of data. Due to a lack of authority over the sample methods used in the past, working with historical datasets exacerbates these difficulties. However, in order to make the best use of the information we already have, sample data from previous sites should be seen through this lens.

Reduction of Organic Compounds That Have Been Chlorinated

Chlorinated volatile organic compounds are among the most difficult organic contaminants to remove from the environment. The focus of this book is on methane and chlorinated ethenes. These compounds have seen considerable application as solvents in the electronics manufacturing and dry cleaning industries. Because of this, their dechlorination processes have been well studied and are well known. Substitution, dehydrohalogenation, reduction, oxidation, and elimination processes are all used to break down chlorinated ethenes and methanes. The same class of chlorinated ethene compounds has also been referred to as "-ethylene" in other studies.

Both chlorine-based ethenes and methanes can go through biologically-mediated chlorine removal under environmentally relevant circumstances, in addition to abiotic reductions by decreased metal ions; nevertheless, excessive levels of pollutants may be harmful to microorganisms and diminish the efficiency of this process. Figure 1 depicts the two other routes that PCE may take, one using triple-bonded ethynes (also called acetylenes or ethylenes), and the other involving double-bonded ethynes. compared to the double-bonded pathway, which is predominantly mediated by widespread soil bacteria, the triple-bonded approach involves an association with the zero-valent iron which sets up the permeable reactivity restriction.

Summary

In order to improve the effectiveness of site management, this study set out to determine whether or not predictive machine learning algorithms may benefit from using data collected from old monitoring wells. Several methods of dimensionality reduction were used to the raw, actual dataset, including basic correlation analysis and the analysis of principal components.

Researching how much data is needed to produce accurate forecasts regarding subsurface pollutants was the research's secondary objective, which was accomplished by creating a realistic synthetic dataset. Prophet, damped Holt's method, and artificial neural network autoregression were evaluated using the fictional dataset. Given

Figure 1. Perchloroethene (PCE) and its transition products' reductive dechlorination routes are shown in Figure 1. On the right is the microbially mediated route, while on the left is the abiotic pathway.

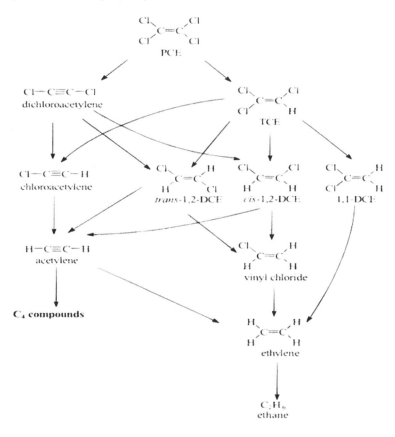

the exploratory nature of the objectives, it is crucial to evaluate the usefulness of algorithms for machine learning due to their continued effect on modern data analytics.

Instead of building vehicle regulation algorithms, this study makes use of a data-driven strategy to train forecasting models using publicly known pollutant amounts. Predictions were made using Prophet and a modified exponentially smoothing technique and then compared to the findings of a realistic synthetic dataset built for a location with historical pollutants. The effects of varying the training data set size and temporal data density are looked at in order to identify possible gains in model performance. Prophet is also used to assess the benefits of employing regressors to enhance the accuracy of forecasts at downgradient wells, utilising trained data from multiple observation wells. The method for forecasting will provide a new tool for developing conceptual site models and managing the site plans, increasing flexibility in decision-making and lowering the cost of monitoring and remediation in a variety of contexts thanks to the computational efficiency of the underlying methodology. As the number and quality of data increases, we may get a deeper understanding of contamination transfer and uncover practical uses that may enhance current management of sites.

REFERENCES

Adamson, D. T., Anderson, R. H., Mahendra, S., & Newell, C. J. (2015). Evidence of 1,4-Dioxane Attenuation at Groundwater Sites Contaminated with Chlorinated Solvents and 1,4-Dioxane. *Environmental Science & Technology*, *49*(11), 6510–6518. doi:10.1021/acs.est.5b00964

Aguilera, H., Guardiola-Albert, C., Naranjo-Fernández, N., & Kohfahl, C. (2019). Towards Flexible Groundwater-Level Prediction for Adaptive Water Management: Using Facebook's Prophet Forecasting Approach. *Hydrological Sciences Journal*, *64*(12), 1504–1518. doi:10.1080/02626667.2019.1651933

Aziz, J. J., Ling, M., Rifai, H. S., Newell, C. J., & Gonzales, J. R. (2003). MAROS: A Decision Support System for Optimizing Monitoring Plans. *Ground Water*, *41*(3), 355–367. doi:10.1111/j.1745-6584.2003.tb02605.x

Babbar-Sebens, M., & Minsker, B. (2008). Standard Interactive Genetic Algorithm— Comprehensive Optimization Framework for Groundwater Monitoring Design. *Journal of Water Resources Planning and Management*, *134*(6), 538–547. doi:10.1061/(asce)0733-9496(2008)134:6(538)

Capozzi, S. L., Rodenburg, L. A., Krumins, V., Fennell, D. E., & Erin Mack, E. (2018). Using Positive Matrix Factorization to Investigate Microbial Dehalogenation of Chlorinated Benzenes in Groundwater at a Historically Contaminated Site. *Chemosphere*, *211*(November), 515–523. doi:10.1016/j.chemosphere.2018.07.180

Chapman, S. W., & Parker, B. L. (2005). Plume Persistence Due to Aquitard Back Diffusion Following Dense Nonaqueous Phase Liquid Source Removal or Isolation. *Water Resources Research*, *41*(12), 1–16. doi:10.1029/2005WR004224

Cherry, J. A., & Freeze, R. A. (1979). *Groundwater*. Prentice Hall.

Elder, Benson, & Eykholt. (2002). Effects of Heterogeneity on Influent and Effluent Concentrations from Horizontal Permeable Reactive Barriers. *Water Resources Research*, *38*(8), 27-1-27–19. https://doi.org/. doi:10.1029/2001wr001259

Farrell, D. M., Minsker, B. S., Tcheng, D., Searsmith, D., Bohn, J., & Beckman, D. (2007). Data Mining to Improve Management and Reduce Costs of Environmental Remediation. *Journal of Hydroinformatics*, *9*(2), 107–121. doi:10.2166/hydro.2007.004

Gleick, P. H. (1993). *Water in Crisis: A Guide to the World's Fresh Water Resources.* Environment Pacific Institute for Studies in Development, and Stockholm Environment Institute.

Compilation of References

Abadi, M., Agarwal, A., Barham, P., Brevdo, E., Chen, Z., Citro, C., Corrado, G. S., Davis, A., Dean, J., Devin, M., Ghemawat, S., Goodfellow, I., Harp, A., Irving, G., Isard, M., Jia, Y., Jozefowicz, R., Kaiser, L., Kudlur, M., & Zheng, X. (2016). TensorFlow: A System for Large-Scale Machine Learning. *Journal Name: Proceedings of the 12th USENIX Symposium on Operating Systems Design and Implementation* (OSDI '16) .

Abadi, M., Agarwal, A., Barham, P., Brevdo, E., Chen, Z., Citro, C., Corrado, G. S., Davis, A., Dean, J., Devin, M., Ghemawat, S., Goodfellow, I., Harp, A., Irving, G., Isard, M., Jia, Y., Jozefowicz, R., Kaiser, L., Kudlur, M., & Zheng, X. (2016). *TensorFlow: Large-Scale Machine Learning on Heterogeneous Distributed Systems* (arXiv:1603.04467). arXiv. https://arxiv.org/abs/1603.04467.

Abbes, H., & Gargouri, F. (2016). Big Data Integration: A MongoDB Database and Modular Ontologies based Approach. *Knowledge-Based and Intelligent Information & Engineering Systems: Proceedings of the 20th International Conference KES-2016,* (pp. 446–455). Science Direct. 10.1016/j.procs.2016.08.099

Abinaya, P., Kumar, V. S., Balasubramanian, P., & Menon, V. K. (2016). Measuring stock price and trading volume causality among Nifty50 stocks: The Toda Yamamoto method. In *2016 International Conference on Advances in Computing, Communications and Informatics (ICACCI)* (pp. 1886-1890). IEEE. 10.1109/ICACCI.2016.7732325

Abirami, A., & Palanikumar, S. A hybrid big-bang big-crunch optimization and deliberated deep reinforced learning mechanisms for cyber-attack detection. Computers and Electrical Engineering, Volume: 109, Part B, 108773, 2023, ISSN 0045-7906, https://doi.org/ doi:10.1016/j.compeleceng.2023.108773

Abirami, T., Priakanth, P., & Madhuvanthi, T. (2022). Effective Face Mask and Social Distance Detection with Alert System for Covid-19 Using YOLOv5 Model. In Advances in Parallel Computing Algorithms, Tools and Paradigms (pp. 80-85). IOS Press. doi:10.3233/APC220011

Adamson, D. T., Anderson, R. H., Mahendra, S., & Newell, C. J. (2015). Evidence of 1,4-Dioxane Attenuation at Groundwater Sites Contaminated with Chlorinated Solvents and 1,4-Dioxane. *Environmental Science & Technology, 49*(11), 6510–6518. doi:10.1021/acs.est.5b00964

Adek, R. T., & Ula, M. (2020). A Survey on The Accuracy of Machine Learning Techniques for Intrusion and Anomaly Detection on Public Data Sets. *2020 International Conference on Data Science, Artificial Intelligence, and Business Analytics (DATABIA)*. IEEE. 10.1109/DATABIA50434.2020.9190436

Agarwal, S., Verma, P. K., & Khan, M. A. (2017). An Optimized Palm Print Recognition Approach using Gabor filter", *International Conference on Computing, Communication and Networking Technologies (ICCCNT)*, Delhi, India. 10.1109/ICCCNT.2017.8203919

Agirre-Basurko, E., Ibarra-Berastegi, G., & Madariaga, I. (2006). Regression and multilayer perceptron-based models to forecast hourly O3 and NO2 levels in the Bilbao area. *Environmental Modelling & Software*, *21*(4), 430–446. doi:10.1016/j.envsoft.2004.07.008

Agrawal, P., Arya, R., Bindal, A., Bhatia, S., Gagneja, A., Godlewski, J., Low, Y., Muss, T., Paliwal, M. M., Raman, S., Shah, V., Shen, B., Sugden, L., Zhao, K., & Wu, M.-C. (2019). Data Platform for Machine Learning. *Proceedings of the 2019 International Conference on Management of Data*, (pp. 1803–1816). ACM. 10.1145/3299869.3314050

Aguilera, H., Guardiola-Albert, C., Naranjo-Fernández, N., & Kohfahl, C. (2019). Towards Flexible Groundwater-Level Prediction for Adaptive Water Management: Using Facebook's Prophet Forecasting Approach. *Hydrological Sciences Journal*, *64*(12), 1504–1518. doi:10.1080/02626667.2019.1651933

Ahila, Dahan, Alroobaea, Alghamdi, Mohammed, Hajjej, Alsekait, & Raahemifar. (2023). A smart IoMT based architecture for E-healthcare patient monitoring system using artificial intelligence algorithms. *Frontires-Sec. Computational Physiology and Medicine*.

Aishwarya, B., Pathak, A., & Hattiambire, S. (2021). AI Medical Chatbot. *Journal of Emerging Technologies and Innovative Research*, *8*(3), 61–64.

Aishwarya, R., & Chawla, V. (2020). Chatbots in Marketing - A morphology of literature. *Proceedings of the European Marketing Academy*, *64187*, 1–11.

Akarsh, Sahoo, & Raj. (n.d.). *Privacy preserving Federated Learning framework for IoMT based big data analysis using edge computing*. Academic Press.

Akrivopoulos, O., Amaxilatis, D., Antoniou, A., & Chatzigiannakis, I. (2017). Design and Evaluation of a Person-Centric Heart Monitoring System over Fog Computing Infrastructure. In *Proceedings of the First International Workshop on Human-centered Sensing, Networking, and SystemsHumanSys'17*. ACM. 10.1145/3144730.3144736

Akshay, S. (2019). Aswathy Rames, Ashika P, "Visual Search Capability using Heatmaps. *International Journal of Engineering and Advanced Technology*, *8*(5), 1811–1814.

Al Hamid, Rahman, Hossain, Almogren, & Alamri. (2017). A Security Model for Preserving the Privacy of Medical Big Data in a Healthcare Cloud Using a Fog Computing Facility With Pairing-Based Cryptography. *IEEE Access*, *5*, 22313-22328. doi:10.1109/ACCESS.2017.2757844

Alagiah, M., & Joseph, B. (2020). Smart Airline Baggage Tracking and Theft Prevention with Blockchain Technology. *Test Engineering and Management, 83*, 3436–3440.

Albawi, S., Mohammed, T. A., & Al-Zawi, S. (2017). Understanding of a convolutional neural network. *2017 International Conference on Engineering and Technology (ICET)*, Antalya, Turkey. 10.1109/ICEngTechnol.2017.8308186

Albersmeyer, J., & Diehl, M. (2010). The Lifted Newton Method and Its Application in Optimization. *SIAM Journal on Optimization, 20*(3), 1655–1684. doi:10.1137/080724885

Alexandros Koliousis, Ilias Katsaroumpas, Peter Pietzuch, and Vladimir Vlassov Title: "Distributed Deep Learning Using TensorFlow and Horovod" IEEE Transactions on Parallel and Distributed Systems Volume: 30 Issue: 7 Year of Publication: 2019 Pages: 1533-1545

Alexey, A. B. (n.d.). *Darknet.* Github repository. https://github.com/AlexeyAB/darknet

Alfaro, J. C., Aledo, J. A., & Gámez, J. A. (2020). *Averaging-Based Ensemble Methods for the Partial Label Ranking Problem.*, doi:10.1007/978-3-030-61705-9_34

Ali, M., Sheikh, S., & Sohail, Y. (2019). Reduction of Food Wastage through Android Application. *Make You Smile, 10*(10).

Al-kahtani, M. S., & Karim, L. (2017). An Efficient Distributed Algorithm for Big Data Processing. *Arabian Journal for Science and Engineering, 42*(8), 3149–3157. doi:10.100713369-016-2405-y

Aluminum Alloys 101. (2020). https://www.mercalloy.com/aluminum-alloys-101/

Alvarez, S. (2020). *Tesla Model Y single-piece rear casts spotted in Fremont factory.* https://www.teslarati.com/tesla-model-y-unibody-casts-sighting-video/

Alzubaidi, L., Zhang, J., Humaidi, A. J., Al-Dujaili, A., Duan, Y., Al-Shamma, O., Santamaría, J., Fadhel, M. A., Al-Amidie, M., & Farhan, L. (2021). Review of deep learning: Concepts, CNN architectures, challenges, applications, future directions. *Journal of Big Data, 8*(1), 53. doi:10.118640537-021-00444-8 PMID:33816053

Ameet Talwalkar, Virginia Smith, Michael Jordan Title: "Distributed Machine Learning: Challenges and Opportunities" Journal Name: IEEE Big Data Volume: N/A Issue: N/A Year of Publication: 2016 Pages: 1-10

Ananthi, G., Raja Sekar, J., Apsara, D., Gajalakshmi, A. K., & Tapthi, S. (2021). Enhanced Palmprint Identification Using Score Level Fusion [IJARSCT]. *International Journal of Advanced Research in Science, Communication and Technology, 4*(3), 76–81. doi:10.48175/IJARSCT-V4-I3-011

Ananthi, G., Raja Sekar, J., & Arivazhagan, S. (2022). Ensembling Scale Invariant and Multiresolution Gabor Scores for Palm Vein Identification. *Information Technology and Control, 51*(4), 704–722. doi:10.5755/j01.itc.51.4.30858

Ananthi, G., Raja Sekar, J., & Arivazhagan, S. (2022). Human palm vein authentication using curvelet multiresolution features and score level fusion. *The Visual Computer*, *38*(6), 1901–1914. doi:10.100700371-021-02253-9

Ananthi, G., Raja Sekar, J., & Lakshmipraba, N. (2018). PALM DORSAL SURFACE AND VEIN PATTERN BASED AUTHENTICATION SYSTEM. *International Journal of Pure and Applied Mathematics*, *118*(11), 767–773.

Andrade, D., & Trabasso, L. G. (2017). An OpenCL framework for high performance extraction of image features. *Journal of Parallel and Distributed Computing*, *109*, 75–88. doi:10.1016/j.jpdc.2017.05.011

Andresen, B. (2005). *Die Casting Engineering: A Hydraulic, Thermal, and Mechanical Process*. Marcel Dekker.

Androutsellis-Theotokis, S., & Spinellis, D. (2004). A survey of peer-to-peer content distribution technologies. *ACM Computing Surveys*, *36*(4), 335–371. doi:10.1145/1041680.1041681

Anwar, S. M., Majid, M., Qayyum, A., Awais, M., Alnowami, M., & Khan, M. K. (2018, November). Medical image analysis using convolutional neural networks: A review. *Journal of Medical Systems*, *42*(11), 1–13. doi:10.100710916-018-1088-1 PMID:30298337

Apparao, K. C., & Birru, A. K. (2017). Optimization of Die casting process based on Taguchi approach. *Materials Today: Proceedings*, *4*(2), 1852–1859. doi:10.1016/j.matpr.2017.02.029

Ariyo, A. A., Adewumi, A. O., & Ayo, C. K. (2014). Stock price prediction using the ARIMA model. In *2014 UKSim-AMSS 16th International Conference on Computer Modelling and Simulation* (pp. 106-112). IEEE. 10.1109/UKSim.2014.67

Arora, M., Tuchen, S., Nazemi, M., & Blessing, L. (2021). Airport Pandemic Response: An Assessment of Impacts and Strategies after One Year with COVID-19. *Transportation Research Interdisciplinary Perspectives*, *100449*, 100449. doi:10.1016/j.trip.2021.100449 PMID:34458721

Arulkumaran, K., Deisenroth, M. P., Brundage, M., & Bharath, A. A. (2017). Deep Reinforcement Learning: A Brief Survey. *IEEE Signal Processing Magazine*, *34*(6), 26–38. doi:10.1109/MSP.2017.2743240

Aziz, J. J., Ling, M., Rifai, H. S., Newell, C. J., & Gonzales, J. R. (2003). MAROS: A Decision Support System for Optimizing Monitoring Plans. *Ground Water*, *41*(3), 355–367. doi:10.1111/j.1745-6584.2003.tb02605.x

Babbar-Sebens, M., & Minsker, B. (2008). Standard Interactive Genetic Algorithm—Comprehensive Optimization Framework for Groundwater Monitoring Design. *Journal of Water Resources Planning and Management*, *134*(6), 538–547. doi:10.1061/(asce)0733-9496(2008)134:6(538)

Baby, K. (2014). *Big Data: An Ultimate Solution in Health Care*.

Badrinarayanan, V., Kendall, A., & Cipolla, R. (2017). SegNet: A Deep Convolutional Encoder-Decoder Architecture for Image Segmentation. IEEE Transactions on Pattern Analysis and Machine Intelligence, (pp. 2481-2495). IEEE. doi: . 2644615 doi:10.1109/tpami.2016

Baier, L., Johren, F., & Seebacher, S. (2019). Challenges in the deployment and operation of machine learning in practice. *Proceedings of the 27th European Conference on Information Systems (ECIS).*

Baki, T. A., Noordin, B., Mohamed, N., Idrus, S. M., & Rasid, S. Z. A. (2022). Digitalization of Airside Operations Process to Improve Airport Operations For The Case of Malaysia Airports. *2022 4th International Conference on Smart Sensors and Application (ICSSA)*, (pp. 130–134). IEEE. 10.1109/ICSSA54161.2022.9870954

Balasubramaniam, S., Kannan, S., & Shivpuri, R. (1999). *Improving the Quality in Die Casting Production Using Statistical Analysis Procedures.* Presented at the 1999 NADCA World of Die Casting, Cleveland, OH. Available: http://www.diecasting.org/archive/transactions/T99-071.pdf

Baran, P. (1962). *On Distributed Communications Networks.* RAND Corporation. doi:10.7249/P2626

Basjaruddin, N. C., Ramadhan, S., Adinugraha, F., & Kuspriyanto, K. (2019). Baggage Tracing at Airports using Near Field Communication. *2019 International Conference on Advanced Mechatronics, Intelligent Manufacture and Industrial Automation (ICAMIMIA)*, (pp. 109–113). IEEE. 10.1109/ICAMIMIA47173.2019.9223350

Batres-Estrada, B. (2015). *Deep learning for multivariate financial time series.* Academic Press.

Beheshti, N., & Johnsson, L. (2020). Squeeze U-Net: A Memory and Energy Efficient Image Segmentation Network. *IEEE/CVF Conference on Computer Vision and Pattern Recognition Workshops*, (pp. 1495-1504). IEEE. .10.1109/CVPRW50498.2020.00190

Bekeneva, Y., Petukhov, V., & Frantsisko, O. (2020). Local image processing in distributed monitoring system. *Journal of Physics: Conference Series, 1679*(3), 032048. doi:10.1088/1742-6596/1679/3/032048

Ben-Nun, T., & Hoefler, T. (2018). *Demystifying Parallel and Distributed Deep Learning: An In-Depth Concurrency Analysis* (arXiv:1802.09941). arXiv. https://arxiv.org/abs/1802.09941

Bhunia, S. S., Dhar, S. K., & Mukherjee, N. (2014). iHealth: A fuzzy approach for provisioning intelligent health-care system in smart city. *2014 IEEE 10th International Conference on Wireless and Mobile Computing, Networking and Communications (WiMob)*, 187-193.

Bischl, B., Binder, M., Lang, M., Pielok, T., Richter, J., Coors, S., Thomas, J., Ullmann, T., Becker, M., Boulesteix, A., Deng, D., & Lindauer, M. (2023). Hyperparameter optimization: Foundations, algorithms, best practices, and open challenges. *WIREs Data Mining and Knowledge Discovery, 13*(2). doi:10.1002/widm.1484

Blei, D. M. (2012). Probabilistic topic models. *Communications of the ACM, 55*(4), 77–84. doi:10.1145/2133806.2133826

Blondheim, D., Jr. (2018). *Unsupervised Machine Learning and Statistical Anomaly Detection Applied to Thermal Images.* Available: http://www.diecasting.org/archive/transactions/T18-071.pdf

Compilation of References

Blondheim, D., Jr. (2020). *Artificial Intelligence, Machine Learning, and Data Analytics: Understanding the Concepts to Find Value in Die Casting Data.* Presented at the NADCA Executive Conference, Clearwater, FL.

Boonyuen, K., Kaewprapha, P., & Srivihok, P. (2018). Daily rainfall forecast model from satellite image using Convolution neural network. *2018 International Conference on Information Technology (InCIT)*, (pp. 1–7). IEEE. 10.23919/INCIT.2018.8584886

Box, G. E., Jenkins, G. M., Reinsel, G. C., & Ljung, G. M. (2015). Time series analysis, control, and forecasting. Academic Press.

Bulat, A., & Tzimiropoulos, G. (2020). Hierarchical Binary CNNs for Landmark Localization with Limited Resources. *IEEE Transactions on Pattern Analysis And Machine Intelligence*, (pp. 343-356). IEEE. doi: . 2018.2866051. doi:10.1109/tpami

Byrd, R. H., Hansen, S. L., Nocedal, J., & Singer, Y. (2016). A Stochastic Quasi-Newton Method for Large-Scale Optimization. *SIAM Journal on Optimization*, *26*(2), 1008–1031. doi:10.1137/140954362

Cai, W., Jin, Y., & Chen, L. (2022). Task-Oriented User Evaluation on Critiquing-Based Recommendation Chatbots. *IEEE Transactions on Human-Machine Systems*, *52*(3), 354–366. doi:10.1109/THMS.2021.3131674

CaiZ.ChenA.LuoY.LiJ. T. "Communication-Efficient Distributed Stochastic Gradient Descent with Pooling Operator" Journal name:SSRN Year of Publication: 2023

Capozzi, S. L., Rodenburg, L. A., Krumins, V., Fennell, D. E., & Erin Mack, E. (2018). Using Positive Matrix Factorization to Investigate Microbial Dehalogenation of Chlorinated Benzenes in Groundwater at a Historically Contaminated Site. *Chemosphere*, *211*(November), 515–523. doi:10.1016/j.chemosphere.2018.07.180

Castro, D., Hickson, S., & Bettadapura, V. (2015). Predicting Daily Activities from Egocentric Images Using Deep Learning. In *Proceedings of the 2015 ACM International Symposium on Wearable ComputersISWC '15*. ACM. 10.1145/2802083.2808398

Cha, J., & Lee, J.-H. (2018). Extracting Topic Related Keywords by Backtracking CNN based Text Classifier. *2018 Joint 10th International Conference on Soft Computing and Intelligent Systems (SCIS) and 19th International Symposium on Advanced Intelligent Systems* (ISIS), (pp. 93-96). IEEE.

Chapman, S. W., & Parker, B. L. (2005). Plume Persistence Due to Aquitard Back Diffusion Following Dense Nonaqueous Phase Liquid Source Removal or Isolation. *Water Resources Research*, *41*(12), 1–16. doi:10.1029/2005WR004224

Chen, T., Li, M., Li, Y., Lin, M., Wang, N., Wang, M., Xiao, T., Xu, B., Zhang, C., & Title, Z. Z. "MXNet: A Flexible and Efficient Machine Learning Library for Heterogeneous Distributed Systems" Journal Name: Proceedings of the 2015 ACM Symposium on Cloud Computing (SoCC '15) Volume: N/A Issue: N/A Year of Publication: 2015 Pages: 1-13

Chen, X., Girshick, R. B., He, K., & Doll, P. (2019). Tensormask: A foundation for dense object segmentation. *CoRR*, abs/1903.12174.

ChenC.-C.YangC.-L.ChengH.-Y. (2019). Efficient and Robust Parallel DNN Training through Model Parallelism on Multi-GPU Platform. *ArXiv:1809.02839 [Cs]*. https://arxiv.org/abs/1809.02839

Cheng, Y., & Feng, L. X. Z. (2018). Appearance-Based Gaze Estimation via Evaluation-Guided Asymmetric Regression. European Conference on Computer Vision, (pp. 105-121). Springer. 10.1007/978-3-030-01264-9_7

Chen, L., Papandreou, G., Kokkinos, I., Murphy, K., & Yuille, A. (2018). DeepLab: Semantic Image Segmentation with Deep Convolutional Nets, Atrous Convolution, and Fully Connected CRFs. *IEEE Transactions on Pattern Analysis and Machine Intelligence*, 40(4), 834–848. doi:10.1109/TPAMI.2017.2699184 PMID:28463186

Chen, Y., Luo, Y., Ding, Y., & Yu, B. (2018). *Automatic Colorization of Images from Chinese Black and White Films Based on CNN. 2018 International Conference on Audio, Language and Image Processing (ICALIP)*, Shanghai, China. 10.1109/ICALIP.2018.8455654

Cherry, J. A., & Freeze, R. A. (1979). *Groundwater*. Prentice Hall.

Cheung, Y., & Peng, Q. (2015). Eye Gaze Tracking with a Web Camera in a Desktop Environment. *IEEE Transactions on Human-Machine Systems*, 45(4), 419–430. doi:10.1109/THMS.2015.2400442

Chi, J., Wang, D., Lu, N., & Wang, Z. (2020). Cornea Radius Calibration for Remote 3D Gaze Tracking Systems. *IEEE Access : Practical Innovations, Open Solutions*, 8, 187634–187647. doi:10.1109/ACCESS.2020.3029300

Chinedu W.O., & Abejide, A.I.(2021). Chatbots applications in education: A systematic review. *Computers and Education: Artificial Intelligence*, 2, 1-10.

Choi, I.-H., Kim, Y. G., & Tran, T. B. H. (2016). *Real-time categorization of driver's gaze zone and head pose - using the convolutional neural network*. Proc. HCI Korea, Korea.

Clearwater, S. H., Cheng, T.-P., Hirsh, H., & Buchanan, B. G. (1989). INCREMENTAL BATCH LEARNING. In *Proceedings of the Sixth International Workshop on Machine Learning* (pp. 366–370). Elsevier. 10.1016/B978-1-55860-036-2.50093-X

Correia, Alencar, & Assis. (2023). Stochastic modeling and analysis of the energy consumption of wireless sensor networks. *IEEE Xplore*.

Cui, H., Zhang, H., Ganger, G. R., Gibbons, P. B., & Xing, E. P. (2016). GeePS. *Proceedings of the Eleventh European Conference on Computer Systems*, (pp. 1–16). ACM. 10.1145/2901318.2901323

Dai, J., Wang, Y., Qiu, X., Ding, D., Zhang, Y., Wang, Y., Jia, X., Zhang, C., Wan, Y., Li, Z., Wang, J., Huang, S., Wu, Z., Wang, Y., Yang, Y., She, B., Shi, D., Lu, Q., Huang, K., & Song, G. (2019). BigDL: A Distributed Deep Learning Framework for Big Data. *Proceedings of the ACM Symposium on Cloud Computing*, (pp. 50–60). ACM. 10.1145/3357223.3362707

Darius, Z., & Sophie, H. (2018). Chatbots – An Interactive Technology for Personalized Communication, Transactions and Services. *IADIS International Journal*, *15*(1), 96–109.

De Gooijer, J. G., & Hyndman, R. J. (2006). 25 years of time series forecasting. *International Journal of Forecasting*, *22*(3), 443–473. doi:10.1016/j.ijforecast.2006.01.001

Dean, J., Corrado, G. S., Monga, R., Chen, K., Devin, M., Le, Q. V., Mao, M. Z., Ranzato, M., Senior, A., Tucker, P., Yang, K., & Ng, A. Y. (n.d.). *Large Scale Distributed Deep Networks*. 11.

Dean, J., Corrado, G., Monga, R., Chen, K., Devin, M., & Mao, M. Marc'Aurelio Ranzato, Andrew Senior, Paul Tucker, Ke Yang, Quoc V. Le, and Andrew Y. Ng Title: "DistBelief: A Framework for Distributed Deep Learning" Journal Name: Proceedings of the 26th International Conference on Neural Information Processing Systems (NIPS '12) Volume: N/A Issue: N/A Year of Publication: 2012 Pages: 1-9

Dean, J., & Ghemawat, S. (2008). MapReduce. *Communications of the ACM*, *51*(1), 107–113. doi:10.1145/1327452.1327492

Devadoss, A.V. & Ligori, T.A.A. (2013). Forecasting of stock prices using multi-layer perceptron. *International Journal of Computing Algorithm, 2*, 440-449.

Dike, H. U., Zhou, Y., Deveerasetty, K. K., & Wu, Q. (2018). Unsupervised Learning Based On Artificial Neural Network: A Review. *2018 IEEE International Conference on Cyborg and Bionic Systems (CBS)*, (pp. 322–327). IEEE. 10.1109/CBS.2018.8612259

Distributed training with TensorFlow . (n.d.). TensorFlow Core. https://www.tensorflow.org/guide/distributed_training

Divya Gupta, Bhatia, & Kumar. (2021). *Resolving Data Overload and Latency Issues in Multivariate Time-Series IoMT Data for Mental Health Monitoring*. IEEE.

Doehler, H. H. (1951). *Die Casting*. McGraw-Hill Book Company.

Dubey, S. R., Singh, S. K., & Chaudhuri, B. B. (2022, September). Activation functions in deep learning: A comprehensive survey and benchmark. *Neurocomput.*, *503*(C), 92–108. doi:10.1016/j.neucom.2022.06.111

Elder, Benson, & Eykholt. (2002). Effects of Heterogeneity on Influent and Effluent Concentrations from Horizontal Permeable Reactive Barriers. *Water Resources Research, 38*(8), 27-1-27–19. https://doi.org/. doi:10.1029/2001wr001259

Elmisery, Rho, & Botvich. (2016). A Fog Based Middleware for Automated Compliance With OECD Privacy Principles in Internet of Healthcare Things. *IEEE Access, 4*, 8418-8441. doi:10.1109/ACCESS.2016.2631546

Faragardi HR. Title: Ethical Considerations in Cloud Computing Systems. Journal name: Proceedings. Year of Publication: 2017

Farki, A., & Noughabi, E. A. (2023). Real-Time Blood Pressure Prediction Using Apache Spark and Kafka Machine Learning. *2023 9th International Conference on Web Research (ICWR)*, 161–166. 10.1109/ICWR57742.2023.10138962

Farrell, D. M., Minsker, B. S., Tcheng, D., Searsmith, D., Bohn, J., & Beckman, D. (2007). Data Mining to Improve Management and Reduce Costs of Environmental Remediation. *Journal of Hydroinformatics*, 9(2), 107–121. doi:10.2166/hydro.2007.004

Fei, L., Zhang, B., Zhang, W., & Teng, S. (2019). Local apparent and latent direction extraction for palmprint recognition. Elsevier on Information science, 473, 59-72. doi:10.1016/j.ins.2018.09.032

Folk, J. (2019). U.S. Aluminum Casting Industry – 2019. *Die Casting Engineer*, 16–19. Available: https://www.diecasting.org/archive/dce/71916.pdf

Forrest, N. (2017). *Iandola, Song Han, Matthew W. Moskewicz, Khalid Ashraf, William J. Dally, Kurt Keutzer, "Squeezenet: Alexnet-Level Accuracy with 50x fewer parameters and <0.5mb Model Size*. ICLR.

Foster, I., & Iamnitchi, A. (2003). *On Death*. Taxes, and the Convergence of Peer-to-Peer and Grid Computing. doi:10.1007/978-3-540-45172-3_11

Fratu, O., Pena, C., Craciunescu, R., & Halunga, S. (2015). Fog computing system for monitoring Mild Dementia and COPD patients - Romanian case study. *2015 12th International Conference on Telecommunication in Modern Satellite, Cable and Broadcasting Services (TELSIKS)*, 123-128.

Fukushima, K. (1980, April). Neocognitron: A self-organizing neural network model for a mechanism of pattern recognition unaffected by shift in position. *Biological Cybernetics*, 36(4), 193–202. doi:10.1007/BF00344251 PMID:7370364

Fydanaki, A., & Geradts, Z. (2018). Evaluating OpenFace: An open-source automatic facial comparison algorithm for forensics. *Forensic Sciences Research*, 3(3), 202–209. doi:10.1080/2 0961790.2018.1523703 PMID:30483670

Garcia-Martin, E., Rodrigues, C. F., Riley, G., & Grahn, H. (2019, December). Estimation of energy consumption I machine learning -. *Journal of Parallel and Distributed Computing*, 134, 75–88. doi:10.1016/j.jpdc.2019.07.007

Genovese, A., Piuri, A., Scotti, V., & Plataniotis, F. (). PalmNet: gabor-PCA convolutional networks for touchless palmprint recognition. *IEEE transaction on Information Forensic and Security, 14,* 3160 - 3174.

Ghoting, A., Krishnamurthy, R., Pednault, E., Reinwald, B., Sindhwani, V., Tatikonda, S., Tian, Y., & Vaithyanathan, S. (2011). SystemML: Declarative machine learning on MapReduce. *2011 IEEE 27th International Conference on Data Engineering*, (pp. 231–242). IEEE. 10.1109/ICDE.2011.5767930

Giri, D., Obaidat, M. S., & Maitra, T. (2017). SecHealth: An Efficient Fog Based Sender Initiated Secure Data Transmission of Healthcare Sensors for e-Medical System. *GLOBECOM 2017 - 2017 IEEE Global Communications Conference*, 1-6.

Gleick, P. H. (1993). *Water in Crisis: A Guide to the World's Fresh Water Resources*. Environment Pacific Institute for Studies in Development, and Stockholm Environment Institute.

Gong, Y.-J., Chen, W.-N., Zhan, Z.-H., Zhang, J., Li, Y., Zhang, Q., & Li, J.-J. (2015). Distributed evolutionary algorithms and their models: A survey of the state-of-the-art. *Applied Soft Computing*, *34*, 286–300. doi:10.1016/j.asoc.2015.04.061

Goodfellow, I., Bengio, Y., Courville, A., & Bengio, Y. (2016). Deep learning: Vol. 1. *No. 2*. MIT Press.

Gropp, W., Lusk, E., Doss, N., & Skjellum, A. (1996). A high-performance, portable implementation of the MPI message passing interface standard. *Parallel Computing*, *22*(6), 789–828. doi:10.1016/0167-8191(96)00024-5

Gu, J., Liu, S., Zhou, Z., Chalov, S. R., & Zhuang, Q. (2022). A Stacking Ensemble Learning Model for Monthly Rainfall Prediction in the Taihu Basin, China. *Water (Basel)*, *14*(3), 492. doi:10.3390/w14030492

Haidar, A., & Verma, B. (2018). Monthly Rainfall Forecasting Using One-Dimensional Deep Convolutional Neural Network. *IEEE Access : Practical Innovations, Open Solutions*, *6*, 69053–69063. doi:10.1109/ACCESS.2018.2880044

Han, Q., McClure, D., Wood, D., & Yang, D. (2017). Statistical Analysis of the Effect of Operational Parameters on the Scrap Rates of Crossmember Casting. *Die Casting Engineer*, 38–43. Available: http://www.diecasting.org/archive/dce/111738.pdf

Han, S., Mao, H., & Dally Title, W. J. "Exploring Hidden Dimensions in Parallelizing Convolutional Neural Networks" Journal Name: Proceedings of the 2016 ACM International Conference on Multimedia (MM '16) Volume: N/A Issue: N/A Year of Publication: 2016 Pages: 689-698

Harini, S., & Ravikumar, A. (2020). Effect of Parallel Workload on Dynamic Voltage Frequency Scaling for Dark Silicon Ameliorating. *2020 International Conference on Smart Electronics and Communication (ICOSEC)*, (pp. 1012–1017). IEEE. 10.1109/ICOSEC49089.2020.9215262

Harini, S., Ravikumar, A., & Keshwani, N. (2022). Malware Prediction Analysis Using AI Techniques with the Effective Preprocessing and Dimensionality Reduction. In J. S. Raj, K. Kamel, & P. Lafata (Eds.), *Innovative Data Communication Technologies and Application* (pp. 153–169). Springer Nature Singapore. doi:10.1007/978-981-16-7167-8_12

Hassanpour, M., & Malek, H. (2020). Learning Document Image Features with SqueezeNet Convolutional Neural Network. *International Journal of Engineering*, *33*(7). doi:10.5829/ije.2020.33.07a.05

Hazratifard, Gebali, & Mamun. (2022). Using Machine Learning for Dynamic Authentication in Telehealth: A Tutorial. *Sensors*, *22*(19).

Heaton, J. B., Polson, N. G., & Witte, J. H. (2016). Deep learning in finance. *arXiv preprint arXiv:1602.06561.*

He, K., Zhang, X., Ren, S., & Sun, J. (2016). Deep residual learning for image recognition. In *The IEEE Conference on Computer Vision and Pattern Recognition (CVPR).*

Herman, E. A. (2012). *Die Casting Process Control E-410.* North American Die Casting Association.

Herman, E. A., & Kirkman, J. S. (2011). *Designing Die Casting Dies Series - E-506.* North American Die Casting Association.

How the pytorch freeze network in some layers, only the rest of the training ? (2019, February 26). PyTorch Forums. https://discuss.pytorch.org/t/how-the-pytorch-freeze-network-in-some-layers-only-the-rest-of-the-training/7088?page=2

Hsu, Q.-C., & Do, A. T. (2013). Minimum Porosity Formation in Pressure Die Casting by Taguchi Method. *Mathematical Problems in Engineering, 2013,* 1–9. doi:10.1155/2013/920865

Hubel, D. H., & Wiesel, T. N. (1968). Receptive fields and functional architecture of monkey striate cortex. *The Journal of Physiology, 195*(1), 215–243. doi:10.1113/jphysiol.1968.sp008455 PMID:4966457

Hung, P. D., Hanh, T. D., & Diep, V. T. (2018). Breast Cancer Prediction Using Spark MLlib and ML Packages. *Proceedings of the 2018 5th International Conference on Bioinformatics Research and Applications,* (pp. 52–59). ACM. 10.1145/3309129.3309133

InamdarM.MehendaleN. (2020). Real-time face mask identification using facemasknet deep learning network. Available at SSRN 3663305. doi:10.2139/ssrn.3663305

Jain, H., & Jain, R. (2017). Big data in weather forecasting: Applications and challenges. *2017 International Conference on Big Data Analytics and Computational Intelligence (ICBDAC),* (pp. 138–142). IEEE. 10.1109/ICBDACI.2017.8070824

Jamshidi, Moztarzadeh, Jamshid, Abdelgawad, & Hauer. (2023). Future of Drug Discovery: The Synergy of Edge Computing, Internet of Medical Things, and Deep Learning. *Internet of Things and Internet of Everything: Current Trends, Challenges, and New Perspectives.*

Jason Dai, Ding Ding, Dongjie Shi, Shengsheng Huang, Jiao Wang, Xin Qiu, Kai Huang, Guoqiong Song, Yang Wang, Qiyuan Gong, Jiaming Song, Shan Yu, Le Zheng, Yina Chen, Junwei Deng, Ge Song Title: BigDL 2.0: Seamless Scaling of AI Pipelines from Laptops to Distributed Cluster, Journal name: arXiv Volume:2204.01715 Year of Publication:2022

Jeroen G. S. Overschie, Ahmad Alsahaf and George Azzopardi, " fseval: A Benchmarking Framework for Feature Selection and Feature Ranking Algorithms, Journal of Open Source software,Volume:7(79) Year of Publication: 2023

Ji Liu, Zhihua Wu, Danlei Feng, Minxu Zhang, Xinxuan Wu, Xuefeng Yao, Dianhai Yu, Yanjun Ma, Feng Zhao and Dejing Dou Title:"HeterPS: Distributed deep learning with reinforcement learning based scheduling in heterogeneous environments" Journal name:Future Generation Computer Systems,Volume:148,Year of Publication:2023,Pages 106-117

Jia, H. (2016). Investigation into the effectiveness of long short-term memory networks for stock price prediction. *arXiv preprint arXiv:1603.07893.*

Jiang, Guo, Khan, Cui, & Lin. (2023). *Energy-saving Service Offloading for the Internet of Medical Things Using Deep Reinforcement Learning.* ACM.

Jia, W., Hu, R.-X., Lei, Y.-K., Zhao, Y., & Gui, J. (2014). Histogram of oriented lines for palmprint recognition. *IEEE Transactions on Systems, Man, and Cybernetics, 44*(3), 385–395. doi:10.1109/TSMC.2013.2258010

Jia, X., He, D., Kumar, N., & Choo, K. K. R. (2018). Authenticated key agreement scheme for fog-driven IoT healthcare system. *Wireless Networks.* Advance online publication. doi:10.100711276-018-1759-3

Ji, G., & Ling, X. (n.d.). Ensemble Learning Based Distributed Clustering. In *Emerging Technologies in Knowledge Discovery and Data Mining* (pp. 312–321). Springer Berlin Heidelberg. doi:10.1007/978-3-540-77018-3_32

Jignesh Chowdary, G., Punn, N. S., Sonbhadra, S. K., & Agarwal, S. (2020, December). Face mask detection using transfer learning of inceptionv3. In *International Conference on Big Data Analytics* (pp. 81-90). Springer. 10.1007/978-3-030-66665-1_6

Jimenez-Perez, G. (2019). *Alejandro Alcaine, Oscar Camara, "U-Net Architecture for the Automatic Detection and Delineation of the Electrocardiogram* (Vol. 46). Computing in Cardiology.

Jin, Y. (2022, January 19). Surveillance, security, and AI as technological acceptance. *AI & Society.* doi:10.100700146-021-01331-9

John, J., Ravikumar, A., & Abraham, B. (2021). Prostate cancer prediction from multiple pretrained computer vision model. *Health and Technology, 11*(5), 1003–1011. doi:10.100712553-021-00586-y

Jovanovic, M., Baez, M., & Casati, F. (2021). Chatbots as Conversational Healthcare Services. *IEEE Internet Computing, 25*(3), 44–51. doi:10.1109/MIC.2020.3037151

Kaelbling, L. P., Littman, M. L., & Moore, A. W. (1996). Reinforcement Learning: A Survey. *Journal of Artificial Intelligence Research, 4*, 237–285. doi:10.1613/jair.301

Kannan, V., Vijaykumar, N., & Title, G. J. "Towards Distributed Training of Deep Learning Models on Heterogeneous Computing Platforms" Journal Name: *Proceedings of the 33rd IEEE International Parallel and Distributed Processing Symposium Workshops (IPDPSW '19),* 2019, Pages: 1109-1116

Kazi, S., Bagasrawala, M., Shaikh, F., & Sayyed, A. (2018). Smart E-Ticketing System for Public Transport Bus. *2018 International Conference on Smart City and Emerging Technology (ICSCET).* (pp. 1-7). IEEE. 10.1109/ICSCET.2018.8537302

Kebira Azbeg, Ouchetto, & Andaloussi. (2022). *BlockMedCare: A healthcare system based on IoT, Blockchain and IPFS for data management security.* Elsevier B.V.

Khandelwal, P., Khandelwal, A., Agarwal, S., Thomas, D., Xavier, N., & Raghuraman, A. (2020). Using computer vision to enhance safety of workforce in manufacturing in a post covid world. arXiv preprint arXiv:2005.05287.

Khan, M. J., Yousaf, A., Abbas, A., & Khurshid, K. (2018). Deep learning for automated forgery detection in hyperspectral document images. *Journal of Electronic Imaging*, *27*(5), 053001. doi:10.1117/1.JEI.27.5.053001

Khan, N., & Efthymiou, M. (2021). The use of biometric technology at airports: The case of customs and border protection (CBP). *International Journal of Information Management Data Insights*, *1*(2), 100049. doi:10.1016/j.jjimei.2021.100049

Kong, A., Zhang, D., & Kamel, M. (2006). Palmprint identification using feature-level fusion. *Science Direct*, *39*(3), 478–487.

Kováčiková, K., Remencová, T., Sedláčková, A. N., & Novák, A. (2022). The impact of Covid-19 on the digital transformation of the airports. *Transportation Research Procedia*, *64*, 84–89. doi:10.1016/j.trpro.2022.09.011

Krizhevsky, A., Sutskever, I., & Hinton, G. E. (2012). Imagenet classification with deep convolu- tional neural networks. In F. Pereira, C. J. C. Burges, L. Bottou, & K. Q. Weinberger (Eds.), Advances in Neural Information Processing Systems (Vol. 25, pp. 1097–1105). Curran Associates, Inc.

Kulkarni, C. S. (2017). Bank Chat Bot–An intelligent assistant system using NLP and machine learning. *International Research Journal of Engineering and Technology*, *4*(5), 2374–2377.

Kumar, A., Kalia, A., & Kalia, A. (2022). ETL-YOLO v4: A face mask detection algorithm in era of COVID-19 pandemic. *Optik (Stuttgart)*, *259*, 169051. doi:10.1016/j.ijleo.2022.169051 PMID:35411120

Kumar, A., Kalia, A., Sharma, A., & Kaushal, M. (2021). A hybrid tiny YOLO v4-SPP module based improved face mask detection vision system. *Journal of Ambient Intelligence and Humanized Computing*, 1–14. PMID:34691278

Kumar, A., Kalia, A., Verma, K., Sharma, A., & Kaushal, M. (2021). Scaling up face masks detection with YOLO on a novel dataset. *Optik (Stuttgart)*, *239*, 166744. doi:10.1016/j.ijleo.2021.166744

Kwon, D., Kim, H., Kim, J., Suh, S. C., Kim, I., & Kim, K. J. (2019). A survey of deep learning-based network anomaly detection. *Cluster Computing*, *22*(S1), 949–961. doi:10.100710586-017-1117-8

Lahiri, A., Agarwalla, A., & Biswas, P. K. (2018). Unsupervised Domain Adaptation for Learning Eye Gaze from a Million Synthetic Images. *11th Indian Conference on Computer Vision, Graphics and Image Processing*. ACM. . 3293423, 2018.10.1145/3293353.3293423

Landry, J., Maltais, J., Deschênes, J.-M., Petro, M., Godmaire, X., & Fraser, A. (2018). *Inline Integration of Shotblast Resistant Laser Marking in a Die Cast Cell*. Available: https://www.diecasting.org/archive/transactions/T18-123.pdf

Lecun, Y., Bottou, L., Bengio, Y., & Haffner, P. (1998, November). Gradient-based learning applied to document recognition. *Proceedings of the IEEE, 86*(11), 2278–2324. doi:10.1109/5.726791

Lee, C. (2018). Automatic Question Generation from Children's Stories for Companion Chatbot. *IEEE International Conference on Information Reuse and Integration*, (pp. 491-494). IEEE. 10.1109/IRI.2018.00078

Lemley, J., Kar, A., Drimbarean, A., & Corcoran, P. (2019). Convolutional Neural Network Implementation for Eye- Gaze Estimation on Low-Quality Consumer Imaging Systems. *IEEE Transactions on Consumer Electronics,* (pp. 179-187). IEEE. doi: . 2019.2899869. doi:10.1109/tce

Leu, J.-S., Su, K.-W., & Chen, C.-T. (2014). Ambient mesoscale weather forecasting system featuring mobile augmented reality. *Multimedia Tools and Applications, 72*(2), 1585–1609. doi:10.100711042-013-1462-4

Levitin, G., & Dai, Y.-S. (2007). Service reliability and performance in grid system with star topology. *Reliability Engineering & System Safety, 92*(1), 40–46. doi:10.1016/j.ress.2005.11.005

Li, M., Andersen, D. G., Smola, A., & Title, K. Y. "Scaling Distributed Machine Learning with the Parameter Server" Journal Name: Proceedings of the 11th USENIX Symposium on Operating Systems Design and Implementation (OSDI '14) Volume: N/A Issue: N/A Year of Publication: 2014 Pages: 583-598

Li, M., Zhou, L., Yang, Z., Li, A., Xia, F., Andersen, D. G., & Smola, A. (n.d.). *Parameter Server for Distributed Machine Learning*. 10.

Li, S., Ning, X., Yu, L., Zhang, L., Dong, X., Shi, Y., & He, W. (2020, May). Multi-angle head pose classification when wearing the mask for face recognition under the COVID-19 coronavirus epidemic. In *2020 international conference on high performance big data and intelligent systems (HPBD&IS)*, (pp. 1-5). IEEE.

Liang Shen, Zhihua Wu, WeiBao Gong, Hongxiang Hao, Yangfan Bai, HuaChao Wu, Xinxuan Wu, Jiang Bian, Haoyi Xiong, Dianhai Yu, Yanjun Ma Title:"SE-MOE: A Scalable And Efficient Mixture-Of-Experts Distributed Training And Inference System" Journal name: arXiv Volume:2205.10034 Year of Publication:2023

Li, M. (2014). Scaling Distributed Machine Learning with the Parameter Server. *Proceedings of the 2014 International Conference on Big Data Science and Computing - BigDataScience '14*. ACM. 10.1145/2640087.2644155

Lin, G. (2016). RefineNet: Multi-Path Refinement Networks for High-Resolution Semantic Segmentation. arXiv:1611.06612.

Lin, J. T., Shih, P.-H., Huang, E., & Chiu, C.-C. (2015). Airport baggage handling system simulation modeling using SysML. *2015 International Conference on Industrial Engineering and Operations Management (IEOM)*, (pp. 1–10). IEEE. 10.1109/IEOM.2015.7093764

Lin, M.-S., Chang, M.-S., Chen, D.-J., & Ku, K.-L. (2001). The distributed program reliability analysis on ring-type topologies. *Computers & Operations Research*, 28(7), 625–635. doi:10.1016/S0305-0548(99)00151-3

Liu, S., Qi, L., Qin, H., Shi, J., & Jia, J. (2018). Path aggregation network for instance segmentation. *CoRR*, abs/1803.01534.

Liu, Xu, Z., Sun, C., Wang, B., Wang, X., Wong, D. F., & Zhang, M. (2017). Content-oriented user modeling for personalized response ranking in chatbots. *IEEE/ACM Transactions on Audio, Speech, and Language Processing*, 26(1), 122–133. doi:10.1109/TASLP.2017.2763243

Liu, Y., & Kumar, A. (2020). Contactless palmprint identification using deeply learned residual features. *IEEE Transaction on Biometric, Behavior and Identity Science*, 2(2), 172–181. doi:10.1109/TBIOM.2020.2967073

Li, X., Yuen, K. F., Wang, X., & Wong, Y. D. (2021). Contactless technologies adoption during the coronavirus pandemic: A combined technology acceptance and health belief perspective. *Technology Analysis and Strategic Management*, 1–14. doi:10.1080/09537325.2021.1988919

Loey, M., Manogaran, G., Taha, M. H. N., & Khalifa, N. E. M. (2021a). A hybrid deep transfer learning model with machine learning methods for face mask detection in the era of the COVID-19 pandemic. *Measurement*, 167, 108288. doi:10.1016/j.measurement.2020.108288 PMID:32834324

Loey, M., Manogaran, G., Taha, M. H. N., & Khalifa, N. E. M. (2021b). Fighting against COVID-19: A novel deep learning model based on YOLO-v2 with ResNet-50 for medical face mask detection. *Sustainable Cities and Society*, 65, 102600. doi:10.1016/j.scs.2020.102600 PMID:33200063

Lu, F., Gao, Y., & Chen, X. (2016). Estimating 3D Gaze Directions Using Unlabeled Eye Images via Synthetic Iris Appearance Fitting. *IEEE Transactions on Multimedia*, 18(9), 1772–1782. doi:10.1109/TMM.2016.2576284

Lu, G., Zhang, D., & Wang, K. (2003). Palmprint recognition using eigen palms features. *Pattern Recognition Letters*, 24(9-10), 1463–1467. doi:10.1016/S0167-8655(02)00386-0

Madhu, D. (2017). A novel approach for medical assistance using trained chatbot. *International Conference on Inventive Communication and Computational Technologies*, (pp. 243-246). IEEE. 10.1109/ICICCT.2017.7975195

Maggiori, E., Tarabalka, Y., Charpiat, G., & Alliez, P. (2017, February). Convolutional neural networks for large-scale remote-sensing image classification. *IEEE Transactions on Geoscience and Remote Sensing*, 55(2), 645–657. doi:10.1109/TGRS.2016.2612821

Mahenge, S. F., Wambura, S., & Jiao, L. (2022). *RCNN-GAN: An Enhanced Deep Learning Approach Towards Detection of Road Cracks*. In 2022 The 6th International Conference on Compute and Data Analysis (ICCDA 2022). Association for Computing Machinery, New York, NY, USA. 10.1145/3523089.3523104

Marita, S. (2021). My Chatbot Companion- a Study of Human-Chatbot Relationships. *International Journal of Human-Computer Studies*, 149, 102601. doi:10.1016/j.ijhcs.2021.102601

Martinez, Monton, Vilajosana, & Prades. (2015). Modeling power consumption for IoT devices. *IEEE Xplore*.

Massaro, A., & Rossetti, S. (2021). Comparing proximity for couples of close airports. Case studies on city-airports in the pre COVID-19 era. *Journal of Air Transport Management, 91*, 101977. doi:10.1016/j.jairtraman.2020.101977

Matkowski, W.M., Chai, T., Kong, A.W.K. (2020). Palmprint recognition in uncontrolled and uncooperative environment. *IEEE transaction on Information Forensic and Security, 15*, 1601 – 1615.

Ma, X., Yao, T., Hu, M., Dong, Y., Liu, W., Wang, F., & Liu, J. (2019). A Survey on Deep Learning Empowered IoT Applications. *IEEE Access : Practical Innovations, Open Solutions, 7*, 181721–181732. doi:10.1109/ACCESS.2019.2958962

Melesse, D., Khalil, M., Kagabo, E., Ning, T., & Huang, K. (2020). Appearance-Based Gaze Tracking Through Supervised Machine Learning. 15th IEEE International Conference on Signal Processing, (pp. 467-471). IEEE. . 9321075, 2020.10.1109/ICSP48669.2020.9321075

Menon, V. K., Vasireddy, N. C., Jami, S. A., Pedamallu, V. T. N., Sureshkumar, V., & Soman, K. P. (2016, June). Bulk price forecasting using spark over nse data set. In *International Conference on Data Mining and Big Data* (pp. 137-146). Springer. 10.1007/978-3-319-40973-3_13

Midson, S. (2014). Report on the 2014 Die Casting Benchmarking Survey Part 2 of 3: Operations. In *Report on the 2014 Die Casting Benchmarking Survey*. North American Die Casting Association.

Ming Zhou, Ziyu Wan, Hanjing Wang, Muning Wen, Runzhe Wu, Ying Wen, Yaodong Yang, Weinan Zhang, Jun Wang Title:"MALib: A Parallel Framework for Population-based Multi-agent Reinforcement Learning", Journal name: arXiv Volume:2106.07551 Year of Publication:2022

Mohindru, G., Mondal, K., & Banka, H. (2022). Performance Analysis of Software Enabled Accelerator Library for Intel Architecture (pp. 465–472). doi:10.1007/978-981-16-3690-5_40

Mondal, P., Shit, L., & Goswami, S. (2014). Study of effectiveness of time series modeling (ARIMA) in forecasting stock prices. *International Journal of Computer Science. Engineering and Applications, 4*(2), 13.

Mudasir Khan, Shah, Khan, ul Islam, Ahmad, Khan, & Lee. (2023). IoMT-Enabled Computer-Aided Diagnosis of Pulmonary Embolism from Computed Tomography Scans Using Deep Learning. *Artificial Intelligence and Advances in Smart IoT*.

N, R., S, S., & S, K. (2016). Comparison of Decision Tree Based Rainfall Prediction Model with Data Driven Model Considering Climatic Variables. *Irrigation & Drainage Systems Engineering, 05*(03). doi:10.4172/2168-9768.1000175

NADCA Product Specification Standards for Die Casting. (2018). 10th ed.). North American Die Casting Association.

Nagrath, P., Jain, R., Madan, A., Arora, R., Kataria, P., & Hemanth, J. (2021). SSDMNV2: A real time DNN-based face mask detection system using single shot multibox detector and MobileNetV2. *Sustainable Cities and Society*, *66*, 102692. doi:10.1016/j.scs.2020.102692 PMID:33425664

Naqvi, R., Arsalan, M., Batchuluun, G., Yoon, H., & Park, K. (2018). Deep learning-based gaze detection system for automobile drivers using a NIR camera sensor. *Sensors (Basel)*, *18*(2), 456. doi:10.339018020456 PMID:29401681

Natarajan, Lokesh, Flammini, Premkumar, Venkatesan, & Gupta. (2023). *A Novel Framework on Security and Energy Enhancement Based on Internet of Medical Things for Healthcare 5.0*. MDPI.

Nazli Tekin, Axar, Aris, Uluagac, & Gungor. (2023). *Energy consumption of on-device machine learning models for IoT intrusion detection*. Elsevier.

Nelson, D. M., Pereira, A. C., & de Oliveira, R. A. (2017, May). Stock market's price movement prediction with LSTM neural networks. In *2017 International joint conference on neural networks (IJCNN)* (pp. 1419-1426). IEEE. 10.1109/IJCNN.2017.7966019

Neumeyer, L., Robbins, B., Nair, A., & Kesari, A. (2010). S4: Distributed Stream Computing Platform. *2010 IEEE International Conference on Data Mining Workshops*, (pp. 170–177). IEEE. 10.1109/ICDMW.2010.172

Noh, H., Hong, S., & Han, B. (2015). Learning deconvolution network for semantic segmentation. *CoRR*. abs/1505.04366.

Opitz, D. W., & Maclin, R. F. (n.d.). An empirical evaluation of bagging and boosting for artificial neural networks. *Proceedings of International Conference on Neural Networks (ICNN'97)*, (pp. 1401–1405). IEEE. 10.1109/ICNN.1997.613999

Orriols-Puig, A., Casillas, J., & Bernado-Mansilla, E. (2009). Fuzzy-UCS: A Michigan-Style Learning Fuzzy-Classifier System for Supervised Learning. *IEEE Transactions on Evolutionary Computation*, *13*(2), 260–283. doi:10.1109/TEVC.2008.925144

Peteiro-Barral, D., & Guijarro-Berdiñas, B. (2013). A survey of methods for distributed machine learning. *Progress in Artificial Intelligence*, *2*(1), 1–11. doi:10.100713748-012-0035-5

Petrovic, A., Zivkovic, M., & Bačanin, D. N. (2020): Singibot - A Student Services Chatbot. *Proceedings of International Scientific Conference on Information Technology and Data Related Research*, (pp. 318-323). IEEE.

Pophale, S., Gandhi, H., & Gupta, A. K. (2021). Emotion Recognition Using Chatbot System, In: V.K. Gunjan, & J.M. Zurada (eds) *Proceedings of International Conference on Recent Trends in Machine Learning, IoT, Smart Cities and Applications. Advances in Intelligent Systems and Computing*, (pp. 1-9). IEEE.

Prabowo, Y. D. (2018). LSTM And Simple RNN Comparison In The Problem Of Sequence To Sequence On Conversation Data Using Bahasa Indonesia. *The 1st 2018 INAPR International Conference*, (pp. 51-56). IEEE.

Compilation of References

Product Design for Die Casting E-606. (2009). (6th ed., Vol. E-606). North American Die Casting Association.

Putri, L. F. O., Sudrajad, A. J., & Nastiti, V. R. S. (2022). Classification of Face Mask Detection Using Transfer Learning Model DenseNet169. *Jurnal RESTI, 6*(5), 790–796.

Qi, Chiaro, Giampaolo, & Piccialli. (2023). *A blockchain-based secure Internet of medical things framework for stress detection.* Elsevier.

Ramgopal, M., Roopesh, M. S., Chowdary, M. V., Madhav, M., & Shanmuga, K. (2023). Masked Facial Recognition in Security Systems Using Transfer Learning. *SN Computer Science, 4*(1), 1–7. PMID:36311350

Ramli, S. N., Ahmad, R., Abdollah, M. F., & Dutkiewicz, E. (2013). A biometric-based security for data authentication in Wireless Body Area Network (WBAN). *2013 15th International Conference on Advanced Communications Technology (ICACT),* 998-1001.

Ranoliya, N., Raghuwanshi, Singh. S.(2017). Chatbot for university related FAQs. *International Conference on Advances in Computing, Communications, and Informatics,* (pp. 1525-1530). ACM.

Ravikumar, A., & Sriraman, H. (2023b). Acceleration of Image Processing and Computer Vision Algorithms [Chapter]. Handbook of Research on Computer Vision and Image Processing in the Deep Learning Era. IGI Global. doi:10.4018/978-1-7998-8892-5.ch001

Ravikumar, A., & Sriraman, H. (2023a). A Novel Mixed Precision Distributed TPU GAN for Accelerated Learning Curve. *Computer Systems Science and Engineering, 46*(1), 1. doi:10.32604/csse.2023.034710

Ravikumar, A., & Sriraman, H. (2023a). Computationally Efficient Neural Rendering for Generator Adversarial Networks Using a Multi-GPU Cluster in a Cloud Environment. *IEEE Access : Practical Innovations, Open Solutions, 11,* 1–1. doi:10.1109/ACCESS.2023.3274201

Ravikumar, A., & Sriraman, H. (2023b). Attenuate Class Imbalance Problem for Pneumonia Diagnosis Using Ensemble Parallel Stacked Pre-Trained Models. *Computers. Materials & Continua, 75*(1), 1. doi:10.32604/cmc.2023.035848

Ravikumar, A., & Sriraman, H. (2023c). Real-time pneumonia prediction using pipelined spark and high-performance computing. *PeerJ. Computer Science, 9,* e1258. doi:10.7717/peerj-cs.1258 PMID:37346542

Ravikumar, A., Sriraman, H., Lokesh, S., & Maruthi Sai Saketh, P. (2023). Identifying Pitfalls and Solutions in Parallelizing Long Short-Term Memory Network on Graphical Processing Unit by Comparing with Tensor Processing Unit Parallelism. In S. Smys, K. A. Kamel, & R. Palanisamy (Eds.), *Inventive Computation and Information Technologies* (pp. 111–125). Springer Nature Singapore. doi:10.1007/978-981-19-7402-1_9

Ravikumar, A., Sriraman, H., Saketh, P. M. S., Lokesh, S., & Karanam, A. (2022). Effect of neural network structure in accelerating performance and accuracy of a convolutional neural network with GPU/TPU for image analytics. *PeerJ. Computer Science, 8,* e909. doi:10.7717/peerj-cs.909 PMID:35494877

Redmon, J., Divvala, S., Girshick, R., & Farhadi, A. (2016). You only look once: Unified, real-time object detection. In *Proceedings of the IEEE conference on computer vision and pattern recognition* (pp. 779-788). IEEE. 10.1109/CVPR.2016.91

Robin, M., John, J., & Ravikumar, A. (2021). Breast Tumor Segmentation using U-NET. *2021 5th International Conference on Computing Methodologies and Communication (ICCMC)*, 1164–1167. 10.1109/ICCMC51019.2021.9418447

Rodriguez-Martinez, I., Lafuente, J., Santiago, R. H. N., Dimuro, G. P., Herrera, F., & Bustince, H. (2022, August). Replacing pooling functions in Convolutional Neural Networks by linear combinations of increasing functions. *Neural Networks*, *152*, 380–393. doi:10.1016/j.neunet.2022.04.028 PMID:35605303

Rolim, C. O., Koch, F. L., Westphall, C. B., Werner, J., Fracalossi, A., & Salvador, G. S. (2010). A Cloud Computing Solution for Patient's Data Collection in Health Care Institutions. *2010 Second International Conference on eHealth, Telemedicine, and Social Medicine*, 95-99. 10.1109/eTELEMED.2010.19

Roondiwala, M., Patel, H., & Varma, S. (2017). Predicting stock prices using LSTM. *International Journal of Scientific Research*, *6*(4), 1754–1756.

Rossmann. (2020). The Impact of Chatbots on Customer Service Performance. In: Spohrer, J., Leitner, C. (eds) Advances in the Human Side of Service Engineering. AHFE 2020. Advances in Intelligent Systems and Computing, 1-7. Springer. doi:10.1007/978-3-030-51057-2_33

Roy, B., Nandy, S., Ghosh, D., Dutta, D., Biswas, P., & Das, T. (2020). MOXA: A deep learning based unmanned approach for real-time monitoring of people wearing medical masks. *Transactions of the Indian National Academy of Engineering*, *5*(3), 509–518. doi:10.100741403-020-00157-z

Russakovsky, O., Deng, J., Su, H., Krause, J., Satheesh, S., Ma, S., Huang, Z., Karpathy, A., Khosla, A., Bernstein, M., Berg, A. C., & Fei-Fei, L. (2015). ImageNet Large Scale Visual Recogni- tion Challenge. *International Journal of Computer Vision*, *115*(3), 211–252. doi:10.100711263-015-0816-y

S, D., & Ravikumar, A. (2015). A Study from the Perspective of Nature-Inspired Metaheuristic Optimization Algorithms. *International Journal of Computer Applications, 113*(9), 53–56. doi:10.5120/19858-1810

Salman, A., Adiono, T., Abdurrahman, I., Aditya, Y., & Chandra, Z. (2021). *Aircraft Passenger Baggage Handling System with RFID Technology.*, doi:10.1109/ISESD53023.2021.9501689

Sandha, S. S., Aggarwal, M., Fedorov, I., & Srivastava, M. Title: MANGO: A Python Library for Parallel Hyperparameter Tuning IEEE Proceedings ICASSP 2020, Year of Publication: 2021

Saravanan, Sreelatha, Atyam, Madiajagan, Saravanan, Kumar, & Sultana. (2023). Design of a deep learning model for radio resources allocation in 5G for massive IoT device. In *Sustainable energy technologies, and assessments*. Elsevier.

Sasibhooshan, R., Kumaraswamy, S., & Sasidharan, S. (2023). Image caption generation using Visual Attention Prediction and Contextual Spatial Relation Extraction. *Journal of Big Data*, *10*(1), 18. doi:10.118640537-023-00693-9

Selvin, S., Vinayakumar, R., Gopalakrishnan, E. A., Menon, V. K., & Soman, K. P. (2017, September). *Stock price prediction using LSTM, RNN and CNN-sliding window model. In 2017 international conference on advances in computing, communications and informatics (icacci).* IEEE.

Sergeev, A., & Del Balso, M. (2018). *Horovod: Fast and easy distributed deep learning in TensorFlow* (arXiv:1802.05799). arXiv. https://arxiv.org/abs/1802.05799

Sergeev, A., Del Balso, M., Johnson, M., Ramanujam, N., Wang, T., Wang, Z., & Re, C. H. "Horovod: Fast and Easy Distributed Deep Learning in TensorFlow", Proceedings of the 2018 ACM SIGMOD International Conference on Management of Data (SIGMOD '18), Year of Publication: 2018,Pages: 27-39

Shahid, N., Rappon, T., & Berta, W. (2019). Applications of artificial neural networks in health care organizational decision-making: A scoping review. *PLoS One*, *14*(2), e0212356. doi:10.1371/journal.pone.0212356 PMID:30779785

Shin, C., Lee, G., Kim, Y., Hong, J., Hong, S.-H., Kang, H., & Lee, Y. (2018). Evaluation of gaze depth estimation using a wearable binocular eye tracker and machine learning. *Journal of the Korea Computer Graphics Society*, *24*(1), 19–26.

Shin, J.-Y., Ro, Y., Cha, J.-W., Kim, K.-R., & Ha, J.-C. (2019). Assessing the Applicability of Random Forest, Stochastic Gradient Boosted Model, and Extreme Learning Machine Methods to the Quantitative Precipitation Estimation of the Radar Data: A Case Study to Gwangdeoksan Radar, South Korea, in 2018. *Advances in Meteorology*, *2019*, 1–17. doi:10.1155/2019/6542410

Siddharth. (2015). An E-Commerce Website based Chatbot. *International Journal of Computer Science and Information Technologies*, *6*(2), 1483–1485.

Simm, J., Arany, A., Zakeri, P., Haber, T., Wegner, J. K., Chupakhin, V., Ceulemans, H., & Moreau, Y. (2017). Macau: Scalable Bayesian factorization with high-dimensional side information using MCMC. *2017 IEEE 27th International Workshop on Machine Learning for Signal Processing (MLSP)*, (pp. 1–6). IEEE. 10.1109/MLSP.2017.8168143

Simonyan K. & Zisserman, A. (2014). Very deep convolutional networks for large-scale image recognition. *CoRR*, abs/1409.1556.

Siyuan Zhuang, Zhuohan Li, Danyang Zhuo, Stephanie Wang, Eric Liang, Robert Nishihara, Philipp Moritz, Ion Stoica, Title:Hoplite: efficient and fault-tolerant collective communication for task-based distributed systems SIGCOMM 2021 Year of Publication: 2021 Pages 641–656

Sk, O., Santosh, K., Halder, C., Das, N., & Roy, K. (2017). Word-Level Multi-Script Indic Document Image Dataset and Baseline Results on Script Identification. *International Journal of Computer Vision and Image Processing*, *7*(2), 81–94. doi:10.4018/IJCVIP.2017040106

Sonntag, D., & Profitlich, H.-J. (2019). An architecture of open-source tools to combine textual information extraction, faceted search and information visualisation. *Artificial Intelligence in Medicine*, *93*, 13–28. doi:10.1016/j.artmed.2018.08.003 PMID:30195983

Sufian, A. Ghosh, A. Naskar, A., & Sultana, F. (2019). Bdnet: Bengali handwritten nu- meral digit recognition based on densely connected convolutional neural networks. *CoRR*, abs/1906.03786.

Sultana, F., Sufian, A., & Dutta, P. (2018). Advancements in image classification using convolu- tional neural network. In *2018 Fourth International Conference on Research in Computa- tional Intelligence and Communication Networks (ICRCICN)*, (pp. 122–129). IEEE.

Su, M., Wu, C., Huang, K., Hong, Q., & Wang, H. (2017). A chatbot using LSTM-based multi- layer embedding for elderly care. *2017 International Conference on Orange Technologies*, (pp. 70-74). IEEE. 10.1109/ICOT.2017.8336091

Sun, Kopper, Karkare, Paffenroth, & Apelian. (2020). Machine Learning Pathway for Harnessing Knowledge and Data in Material Processing. *Inter Metalcast*. doi:10.1007/s40962-020-00506-2

Sun, X., Zhang, P., Sookhak, M., Yu, J., & Xie, W. (2017). Utilizing fully homomorphic encryption to implement secure medical computation in smart cities. *Personal and Ubiquitous Computing*, *21*(5), 831–839. doi:10.100700779-017-1056-7

Szegedy, C., Liu, W., Jia, Y., Sermanet, P., Reed, S., Anguelov, D., Erhan, D., Vanhoucke, V., & Rabinovich, A. (2015). Going deeper with convolutions. In *The IEEE Conference on Computer Vision and Pattern Recognition (CVPR)*. IEEE.

Tan, W., Wei, T., & Mailthody Title, V. S. "Deep Learning with COTS HPC Systems: Distributed Strategies and Frameworks" Journal Name: Proceedings of the 2017 ACM International Conference on Supercomputing (ICS '17) Volume: N/A Issue: N/A Year of Publication: 2017 Pages: 56-67

Tang, W., Zhang, K., Zhang, D., Ren, J., Zhang, Y., & Shen, X. S. (2019). Fog-Enabled Smart Health: Toward Cooperative and Secure Healthcare Service Provision. *IEEE Communications Magazine*, *57*(5), 42–48. doi:10.1109/MCOM.2019.1800234

Tao, H., Bhuiyan, M. Z. A., Abdalla, A. N., Hassan, M. M., Zain, J. M., & Hayajneh, T. (2019). Secured Data Collection With Hardware-Based Ciphers for IoT-Based Healthcare. *IEEE Internet of Things Journal*, *6*(1), 410–420. doi:10.1109/JIOT.2018.2854714

Tavana, P., Akraminia, M., Koochari, A., & Bagherifard, A. (2023). An efficient ensemble method for detecting spinal curvature type using deep transfer learning and soft voting classifier. *Expert Systems with Applications*, *213*, 119290. doi:10.1016/j.eswa.2022.119290

Tejedor, E., Becerra, Y., Alomar, G., Queralt, A., Badia, R. M., Torres, J., Cortes, T., & Labarta, J. (2017). PyCOMPSs: Parallel computational workflows in Python. *International Journal of High Performance Computing Applications*, *31*(1), 66–82. doi:10.1177/1094342015594678

TensorFlow. (n.d.). TensorFlow. https://www.tensorflow.org/

Teuwen, J. (2020). *Convolutional neural networks, Elsevier and MICCAI Society Book Series, Handbook of Medical Image Computing and Computer Assisted Intervention.* Academic Press.

Thalagala, S., & Walgampaya, C. (2021). Application of AlexNet convolutional neural network architecture-based transfer learning for automated recognition of casting surface defects. *2021 International Research Conference on Smart Computing and Systems Engineering (SCSE)*, Colombo, Sri Lanka. 10.1109/SCSE53661.2021.9568315

Thusoo, A., Sen Sarma, J., Jain, N., Shao, Z., Chakka, P., Zhang, N., Antony, S., Liu, H., & Murthy, R. (2010). Hive - a petabyte scale data warehouse using Hadoop. *2010 IEEE 26th International Conference on Data Engineering (ICDE 2010)*, (pp. 996–1005). IEEE. 10.1109/ICDE.2010.5447738

Tsoukalas, V. D. (2008, December). Optimization of porosity formation in AlSi9Cu3 pressure die castings using genetic algorithm analysis. *Materials & Design, 29*(10), 2027–2033. doi:10.1016/j.matdes.2008.04.016

Tzutalin. (2015). *LabelImg.* Github. https://github.com/heartexlabs/labelImg

Verbraeken, J., Wolting, M., Katzy, J., Kloppenburg, J., Verbelen, T., & Rellermeyer, J. S. (2021). A Survey on Distributed Machine Learning. *ACM Computing Surveys, 53*(2), 1–33. doi:10.1145/3377454

Vora, S., Rangesh, A., & Trivedi, M. M. (2018). *Driver gaze zone estimation using convolutional neural networks: A general framework and ablative analysis.* Arxiv. https://arxiv.org/abs/1802.02690, 2018.

Wagan, Koo, Siddiqui, Qureshi, Attique, & Shin. (2023). *A Fuzzy-Based Duo-Secure Multi-Modal Framework for IoT Anomaly Detection.* Elsevier.

Wang, Y., Wu, H., Zhang, J., Gao, Z., Wang, J., Yu, P. S., & Long, M. (2021). *PredRNN: A Recurrent Neural Network for Spatiotemporal Predictive Learning.*

Wang, C., Shi, F., Xia, S., & Chai, J. (2016). Realtime 3D eye gaze animation using a single RGB camera. *ACM Transactions on Graphics, 35*(4), 1–14. doi:10.1145/2897824.2925947

Wang, J., Zhu, H., Wang, S. H., & Zhang, Y.-D. (2021). A Review of Deep Learning on Medical Image Analysis. *Mobile Networks and Applications, 26*(1), 351–380. doi:10.100711036-020-01672-7

Wang, Z., Chai, J., & Xia, S. (2021). Realtime and Accurate 3D Eye Gaze Capture with DCNN-Based Iris and Pupil Segmentation. *IEEE Transactions on Visualization and Computer Graphics, 27*(1), 190–203. doi:10.1109/TVCG.2019.2938165 PMID:31478861

Wei, J., Dai, W., Qiao, A., Ho, Q., Cui, H., Ganger, G. R., Gibbons, P. B., Gibson, G. A., & Xing, E. P. (2015). Managed communication and consistency for fast data-parallel iterative analytics. *Proceedings of the Sixth ACM Symposium on Cloud Computing*, (pp. 381–394). ACM. 10.1145/2806777.2806778

Weiss, S. M., & Indurkhya, N. (1995). Rule-based Machine Learning Methods for Functional Prediction. *Journal of Artificial Intelligence Research, 3,* 383–403. doi:10.1613/jair.199

Wilson, S. W. (1995). Classifier Fitness Based on Accuracy. *Evolutionary Computation, 3*(2), 149–175. doi:10.1162/evco.1995.3.2.149

Wood, E., Baltrušaitis, T., Morency, L., Robinson, P., & Bulling, A. (2018). GazeDirector: Fully Articulated Eye Gaze Redirection in Video. *Computer Graphics Forum, 37*(2), 217–225. doi:10.1111/cgf.13355

Wuest, T., Weimer, D., Irgens, C., & Thoben, K.-D. (2016, January). Machine learning in manufacturing: Advantages, challenges, and applications. *Production & Manufacturing Research, 4*(1), 23–45. doi:10.1080/21693277.2016.1192517

Wu, J.-N. (2016). Compression of fully-connected layer in neural network by Kronecker product. *2016 Eighth International Conference on Advanced Computational Intelligence (ICACI),* Chiang Mai, Thailand. 10.1109/ICACI.2016.7449822

Wu, W., Cao, J., Zheng, Y., & Zheng, Y. (2008). WAITER: A Wearable Personal Healthcare and Emergency Aid System. *2008 Sixth Annual IEEE International Conference on Pervasive Computing and Communications (PerCom),* 680-685. 10.1109/PERCOM.2008.115

Xiang-Qian, W., Kuan-Quan, W., & Zhang, D. (2002). Wavelet based palm print recognition. *Intern. Conf. Mach. Learn. Cybern, 3,* 1253–1257.

Xing, E. P., Ho, Q., Xie, P., & Wei, D. (2016). Strategies and Principles of Distributed Machine Learning on Big Data. *Engineering, 2*(2), 179–195. doi:10.1016/J.ENG.2016.02.008

Yadan, O., Adams, K., & Taigman, Y. (2013). *Multi-GPU Training of ConvNets.* Eprint Arxiv.

Yan, B., Pei, T., & Wang, X. (2019). Wavelet Method for Automatic Detection of Eye-Movement Behaviors. *IEEE Sensors Journal, 19*(8), 3085–3091. doi:10.1109/JSEN.2018.2876940

Yang Xiang, Zhihua Wu, Weibao Gong, Siyu Ding, Xianjie Mo, Yuang Liu, Shuohuan Wang, Peng Liu, Yongshuai Hou, Long Li, Bin Wang, Shaohuai Shi, Yaqian Han, Yue Yu, Ge Li, Yu Sun, Yanjun Ma, Dianhai Yu Title: "Nebula-I: A General Framework for Collaboratively Training Deep Learning Models on Low-Bandwidth Cloud Clusters" Journal Name: arXiv Volume:2205.09470 Year of Publication: 2022

Yanping Huang, Youlong Cheng, Ankur Bapna, Orhan Firat, Derek Gilpin, and Mostafa Dehghani,"GPipe: Efficient Training of Giant Neural Networks using Pipeline Parallelism", Year of Publication: 2019

Yeo, C. S., Buyya, R., Pourreza, H., Eskicioglu, R., Graham, P., & Sommers, F. (n.d.). Cluster Computing: High-Performance, High-Availability, and High-Throughput Processing on a Network of Computers. In Handbook of Nature-Inspired and Innovative Computing (pp. 521–551). Kluwer Academic Publishers. doi:10.1007/0-387-27705-6_16

Yifei Wang, Wei Zhang, Jun Yuan, Xiaolong Wang, and Jie Liu Title: "Scalable Distributed DNN Training Using Commodity GPU Cloud Computing" Journal Name: IEEE Transactions on Parallel and Distributed Systems Volume: 30 Issue: 8 Year of Publication: 2019 Pages: 1813-1827

Yim, J., Ju, J., Jung, H., & Kim, J. (2015). Image Classification Using Convolutional Neural Networks With Multi-stage Feature. In J. H. Kim, W. Yang, J. Jo, P. Sincak, & H. Myung (Eds.), *Robot Intelligence Technology and Applications 3. Advances in Intelligent Systems and Computing* (Vol. 345). Springer. doi:10.1007/978-3-319-16841-8_52

Yugank, Sharma, & Gupta. (2022). *An approach to analyse the energy consumption of an IoT system.* Springer.

Zeiler, M. D., & Fergus, R. (2014). Visualizing and understanding convolutional networks. In D. Fleet, T. Pajdla, B. Schiele, and T. Tuytelaars (Eds.), Computer Vision – ECCV 2014 (pp. 818–833). Springer International Publishing. doi:10.1007/978-3-319-10590-1_53

Zhang, R., Isola, P., & Efros, A. A. (2016). Colorful image colorization. *CoRR*, abs/1603.08511.

Zhang, D., Kong, W. K., You, J., & Wong, M. (2003). Online palmprint identification. *IEEE Transaction on Pattern Analysis and Machine*, 25(9), 1041–1050. doi:10.1109/TPAMI.2003.1227981

Zhang, F., & O'Donnell, L. J. (2020). Support vector regression. In *Machine Learning* (pp. 123–140). Elsevier. doi:10.1016/B978-0-12-815739-8.00007-9

Zhang, L., Li, L., Yang, A., Shen, Y., & Yang, M. (2017). Towards contactless palmprint recognition: A novel device, a new benchmark, and a collaborative representation based identification approach. *Pattern Recognition*, 69, 199–212. doi:10.1016/j.patcog.2017.04.016

Zhang, P., Jia, Y., Gao, J., Song, W., & Leung, H. (2020). Short-Term Rainfall Forecasting Using Multi-Layer Perceptron. *IEEE Transactions on Big Data*, 6(1), 93–106. doi:10.1109/TBDATA.2018.2871151

Zhang, S., Ren, X., Luo, L., Guo, T., & Liang, X. (2019). Logging-based identification and evaluation of karst fractures in the eastern Right Bank of the Amu Darya River, Turkmenistan. *Natural Gas Industry B*, 6. Advance online publication. doi:10.1016/j.ngib.2019.01.008

Zhang, S., & Wei, C. (2020). Deep learning network for UAV person re-identification based on residual block. *Science China. Information Sciences*, 63(7), 179203. doi:10.100711432-018-9633-7

Zhang, S., Yao, Z., Xu, S., Xu, S., Huang, J., Wang, Y., Zhang, C., & Zhuang, Y. (2018). Exploiting Data Parallelism in Deep Learning: A Comparative Study of Multi-GPU and Multi-Node Training. *IEEE Transactions on Parallel and Distributed Systems Volume*, 29(11), 2527–2540. doi:10.1109/TPDS.2018.2840098

Zhang, W., Iqbal, S., Wu, S., Zhang, J., Bao, Y., Huang, C., Zhan, J., & Title, D. Q. (2018, November). Scalable Distributed DNN Training Using Commodity GPU Cloud Computing. *Journal Name: IEEE Transactions on Parallel and Distributed Systems Volume*, 29(11), 2427–2442.

Zhao, Y., Man, K. L., Smith, J., Siddique, K., & Guan, S.-U. (2020). Improved two-stream model for human action recognition. *J Image Video Proc.*, *2020*(1), 24. doi:10.118613640-020-00501-x

Zheng, M., Chen, N., Zhu, J., Zeng, X., Qiu, H., Jiang, Y., Lu, X., & Qu, H. Distributed bundle adjustment with block-based sparse matrix compression for super large scale datasets" arXiv:2307.08383 Year of Publication: 2023

Zheng, J., Wang, Q., Zhao, P., & Wu, C. (2009, October). Optimization of high-pressure die-casting process parameters using artificial neural network. *International Journal of Advanced Manufacturing Technology*, *44*(7–8), 667–674. doi:10.100700170-008-1886-6

Zhi, J., Wang, R., Clune, J., & Stanley, K. O. Title:"Fiber: A Platform for Efficient Development and Distributed Training for Reinforcement Learning and Population-Based Methods"Journal name: arXiv Volume:2003.11164 Year of Publication:2020 A. Shafi, J. Hashmi, H. Subramoni and D. Panda, Title:"Efficient MPI-based Communication for GPU-Accelerated Dask Applications" Journal name: 2021 IEEE/ACM 21st International Symposium on Cluster, Cloud and Internet Computing (CCGrid) Year of Publication: 2021, Pages: 277-286

Zhou, X., Gong, W., Fu, W., & Du, F. (2017, May). Application of deep learning in object detection. In *2017 IEEE/ACIS 16th International Conference on Computer and Information Science (ICIS)* (pp. 631-634). IEEE. 10.1109/ICIS.2017.7960069

Zhu, Y., Yao, C., & Bai, X. (2016). Scene text detection and recognition: Recent advances and future trends. *Frontiers of Computer Science*, *10*(1), 19–36. doi:10.100711704-015-4488-0

Zunic, E., Korjenic, K., Hodzic, K., & Donko, D. (2020). Application of Facebook's Prophet Algorithm for Successful Sales Forecasting Based on Real-world Data. *arXiv preprint arXiv:2005.07575.*

About the Contributors

J. Joshua Thomas received his PhD. degree from University Sains Malaysia (USM), School of Computer Sciences, in 2015. He worked as research assistant at the Artificial Intelligence Lab in University Sains Malaysia. His research interests include scheduling algorithms, machine learning algorithms, data analytics, deep learning, and visual analytics, and Chemoinformatics. Dr. J. Joshua has authored several publications in leading international conferences and journals. Some of his research work were published in conferences including, IEEE, ICONIP, IVIC, IV, COMPSE, ICO. He has funded external, internal, short term research grants and industry collaborative projects. He has been invited as plenary speaker at IAIM2019, delivered, conduct Workshop's (IVIC19) at International conferences. He is an Associate Editor for the journal of Energy Optimization and Engineering (IJEOE), and invited as guest editor for JVLC-Elsevier, IJDSA-Springer, IJCC-IGI-Global, IJIRR-Inderscience.

S. Harini serves an as Associate Professor in Distributive Architecture and Parallel Systems at the Vellore Institute of Technology.

V. Pattabiraman obtained his Bachelor's from Madras University and Master's degree from Bharathidasan University. He completed his PhD from Bharathiar University, India. He has a total Professional experience of more than 16 years working in various prestigious institutions. He has published more than 30 papers in various National and International peer reviewed journals and conferences. He visited various countries namely few China, Singapore, Malaysia, Thailand and South Africa etc. for presenting his research contributions as well as to giving key note address. He is currently an Associate Professor and Program-Chair for Master's Programme at VIT University-Chennai Campus, India. His teaching and research expertise covers a wide range of subject area including Data Structures, Knowledge Discovery and Data mining, Database echnologies, Big Data Analytics, Networks and Information security, etc.

* * *

G. Ananthi is currently working as an Assistant Professor (Senior Grade), in the Department of Computer Science and Engineering, Mepco Schlenk Engineering College, Sivakasi. She completed her UG in CSE and PG in CSE at Mepco Schlenk Engineering College respectively on 2001 and 2010. She completed her Ph.D in Information and Communication Engineering under Anna University, Chennai during July 2022. She has 19 years of teaching experience. She has 23 publications in Journals and conferences. She has two published patents and seven granted copyrights. She is a life member in CSI and ISTE. Her areas of specialization are image processing, machine learning and soft computing.

Nikhil Chapre is currently an undergraduate Computer Science student at Vellore Institute of Technology. He was a leading member of OWASP VIT Student Chapter and has mentored many students on Cybersecurity. He is an avid learner and his current research interests lie in the region of Computer Vision and Natural Language Processing.

Chitra Dhawale is a Professor in the Science and Technology Department of Datta Meghe Institute of Education and Research (Deemed to be University). She received her Ph.D. Degree in Computer Science from S.G.B. Amravati University in 2009. She is having 25+ years of teaching and research experience in computer science. Her area of Expertise includes: Data Science, Machine Learning, Deep Learning, Python Programming, R Programming, Tableau. She/he is the author of 02 books, 08 book chapters and 78 research papers.

Mohanraj Elangovan is an Associate Professor/AI and Data Science Department, K.S. Rangasamy College of Technology. He has more than 15 years of teaching experience and published more than 30 articles in reputed journals. His domain of research interest are AI, Wireless networks, ML, DL, etc.

Shenbagalakshmi G. is working as Assistant Professor in the Department of Computer Science and Engineering at Mepco Schlenk Engineering College, Sivakasi. She graduated het Bachelor of Technology in Information Technology at Arulmigu Kalasalingam College of Engineering, Srivilliputhur affiliated to Anna University Chennai, Tamilnadu, India. She secured Master of Engineering in Computer Science and Engineering at Mepco Schlenk Engineering College, Sivakasi affiliated to under Anna University Chennai, Tamilnadu, India. She has completed Ph.D., in Computer Science and Engineering at Anna University, Chennai, Tamilnadu, India. She is having research experience of 5 years and teaching profession for more than 2 years. She has presented 12 papers in National and International Journals,

Conference and Symposiums. Her main area of interest includes Wireless Sensor Network, Internet of Things and Soft Computing.

Pujaa M. is a UG student at Mepco Schlenk Engineering College, Sivakasi, in Department of CSE.

Parvathi R. is a Professor of School of Computing Science and Engineering at VIT University, Chennai since 2011. She received the Doctoral degree in the field of spatial data mining in the same year. Her teaching experience in the area of computer science includes more than two decades and her research interests include data mining, big data and computational biology.

Mekala Ramasamy is an Assistant Professor/Department of Information Science and Engineering. She is a research scholar and having 12 years of teaching experience. Her research interest areas are NLP, ML/DL, AI, etc.

G. Sandhiya is a UG student at Mepco Schlenk Engineering College, Sivakasi, in Department of CSE.

Kalayni Satone is working as an Asst. Professor at Department of Science and Technology, Datta Meghe Institute of Higher Education and Research. Her research domain Deep Learning. She has published numerous papers in various journals and guided post graduation students for project development.

A.T. Anisha Shruti is a UG student at Mepco Schlenk Engineering College, Sivakasi, in Department of CSE.

Azam Siddiqui is a highly skilled software developer and a graduate of the Vellore Institute of Technology in India. He was recognized as the 2nd runner-up in the prestigious WaiDatathon 2021 competition. Currently, he contributes his expertise as a software developer at Hyperzod Tech, specializing in SaaS platform and microservices development.

Agila Harshini T. is an academician, research scholar, currently working as Research Associate in VIT Chennai. Her research domain is deep learning and AI.

Pranjali Ulhe is working as an Asst. Professor at Department of Science and Technology, Datta Meghe Institute of Higher Education and Research. Her research domain Deep Learning. She has published numerous papers in various journals and guided post graduation students for project development.

Kiruthika V. is working as Assistant Professor in the School of Electronics Engineering, Vellore Institute of Technology, Chennai. She has pursued her research studies in the area of Medical Image Processing and Machine Learning. Her area of interests includes Image Processing, Signal Processing, Deep Learning and Machine Learning. She has published eleven papers related to the area of interest in reputed journals and conferences till date. She also reviews manuscripts submitted to peer-review journals and conferences.

Amretha V. M. is a UG student at Mepco Schlenk Engineering College, Sivakasi, in Department of CSE.

Xiaohui Yuan received the B.S. degree in electrical engineering from the Hefei University of Technology in 1996 and the Ph.D. degree in computer science from Tulane University in 2004. He was with the National Institute of Health between 2004 and 2006 and is currently a Professor with the University of North Texas. His research interests include computer vision, artificial intelligence, data mining, and machine learning. He was a recipient of the Ralph E. Powe Junior Faculty Enhancement Award in 2008. He serves as the Editor-in-Chief of the International Journal of Smart Sensor Technologies and Applications and on the Editorial Board of several international journals as well as the Chair of many international conferences.

Index

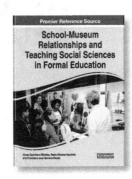
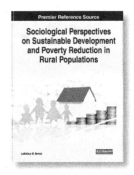